READERS LOVE FAITH MARTIN

'A must read for all crime fiction fans'

'Have become an addict of Faith Martin – love her novels'

'Cracking good read'

'Plenty of action and drama to keep the reader
gripped through to the end'

'I would recommend this to anyone who
enjoys crime fiction'

'Compelling murder mystery'

'Fabulous police procedural'

FAITH MARTIN has been writing for nearly thirty years, under four different pen names, and has published over fifty novels. She began writing romantic thrillers as Maxine Barry, but quickly turned to crime! As Joyce Cato she wrote classic-style whodunits, since she's always admired the golden-age crime novelists. But it was when she created her fictional DI Hillary Greene, and began writing under the name of Faith Martin, that she finally began to become more widely known. Her latest literary characters WPC Trudy Loveday, and city coroner Dr Clement Ryder, take readers back to the 1960s, and the city of Oxford. Having lived within a few miles of the city's dreaming spires for all her life (she worked for six years as a secretary at Somerville College), both the city and the countryside/wildlife often feature in her novels. Although she has never lived on a narrowboat (unlike DI Hillary Greene!) the Oxford canal, the river Cherwell, and the flora and fauna of a farming landscape have always played a big part in her life – and often sneak their way onto the pages of her books.

Also by Faith Martin

A Fatal Mistake
A Fatal Flaw
A Fatal Secret
A Fatal Truth

A Fatal Obsession

FAITH MARTIN

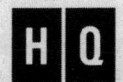

ONE PLACE, MANY STORIES

HQ
An imprint of HarperCollins*Publishers* Ltd
1 London Bridge Street
London SE1 9GF

This paperback edition 2020

2

First published in Great Britain by
HQ, an imprint of HarperCollins*Publishers* Ltd 2018

MIX
Paper from
responsible sources
FSC www.fsc.org **FSC™ C007454**

Typeset by Palimpsest Book Production Ltd, Falkirk, Stirlingshire
Printed and bound in Great Britain by CPI Group (UK) Ltd, Croydon CR0 4YY

For my Mum and Dad – for always believing in me

PROLOGUE

Oxford, July 1955

The body on the bed lay sedate and demurely silent as the middle-aged man looked slowly around the room. It was a lovely room – large, well proportioned and lavishly decorated in tones of blue and silver. One of two large sash windows was partly open, allowing a warm summer breeze to blow in, gently wafting the fine net curtains and bringing with it a faint scent of honeysuckle from the lush and well-tended gardens below.

The man wandered slowly around the opulent bedroom, his eyes greedily taking in everything from the quality of the silk bedsheets to the bottles of expensive perfume on an ornate antique dresser, while being careful not to touch anything. Having been born into a working-class family, he knew nothing about the pedigree of the paintings that adorned the walls. But he would have been willing to bet a week's wages that the sale of just one of them would be more than enough to set him and his family up for life.

He'd never before had cause to visit any of the mansions that proliferated in the swanky streets that stretched between the Woodstock and Banbury Roads in the north of the city, or any of the leafy avenues in the area. So now he took his time, and a considerable amount of pleasure, in looking around him, luxuriating in the deep tread of the plush blue Axminster carpet beneath his feet, which was so reminiscent of walking on mossy lawns.

His eyes turned wistfully to the jewellery box on a walnut bedside table, left carelessly open. Gold, pearls and a few sparkling gemstones winked in the summer sun, making his fingers positively itch.

'Very nice,' he muttered quietly to himself. But he knew better than to slip even a modest ring or two into his pocket. Not this time – and certainly not with *these* people. The man hadn't reached his half century without learning there was one law for the rich, and one for everyone else.

Thoughtfully, his eyes turned once more to the body on the bed. A pretty little thing she was. Young too. Just out of her teens, perhaps?

What a damned shame, he thought vaguely.

Then the breeze caused something on the bedside table to flutter slightly, the movement instantly catching his eye. He walked closer to the bed and the dead girl, again careful where he put his feet, and saw what it was that had been disturbed. It had clearly been deliberately propped up among the pots of face cream and powder compacts, lipsticks and boxes of pills.

Bending ponderously at the waist, the man, who was definitely beginning to run to fat, squinted down at it and read some of the words written there.

And slowly, a large, beaming smile spread over his not particularly attractive face. He gave a long, slow, near-silent whistle and then looked sharply over his shoulder to make sure nobody from the house had come upstairs behind him and could see what he was about to do. Confident he remained alone and unobserved, he reached out for the item and put it safely away in his large inside jacket pocket.

Then he lovingly patted the place over his heart where it lay. For, unless he was very much mistaken, this precious little find was the best bit of luck he'd had for many a year – if not in his whole life. And it was certainly going to make his imminently approaching retirement years far more pleasant than he'd ever previously anticipated.

He walked jauntily to the door, leaving the dead girl behind him without a second thought, and stepped out confidently onto the landing.

Time, he rather thought, to tackle the man of the house.

Chapter One

Oxford, January 1960

Probationary WPC Trudy Loveday shouted, 'Oi, you, stop right there. Police!' at the top of her lungs, and took off at a racing sprint.

Needless to say, the young lad she'd just seen snatch a woman's handbag as she was standing below the clock face on Carfax Tower did nothing of the kind. She just had time to catch a fleeting impression of a panic-stricken young face as he shot a quick look at her over his shoulder, and then took off down The High, like a whippet after a hare.

He nearly got run over by a taxi as he crossed the main road at the intersection but, luckily for Trudy, the traffic that had screeched to a halt to allow him to cross meant she could take advantage of the gap to race across herself, in rather more safety.

On her face, had she but known it, was a look of sheer joy. Sergeant O'Grady had given her the task of trying to find the man responsible for a spate of bag-snatching in the city centre that had been going on since before the Christmas rush, but this was the first time she'd actually caught sight of her quarry in all that time. Though the thief had been active enough, and the list of outraged complaints from housewives and shoppers had grown steadily longer, neither she nor any of her fellow constables walking the beat had yet been lucky enough to be in the right spot at the right time.

Until now.

And a month of pounding the freezing pavements, taking statements from enraged or tearful women, and hiding behind shop doors on increasingly aching feet while keeping her eyes peeled for mischief, had left Trudy with a proper grudge against this particular villain.

Which meant she was in no mood to lose him now.

She was aware that many of the people in the streets were watching her race by with open mouths and round, astonished eyes. Some of the men, indeed, looked as if they were going to try and interfere, and she could only hope and pray that they wouldn't. Although they no doubt meant well, the last thing she needed was for some chivalrous, middle-aged bank manager to try and stop the fleeing thief for her, only to be roughly tossed to the floor, punched, or worse.

The paperwork involved in that was something she definitely didn't want to think about. Not to mention the look of resigned fury that would cross DI Jennings's face when he learned she'd somehow managed to muck up such a simple arrest.

Less than a minute of mad chasing had passed so far, and rather belatedly she remembered her whistle and debated whether or not she should use it.

At nineteen (nearly twenty), Trudy Loveday still remembered her glory days at the track and field events at her school where she'd always won cups on sports day for her racing – be it sprinting or cross-country. And she could still run like the wind, even in her neat black shoes and police uniform, with her leather satchel of accoutrements bouncing on her hip. Moreover, she could tell she was gaining ground on the little villain in front of her, who had to deal with the added obstacle of shouldering pedestrians out of his way as he ran, leaving the pavements rather less clogged for her.

Her legs and arms were pumping away in that satisfying and remembered rhythm that allowed her to eat up the yards, and she was reluctant to alter that flow, but training and good sense told her she must. So, trying not to lose momentum, she reached her hand across her chest, swung the silver whistle on its chain up to her lips, and blew hard on the outward, expelling breath.

The distinctive, loud-pitched whistle promptly resounded in the cold, frost-laden air, and would, she knew, bring any of her colleagues within hearing distance running to her aid. Which might be just as well if the bag-snatcher decided to give up his attempt at a straight flight and tried to lose himself in the city's narrow, medieval back streets, or by dodging in and out of the shops.

But so far he was intent on just running down The High, no doubt confident he could outrun a mere woman. But this hardly made him the first man to underestimate her.

With a confident grin, Trudy put on an extra burst of speed. He was so close now, she could almost feel the moment when she'd rugby-tackle him to the ground, hear him grunt with surprise and then see the look of dismay on his cocky little face as she slipped her handcuffs on him and gave him his caution.

And at that moment, just as she was reaching out and getting ready to grab him, he turned and glanced over his shoulder, saw her and swore. And immediately began to dodge to his right, between two parked cars.

Trudy cast a swift look over her shoulder, saw that the road was clear, then looked ahead as far as Magdalen Bridge, noticing the familiar outline of a red bus chugging along, coming towards her. But she had plenty of time before it reached them.

Anticipating the fleeing thief's intention of crossing the road and trying to lose her down one of the side streets opposite, Trudy gave a final blast on her whistle. This was as much to warn the gaping, watching public to keep out of the way as it was an attempt to attract further help from her colleagues.

Then she leapt sideways.

Her timing, as she'd known it would be, was near perfect, and before he could gain the middle of the road, she was on him, swinging him around and back towards the pavement. She hit him hard, putting all of her slight weight into it. Luckily, at five feet ten, she was a tall girl, and had a long reach.

The thief landed unluckily on his nose on the icy tarmac, and yelped in shock. He was a skinny, wiry specimen, all arms and legs, and already his nose was bleeding profusely. Comically, he was still clutching the lady's handbag he'd snatched back at Carfax.

Trudy felt her police cap fall off as she landed on top of him but, mercifully, her long, wavy, dark-brown hair was held up in such a tight bun by a plethora of hair pins and elastic bands that it remained contained.

Reaching behind her, with one knee firmly positioned in the middle of the thief's back, she groped for her handcuffs. She was vaguely aware of a male voice shouting something only a short distance away, and that the public, who had begun gathering in a curious little knot around her, were now moving back, when the thief beneath her suddenly bucked and twisted violently.

And before she could even open her mouth to begin to caution him, his elbow shot upwards, smacking her firmly in the eye.

'Owwww!' she yelled, one hand going up instinctively to cup her throbbing cheekbone. This provided the bag-snatcher with the opportunity he'd been waiting for, and he gave another massive heave, sending her sprawling.

Nevertheless, she had enough presence of mind to reach out and grab him by the foot as he attempted to get up. He turned, drew back his free leg and was clearly about to kick her in the face when she became aware of another figure looming over her.

'All right, matey, hold it right there! You ain't going nowhere,' a triumphant voice said. And a pair of large male hands came into her view, hauling the bag-snatcher to his feet. 'I'm arresting you for assaulting a police officer in the course of her duty. I must caution you that anything you say will be taken down and may be given in evidence.'

Trudy, her large, dark-brown eyes watering as much in frustration as in pain, watched as PC Rodney Broadstairs – the Lothario of St Aldates police station – slipped his handcuffs onto *her* suspect. Stiffly, she got to her feet. Only now that the adrenaline was wearing off was she beginning to feel the scrapes and bruises she'd sustained in the tackle. Although, fortunately, her gloves, uniform, and the heavy black serge greatcoat she wore over it had saved her from losing any actual skin.

A brief and polite smattering of applause from the public rang out as PC Broadstairs began frogmarching the thief back to the pavement. One member of the public diffidently offered Trudy her cap back, which she took with a smile and a weary word of thanks.

She also retrieved the lady's handbag for evidence.

But the admiring looks from the bystanders and the murmuring of approval for 'the plucky little thing' as she limped grimly after PC Broadstairs and the bag-snatcher did little to improve her now sour mood. Because she knew, after nearly a year's bitter experience, just how things were going to go now.

Broadstairs, having been the one to deliver the caution and put on the cuffs, would be accredited with the arrest. It would be the good-looking PC, not the humble probationary WPC, who would get the nod of approval from her superior officers.

She would no doubt be told to go home to her mum and dad and get some rest, nurse her burgeoning black eye and then type up her report first thing in the morning. Oh, and to go and get the deposition of the woman whose bag had been snatched. And all the time having to endure the whispers and snide asides about how that was all WPCs were good for.

Disconsolately, as she trooped back to St Aldates, she could only hope that DI Jennings wouldn't use her minor injuries as an excuse to put her back on desk duty again.

In front of her, PC Rodney Broadstairs looked over his shoulder at her and winked.

*

As WPC Trudy Loveday wrestled with the desire to swear in a most unladylike manner at her male colleague, five miles away, in the small and pretty village of Hampton Poyle, Sir Marcus Deering had stopped work for his elevenses.

Although he was still nominally in charge of the large chain of department stores that had made his fortune, at the age of sixty-three he now worked two days a week from the study in his large country residence in Oxfordshire. He was confident his managing directors, plus a whole board of other executives, could safely be left to do the bulk of the work without any major mishaps, and now rarely travelled to the main offices in Birmingham.

He sighed with pleasure as his secretary came into the book-lined room with a coffee tray laden with fresh-baked biscuits and that morning's post. A rather portly man, with thinning grey hair, a neatly trimmed moustache and large, hazel-green eyes, Sir Marcus liked to eat.

His appetite, however, instantly fled as he recognised the writing on one large, plain-white envelope. Addressed to him in block capital letters, it had been written in a rather bilious shade of green.

His secretary deposited the tray on his desk and, noticing the way his lips had thinned into a very displeased line, hastily beat a retreat.

Sir Marcus scowled at the pile of correspondence and took a desultory sip of his coffee, telling himself that this latest in a line of recent anonymous letters was nothing more than a nuisance. No doubt written by some crackpot with nothing better to do with his time, it was hardly worth the effort of opening and reading it. He should just consign it straight to the wastepaper basket instead.

But he knew he wouldn't do that. Human nature wouldn't let him. The cat wasn't the only creature curiosity was capable of killing, after all. And so, with a slight sneer of distaste, he snatched the offending envelope from the pile of correspondence, reached for his silver paper knife, and neatly slit it open. He then pulled out the single piece of paper within, knowing what it would say without even having to look at it. For the letters always made the same preposterous, ambiguous, infuriatingly meaningless demand.

He'd received the first one a little under a month ago. Just a few lines, the implication of a veiled threat, and unsigned, of course. Nonsense, through and through, he remembered thinking at the time. It was just one of the many things a man of his standing – a self-made, very wealthy man – had to put up with.

He'd crumpled it up and tossed it away without a second thought.

Then, only a week later, another one had come.

And, oddly enough, it hadn't been more threatening, or more explicit, or even more crudely written. The message had been exactly the same. Which was unusual in itself. Sir Marcus had always assumed that nasty anonymous letters became more and more vile and explicit as time progressed.

Whether it was this anomaly, or sheer instinct, he couldn't now say, but something about it had made him pause. And this time, instead of throwing it away, he'd kept it. Not that it really worried him, naturally.

But he'd kept the one that had come last week too, even though it had said exactly the same thing. And he'd probably slip this one, also, into the top drawer of his desk and carefully lock it. After all, he didn't want his wife finding them. The wretched things would only scare her.

With a sigh, he unfolded the piece of paper and read it.

Yes, as he'd thought – the same wording, almost exactly.

DO THE RIGHT THING. I'M WATCHING YOU. IF YOU DON'T, YOU'LL BE SORRY.

But this letter had one final sentence – something that was new.

YOU HAVE ONE LAST CHANCE.

Sir Marcus Deering felt his heart thump sickeningly in his chest. One last chance? What was that supposed to mean?

With a grunt of annoyance, he threw the paper down onto his desk and stood up, walking over to the set of French windows that gave him a view of a large, well-maintained lawn. A small brook cut across the stretch of grass marking the boundary where the formal flower garden began, and his eyes restlessly followed the skeletal forms of the weeping willows that lined it.

Beyond the house and large gardens, which were so colourful and full of scent in the summer (and the pride and joy of his wife, Martha) came yet more evidence of his wealth and prestige, in the form of the fertile acres being run by his farm manager.

Normally, the experience of looking out over his land soothed Sir Marcus, reassuring him and reminding him of just how far he'd come in life.

It was stupid to feel so bloody . . . well, not frightened by the letters exactly; Sir Marcus wouldn't admit to being quite *that*. But unsettled. Yes, he supposed that was fair. He definitely felt uneasy.

On the face of it, they were nothing. The threat was meaningless and tame. There wasn't even any foul language involved. As far as nasty anonymous notes went, they were rather pathetic really. And yet there was something about them . . .

He gave himself a little mental shake and tramped determinedly back to his desk, sitting down heavily in his chair. And with a look of distaste on his face, he swept the letter into a drawer along with all the others, and locked it firmly.

He had better things to do with his time than worry about such stupid nonsense. No doubt the mentally deficient individual who'd written them was sitting somewhere right this moment, chortling away and imagining he'd managed to put the wind up him.

But Sir Marcus Deering was made of sterner stuff than that!

Do the right thing . . . Surely, it couldn't be referring to the fire, could it? A spasm of anxiety shot through him. That was all so long ago, and had had nothing to do with him. He'd been young, still working in his first executive position, and had no doubt been wet behind the ears; but the fire hadn't even occurred on his watch, and certainly hadn't been his responsibility.

No. It couldn't be about that.

Defiantly, he reached for a biscuit, bit into it, opened the first of his business letters and pondered whether or not he should introduce a new line in wireless sets into his stores. The manager at the Leamington Spa emporium was all for ordering in a large batch of sets in cream Bakelite.

Sir Marcus snorted. Cream! What was wrong with Bakelite that was made to look like good solid mahogany? And what did it matter if it *was* 1960 now, and the start of a whole new exciting decade, as the manager's letter insisted? Would house-wives really fork out their husband's hard-earned money on cream Bakelite?

But at the back of his mind, even as he called in his secretary and began to dictate a reprimand to his forward-thinking executive in the spa town, his mind was furiously churning.

Just what the devil did the letter mean by 'do the right thing'? What *was* the right thing? And what would happen if he, Sir Marcus, *didn't* do the right thing?

Chapter Two

'That you, love?' Barbara Loveday called out as she heard the front door open and shut. 'I'm in the kitchen!'

And Trudy, who was wearily hanging up her things in the tiny hallway, couldn't help but smile. Of course her mother was in the kitchen – Barbara Loveday was rarely anywhere else. Throughout their childhood, she and her older brother, Martin, had spent more time in that tiny, comforting space than anywhere else in the small terraced house in the rather rundown area of Botley they called home.

As a suburb of the city, Botley might lack Headington's lofty hills and smart new housing, or Osney Mead's more bohemian and colourful canal-side charm, but Trudy couldn't imagine living anywhere else. And on a cold, disappointing day, with her bones aching and her eye blackening nicely, she was more than happy to traipse through to the kitchen, where she knew the appetising smell of something tasty cooking, and a warm, loving welcome from her mother could be guaranteed to greet her.

'You're home earl—oh, Trudy, love!' Barbara said helplessly, her face creasing in concern as she saw her daughter's face. 'What happened? Come here.'

For a moment, as her mother's ample form enfolded her and pansy-brown eyes – the mirror image of her own – inspected her face carefully, she didn't mind feeling as if she was about six years old again. It was, after all, very nice to know that someone loved and cared for you, and here, in this little kitchen, with its cracked linoleum floor and cheerful yellow curtains, she felt safe and appreciated once more.

Which was more than could be said of how she'd felt back at the station.

'Here, love, sit down. Let me make you a nice cuppa. I'll put something on that eye. I've got some cream that'll do the trick. I only wish we had a nice bit of beefsteak to put on it.'

Trudy couldn't help but grin – even though it made her face hurt. Because if the Loveday family *had* been able to afford a nice bit of beefsteak, she knew full well they'd never be foolish enough to waste it on her face. It would be cooked and scoffed in no time at all.

'Mum, it's nothing,' she insisted, sitting down at the tiny kitchen table, shoved up against one wall to preserve space, and then looking down as Maggie the cat rubbed against her ankles. She reached down absently to stroke her black-and-white fur. But the loud purring that resulted, Trudy suspected cynically, was more likely intended as a spur for someone to feed her than as an offer of support or sympathy for her human companion.

Trudy was wise to the ways of feline cunning.

'So, what happened this time then?' Barbara demanded,

standing by the sink as she watched the kettle start to boil, hands planted firmly on her ample hips.

Trudy sighed. She really didn't want to get into this fight again. The same old argument about whether or not women belonged in the police force had been running in the family home ever since she'd told her parents what she wanted to do for a living.

'Like I said, Mum, it's nothing. I just slipped and fell on the icy pavement, that's all.'

Well, that wasn't totally a lie, Trudy mused. The pavement *had* been icy. And if she hadn't so much slipped as launched herself into orbit in order to bring down a bag-snatcher . . . well, her mother certainly didn't need to know *that*.

'Don't give me that, Gertrude Mary Loveday,' her mother warned, making Trudy wince. Only her mother ever called her by her detested full first name – and then only when she was in trouble.

Named after one of her dad's sisters, who had died young in the war, Trudy had always insisted on the diminutive, practically from the time she had first learned to talk. And teasing from her schoolmates when they'd discovered her proper Christian name had only reinforced her determination to remain strictly – and only – Trudy.

Now she shot her mum a sharp glance.

'And don't give me that look, neither,' Barbara Loveday shot back crisply. 'You were out chasing villains, weren't you? That's how you got that shiner, my girl. Do you think I'm stupid?'

Trudy resisted the urge to slump over the table and hold her head in her hands. 'Mum, that's my job,' she wailed helplessly. 'That's what the police *do*.'

Barbara sniffed. 'I daresay it is,' she agreed stiffly. 'But why are you one of the ones that's doing it, that's what I can't understand. Silly, I call it. I thought when you went to college to learn to do typewriting and shorthand, you'd become a secretary.' Her mother ploughed on, with the now all-too-familiar lament. 'You'd have been the first in either my family or your dad's to do that! Us Butlers and Lovedays have always worked in shops or factories, or on the buses, like your dad. You'd have been the first one to work in a nice office. Even our Martin works with his hands.'

'He's a carpenter, Mum,' Trudy said wryly. 'He's earning good money and always will. He's got a trade.'

'Yes, that's true enough,' Barbara said, taking time off from berating her daughter to beam with pride at the contemplation of her firstborn. 'I wish he was still living at home, though.'

Trudy smiled. Martin had moved out of the family home over a year ago, to lodge with a friend of the family nearer his work up in Cowley. And, like any other young, fit and good-looking man, very glad he'd been to get out from under his parents' watchful eyes too. Not that Trudy would ever tell them so! While she had a good idea what the rascal got up to of a Saturday night, she rather thought her mum and dad were still in blissful ignorance.

'And you could have been a secretary.' Predictably her mum went straight back on the attack as she heaped three spoonfuls of tea leaves into the teapot and poured boiling water over them. 'Instead of sitting there now, looking like someone who's been dragged through a hedge backwards.'

Trudy bit back a groan. No matter how many times she'd tried to explain to her mother that working in a boring office, doing boring, meaningless clerical work, wasn't for her, Barbara Loveday had never accepted it.

Which was rather ironic really, Trudy thought, fighting back the urge to laugh. For once she'd finished her police training at Eynsham Hall, and been stationed at St Aldates, she'd spent more time typing up reports, filing and making cups of tea for her superiors than any secretary.

It had all been so far removed from what she had thought of as proper police work that she'd despaired of ever being given more responsibility.

So now, just when she'd finally made it onto the beat, and had even managed to get one or two nice little arrests to her name (two shoplifters and a case of minor arson), this disaster with the bag-snatcher had to go and happen! It just wasn't fair!

She could still see the rather guilty look on Sergeant O'Grady's face when he'd seen her black eye, and the uncomfortable look on DI Jennings's face when he'd read her report.

As men, they didn't like to see women get hurt – especially as a result of violence. And while she understood it (and in a way even appreciated the gallantry of it), she also knew, with a growing sense of frustration, that while they maintained that attitude it was going to be almost impossible for her to advance her career.

Because once she'd finished her two-year probationary period in uniform, walking the beat and doing her general duties, the first chance she got she was going to sit her exams and apply to be a TDC – or Temporary Detective Constable.

It wouldn't happen at once, of course. Nor would it be a case of working just another two years or so. More likely she'd have to get in a good four or five years before that could happen.

But she was determined it would. And no man was going to stop her, superior officers or . . . .

'Trudy!'

Her head shot up as she realised her mother had been giving her the usual lecture, and she'd been caught out, letting her mind wander.

'Sorry, Mum,' she muttered.

Barbara sighed wearily. 'What's wrong with settling down with a nice young man and having a couple of young 'uns, that's what I'd like to know?' she added stubbornly.

Trudy was about to tell her roundly that there would be plenty of time for all that, but then her mother's face crumpled. 'Oh, Trudy, love, it just scares me so, you being out there on your own, walking down dark streets and dressed in that uniform. There are plenty of louts out there who don't care for the police sticking their noses in their business. What if you get really hurt next time?'

Trudy got up and hugged her mother hard. 'Please, try not to worry, Mum,' she said uselessly. 'They train us how to cope with stuff like that. And besides, I've got my truncheon.'

But of course her mother worried – how could she not? And her dad did too. Although more easy-going and tolerant than his wife, and less inclined to lecture her, she was well aware he would have preferred her to find another job. Any other job – even if it was only as a clippie on one of his beloved buses.

She could still remember how he'd laughed when, as a little girl listening to his stories of life as a bus driver for the City of Oxford Motor Services, she'd told him she wanted to drive buses too, when she grew up.

Not that that was an option either, Trudy thought with a brief grin. Who'd ever heard of a woman bus driver?

Still, she knew both her parents agreed anything would be better than their 'little girl' working as a serving WPC.

And although she sometimes felt conscience-stricken that she was causing them so much worry and grief, she also knew there was little she could realistically do about it. She'd just have to wait for their anxiety and fears to wear off – which they would have to do eventually, right? And who knew – maybe a little further down the line, when she'd got her sergeant's stripes and they were feeling as proud as punch of her, they'd look back on days like this and laugh.

Chapter Three

Dr Clement Ryder reached for the claret jug and swore loudly as his hand began to twitch.

It was dark outside, it had been a long and tiring day, and after going out for a quick and rather unsatisfying meal of sausages and mash in his local pub, he felt like he deserved a decent nightcap by his own fireside. Having a nightcap at all was a rare occurrence for him, since he seldom drank alone. Now he realised he probably shouldn't have bothered, since he couldn't seem to hold the glass straight, damn it.

At least, he thought grimly, the shakes hadn't started until after he'd left the office. And so far, praise be, he'd never had an attack of them while actually in court. Which meant the humiliating moment when he'd have to come clean about his condition to his staff and superiors could be put off a while longer yet.

Which was just as well. Clement had no intention of telling anyone anything, if he could help it.

At fifty-seven, Clement was beginning to feel the cold more

and more, he'd noticed. Luckily, his thick-walled Victorian house overlooking South Parks Road was relatively draught-proof, and as he carefully poured out a small measure of his third-best claret, he was pleased to note that he didn't spill a drop.

He smiled sourly, but knew he should be grateful for even small victories.

So far, the shaking palsy that had begun to stalk him a little over five years ago hadn't become a major issue in his new life. Even though it had, obviously, put paid to his old one.

Born to middle-class parents in a suburb of Cheltenham, Clement had earned a scholarship to Oxford, where he'd studied medicine. From there he'd gone on to a residency at a major London hospital, culminating, after years of hard graft and more study, in a surgical position at the same hospital.

He'd then gone on to specialise in heart surgery, and by the age of forty had smugly assumed his life would continue in the same vein.

Of course, it hadn't. His children had grown rapidly and, with a thirst for independence, had left home at the first opportunity. Which, as it turned out, was just as well since Angela, his wife, had died before she could reach her fiftieth birthday.

And, as if that hadn't been enough of a blow, two years later, while preparing for surgery, he'd noticed a slight tremble in his left hand when he'd been scrubbing up.

Naturally, he'd dismissed it as probably nothing. The surgery had gone well, but two weeks later, he'd felt a slight weakness in his arm when he'd been lifting a half pint of beer at a retirement party for one of his colleagues.

Again, he'd dismissed it – but perhaps not quite so quickly, and with an added sense of unease and foreboding.

Over the next year, he monitored himself closely, noting down every little incident, every little unexplained tremble or weakness of limb. And, of course, he'd done his research.

He found that, way back in the mists of time, '*paralysis agitans*' had been known to physicians. But it was only in 1817 that James Parkinson had published 'An Essay in the Shaking Palsy', which best described the familiar characteristics of people suffering from this condition, detailing the resting tremor, abnormal posture and gait, paralysis and diminished muscle strength, and the way the disease progressed over time.

At first, Clement had not accepted it. There were other possible causes of his symptoms, after all. But one thing became immediately clear – he could not continue operating on people until he knew for sure.

And so he'd taken a few weeks of leave and, under a false name, booked himself into a little clinic he knew of in the south of France, where he'd ordered and overseen a series of tests he'd had run on himself. And when the results came in, he knew they effectively meant the end of his world.

Clement sighed heavily now as he took a large gulp of the claret. He was vaguely aware that, since he'd ceased operating, he had slowly grown used to becoming a social drinker – in a minor way. Fastidious about not touching alcohol for so many years, it made a nice change to be able to indulge now and then.

But, he thought now, with a snort of amusement, if people *did* begin to detect the odd whiff of alcohol on his breath, getting a reputation for being a bit of a lush could be a positive bonus. It would help explain the odd stumble or two, or a bout of clumsy shaking.

Now how was that for irony? A man who'd always been

careful not to imbibe too much being taken for a lush? Still, it was better than being thrown on the scrap heap.

Outside, the hail passed, but he continued to stare into the fire, his mind drifting back over the years.

The loss of so much in such a short space of time might have broken a lesser man. But Clement Ryder had never been the sort of man to let life kick him when he was down. So, after tendering his immediate resignation, he had looked around for something to fill his time.

He'd returned to Oxford, but had no desire to teach. Instead, he'd simply sat down one day and asked himself what he *did* – and *didn't* – want from life.

He certainly didn't want to leave the world of medicine altogether, but he was wise enough – and knew himself well enough – to know that becoming a GP or consultant at some hospital would soon drive him insane. Surgeons were lofty individuals with very healthy egos, and heart and brain surgeons, especially, were used, quite literally, to holding the balance of life and death in their hands.

As ugly and appalling as it sounded, he knew he couldn't bear to become something less than he'd once been. He also felt he needed a complete change of direction – the challenge of some-thing new, something that could grab his interest, and which would prevent him from slipping into self-pity or bitterness. In short, he needed another major and rewarding goal to aim for.

So, after some thought and investigation, he'd studied law, and retrained to become a coroner.

And it was the coroner's court that had now been his home, and his world, for the last few years. There, his sharp mind, medical knowledge, newly acquired legal training and natural, dogged determination to find out the truth had become vital assets.

He prided himself – with some justification – on just how quickly he'd come to grips with his new role. After barely a year, he was confident he could tell when witnesses were lying or fudging. He had developed a sixth sense for what the police were thinking and wanted from him – and formed his own opinion as to whether or not to give it to them. And while this latter trait might not have endeared him overmuch to the local constabulary, no one had any doubt that, when Dr Clement Ryder was presiding, a case wouldn't be allowed to get out of hand.

He was both thorough and competent, and didn't need to be told his name was both feared and respected by those that mattered – he simply took it for granted!

Which was why the thought of their pity, or glee, should his medical condition became known, was anathema to him. And why he was so determined to keep it a secret for as long as humanly possible. Besides, they'd be bound to try and oust him from his office, and he was damned if he was going to restart his life a third time. No, they'd have to drag him from the coroner's court by the scruff of his neck, kicking and screaming.

And it would take someone with far more guts than any of his clerks, or those namby-pambies at the Town Hall to do that!

With a grunt of amusement, Clement drank the last of his claret. He had court tomorrow and would be glad of a good night's sleep. He'd be damned if he'd let his illness affect his professionalism.

He got slowly to his feet – and at six-feet-one he had some way to rise from the chair. In the window he caught a glimpse of his reflection as he passed – his hair now fully silver/white, without even a hint of the dark brown it had once been. Rather watery grey eyes matched the rainwater running down the glass.

With some satisfaction, he noticed that his hand had stopped trembling. For now, anyway. With a sense of relief, he gave a mild, self-satisfied grunt.

Just as he suspected, there were still many good years left in him yet. Which was just as well. Only last year he'd had to steer a jury which had obviously been intent on bringing in an accidental verdict towards an open verdict instead, leaving the way clear for the police to pursue the case further and eventually arrest the guilty party for negligent manslaughter.

As a surgeon who had once had the power of life and death over people, Clement Ryder had no qualms about sitting in judgement over witnesses he knew to be guilty. *And* making sure they got their just deserts. On his watch, nobody got away with anything!

Naturally, such an attitude hadn't earned him many friends, but then Clement had never been a man who'd needed the approbation of others. Which was probably just as well, since his friends – real, true friends – were few.

The grandfather clock in the small hallway struck eleven as he tramped past it on his way to the stairs. Tomorrow the inquest on a schoolgirl who'd died after being struck by a car in St Giles would open.

Her grieving family would all be in attendance. It was going to be grim.

Chapter Four

Trudy's black eye had paled into a mere smudge of yellow when, five days after catching the bag-snatcher (and losing the collar to the golden-haired, blue-eyed boy, Rodney Broadstairs), she returned from the Records Office and saw that something had caused a stir in the main office.

Sidling over to Rodney, who was sitting at a desk, painstakingly typing out a report with his two forefingers, she whispered, 'What's up?'

She nodded at the portly, prosperous-looking man with a neat moustache who was being ushered very civilly into Jennings's private office by Sergeant O'Grady.

'Dunno,' Rodney said vaguely. 'Some bigwig not happy about some poison-pen letters or something.'

Trudy sighed.

Knowing that pumping him for further information would be useless, since Rodney tended to be able to deal with only one thing at a time, Trudy sauntered casually towards the DI's slightly open door, a file in hand for camouflage.

Much to her chagrin, after her recent stint of roughhousing with the purse-snatcher, DI Jennings had promptly assigned her to Records and filing work. Now, opening the filing-cabinet drawer nearest to Jennings's office (and pretending to search diligently for the right spot to deposit the file), she let her ears flap unashamedly.

Inside the office, Sir Marcus Deering, slightly red-faced and breathing a touch heavily, slapped a piece of paper down onto the desk and snapped, 'There!' He took a long, shaky breath. 'Just you read *that* and then tell me I'm overreacting,' he challenged.

Jennings, at not quite forty years of age, made vaguely appeasing sounds. A slender man with thinning fair hair and a nose just big enough to make him feel self-conscious about it, he shifted uncomfortably in his seat.

When Sir Marcus Deering had first telephoned to say he would be calling in and expected to see someone senior, he'd known he'd have to be careful. Naturally, his superiors would expect him to treat the man with kid gloves. The businessman's charitable donations to many local good causes (including the police widows and orphans fund) were very well known. As was the fact that he sat on several boards where his influence spread further than just the Town Hall.

Also, Jennings had no doubt at all that he was a fellow Mason.

Mindful of all this, he cleared his throat carefully and read the green-inked missive in front of him.

YOU HAVE FAILED TO DO THE RIGHT THING. YOU WERE WARNED THAT YOU ONLY HAD ONE MORE CHANCE. NOW YOUR SON WILL DIE. HE WILL DIE AT

EXACTLY TWELVE NOON TOMORROW. PERHAPS THEN YOU WILL DO THE RIGHT THING.

Over his right shoulder, Sergeant O'Grady gave a small sigh. A slightly chubby man with a sandy quiff that tended to flop over his forehead, the Sergeant, at forty-one, had long since given up on any hopes of gaining further promotion. Not that it worried him much. He'd been at the station for years and had it running just as he liked it.

Now he pursed his lips. When the Inspector had told him a local dignitary had been receiving poison-pen letters he hadn't been expecting this. The usual run-of-the-mill stuff tended to accuse the recipients of sexual misbehaviour. More rarely, they included death threats – but nothing this precise. In fact, to Mike O'Grady's mind, there was something uncannily odd about the specific threat. What kind of madman actually told you when he intended to strike?

'I can see that you would find this very distressing, sir,' DI Jennings began diplomatically. 'But first, let me assure you that nearly all anonymous letters are the work of cranks, and any threats made in them are very seldom carried out. What's more, they're usually written by women (rather than men) who either have delusions of grandeur or whopping great inferiority complexes. On the whole, they tend to be a rather sorry, pathetic bunch.'

Sir Marcus, who was nervously fiddling with his hat – a nice homburg in dark grey – snorted impatiently. 'Do you think I'm not aware of all that, man? That's why, when I first started getting these blasted things, I just ignored them. Threw the first one in the bin, where it belonged. But when they kept on coming, all saying the same blessed thing, I started saving them – just in case. But this is the first one that's threatened my son, damn it! That's going too far.'

Jennings slowly sat up a little straighter in his chair. 'You've had others, you say, sir? I don't suppose you brought . . .' He broke off as Sir Marcus grunted and pulled a few sheets of paper from his pocket.

'Yes. Here, read them. All identical, as you can see, except for these last two.'

'Hmmm . . . yes. I can see why they'd make you feel uneasy, Sir Marcus,' the DI conceded. 'Do you have any idea who might have sent them?'

'Not a clue,' Sir Marcus shot back shortly. 'And don't think I haven't wondered. This last month or so, I've done little else.'

'Anybody you had cause to sack recently?' Jennings persisted. 'You're bound to have a disgruntled employee or two in the offing, so to speak?'

'Bound to,' Sir Marcus said offhandedly. 'But I doubt it would run to this, do you?'

Jennings sighed. 'Perhaps not, sir,' he agreed, although secretly he wasn't so sure. Folk did odd things when they got their gander up. 'What about your domestic staff, sir?'

'No, no. Been with me years, all of them,' the millionaire said dismissively. 'Well, the cook and my butler, certainly. The housemaids seem to come and go . . . leave all that sort of thing to my wife.'

'Hmmm. And do you, er . . .' Jennings paused, trying to find a tactful way to put the next question. 'Do you have any idea what our anonymous letter writer means when they urge you to do the right thing?'

Sir Marcus wavered. Again, he thought about the fire. And

again he dismissed it. It was so long ago now, and it definitely hadn't been his fault. 'Er, no. That's what's so frustrating. Why can't this bloody person just say what they mean in straightforward language? Usually these anonymous letters have no trouble doing that, do they?'

And Jennings was forced to agree that Sir Marcus had a point. Your run-of-the-mill nasty letter usually spelt out, in very colourful language indeed sometimes, exactly what was on the writer's mind.

'It's this blasted threat to Anthony that's really thrown me,' Sir Marcus admitted with a heavy sigh. 'The boy just laughs it off, of course, but I'm not so sure.' He leaned forward slightly in his chair and fixed the Inspector with a fierce eye. 'Isn't it the job of the police to protect citizens when their lives are being threatened?'

And there it was, Jennings thought, biting back a groan. Ever since he'd read the letter, he'd just known this would be coming. And of course there was no getting around it. He'd have to waste a certain number of man hours on it.

'Yes, sir, of course it is,' he said soothingly. 'And you can be assured that, come noon tomorrow, Sergeant O'Grady here will be at your house, and will have your son under observation at all times.'

'Yes, well . . . so I should jolly well hope,' Sir Marcus said, a little more mollified now as he leant back in his chair. 'I've told Anthony I want him in the house, and although he kicked up a bit of a fuss about it, he's agreed. Mind you, he says he can take care of himself, and I dare say he can, but, well, when you're dealing with someone a bit cracked, as this blasted idiot obviously is, you never can tell, can you? I dare say Anthony could acquit himself well if it came to a brawl or a bout of fisticuffs,' his father boasted proudly, 'but what if the maniac has a knife? Or worse, a gun?'

'I think that's highly unlikely, Sir Marcus,' Jennings reassured him promptly. But secretly, he had to wonder. A lot of men had brought their service revolvers back with them from the war. They weren't supposed to, of course, but they did. So it wasn't beyond the realms of possibility that the letter writer had the wherewithal to follow up on his threat to kill Sir Marcus's son.

'That's as may be. But until we find out who's been writing these damn letters, how can we be sure?' Sir Marcus demanded fretfully. 'It may well turn out to be some demented old woman who gets a kick out of scaring people, or some weedy little clerk in one of my back offices with a Napoleon complex or bearing a grudge of some kind. But then again it might not! Damn it, man, I can't go around the rest of my life looking over my shoulder!'

'No, sir, of course you can't,' Jennings said, and not without genuine sympathy for his point of view. 'And we'll definitely look into it for you. If you could just provide us with a list of anybody you think might, even by the remotest chance, have some sort of grudge against you or your family, sir?'

The businessman nodded glumly and rose ponderously to his feet. 'Very well, I'll do that. And you'll be at the house tomorrow?' he demanded, drawing out one of his personal visiting cards and placing it on the desk. 'This is the address.'

'Yes, sir, my Sergeant and another constable will be there bright and early,' Jennings promised. 'I take it your son lives with you?'

'At the moment. He has a flat in London, of course, but he's still up with us for Christmas. He likes to attend the Boxing Day hunt,' the older man said, a fond glint coming to his eye as he talked about his son and heir. 'So he always stays on for another couple of weeks to enjoy the gallops. Boy always was horse-mad, and rides every day he's with us.'

Jennings, not one whit interested, nodded vaguely. 'I see, sir. Well, leave it with us. Sergeant, show Sir Marcus out.'

Outside, Trudy stepped smartly away from the filing cabinet and nonchalantly moved back towards a free desk.

Sergeant O'Grady shot her a quick look, lips twitching, as he ushered their visitor out.

Once back in with the DI, he sighed in sympathy. 'It's a bit of a pig, sir, and no mistake,' he said flatly. 'But there's nothing much we can do for him, of course. Sooner or later our letter-writing friend will just get bored and move on to some other target. And as for the chances of anything funny happening tomorrow bang on noon . . .' O'Grady snorted. 'Well, that's about on a par with pigs being seen flying over Brize Norton airbase.'

'No good telling Sir Marcus that, though,' Jennings said with a brief smile. 'And I don't mind telling you, that threat to his son was a bit odd. Naming a specific date and time like that.'

'Yes,' O'Grady agreed uncertainly. 'It's not the usual run-of-the-mill thing, I'll grant you.' And he wondered if his superior had picked up on the slight hesitation when he'd asked Sir Marcus if he had any idea what the letter writer meant by 'doing the right thing'. Because the Sergeant was sure Sir Marcus had definitely looked a bit shifty-eyed then. And if the millionaire didn't have a skeleton or two in his cupboard, he'd eat his hat. The rich, in his experience, always had something they'd prefer to keep quiet about.

'Well, go and hold their hands tomorrow anyway,' Jennings ordered briskly. 'And although I agree that the chances of anything coming of it are virtually nil, take a strapping lad with you just in case. Broadstairs, perhaps. He's handy to have in a scrap.'

'Sir.'

'Oh, and Sergeant . . .'

'Sir?'

'When you go tomorrow, take WPC Loveday with you, will you? All week long she's been giving me long-suffering looks. It's beginning to get on my nerves. She can help question the housemaids or something. They won't know anything, naturally, so it won't matter if she cocks it up.'

O'Grady grinned. 'Good idea, sir. It'll be good practice for her too – honing her questioning skills.'

Jennings shrugged indifferently.

But as he closed the door behind him, Mike O'Grady didn't think it was at all likely that WPC Trudy Loveday would cock anything up. She was a bright enough girl and, being pretty and personable as well, would probably have Sir Marcus's domestic staff quickly eating out of her hand.

Chapter Five

The next morning, Mavis McGillicuddy dunked a soldier into her boiled egg and glanced at the kitchen clock. She had an hour yet before she had to get her granddaughter up for school, which was just as well, since, at ten years old, Marie was fast getting to the stage where her endearingly childish eagerness to please was beginning to transform into something more mutinous.

Not that Mavis minded all the ups and downs that came with child rearing, even at her age. Most women in their early sixties might have thought all that was behind them now, but Mavis was very much aware that without her son and his daughter living with her, she'd be just one more lonely widow.

And she'd much rather be rushed off her feet or dealing with a childish tantrum than sitting twiddling her thumbs.

On the wireless the Prime Minister, Harold Macmillan, was saying something dreary, as he always seemed to be doing, and she was half-tempted to get up and fiddle with the dial to see if she could find something more cheerful to listen to. But nowadays the radio stations seemed to play nothing but all this modern music the youngsters were going for. It was all Be-bop-a-lula this, or Poison Ivy that. And it was getting harder and harder for her to find the music she liked – recordings of the Glenn Miller Band, say, or a nice bit of Vera Lynn.

She looked up as the kitchen door opened and her only child swept in. 'Morning, Mum. Seen my boots anywhere – the ones with the toe-caps? I'm uprooting some old apple trees today, and I don't want . . . oh, I see them.'

The sight of her son, Jonathan, always brought a smile to Mavis's face. At just turned thirty, he was still a handsome lad and looked far younger than his years. He'd inherited his thick, wavy blond hair from her and striking hazel-green eyes from his father. At nearly six feet tall, his work as a landscape gardener kept him fit and lean.

As she fondly watched him pulling on his work boots, she sipped her tea in contentment. Although life had been hard for Mavis in her early years (and during the war, naturally), she had to admit she'd had *some* luck in her life, and never ceased to be thankful for it. Outside the window of their modest, tiny, terraced house, the suburb of Cowley was going about its busy business, with the majority of the men in the neighbourhood flocking into the car works. But, thanks to help from Jonathan's father, Mavis actually owned the little house they lived in, and was the only one in their street not to be renting. She had been able to afford to send Jonathan to the local grammar school, which in turn had led to his being able to do a bit better for himself than his peers, first becoming apprentice to the head gardener at St Edmund Hall, before striking out on his own and setting up his own little business.

Yes, in many ways, Mavis knew, she had been lucky.

'Marie still in bed?' her son asked now, pouring out a mug of tea for himself and peering through the window. The last few days had been wet and relatively mild – perfect for grubbing up stubborn tree roots.

'Yes. She's not happy to be going back to school after the Christmas holidays, though,' Mavis said with a smile. 'So I suspect I'll have a bit of a job getting her up in time. But don't you worry about it, son – I'll not be having any of her tantrums. She'll soon settle down again.'

Absently, Jonathan walked behind her chair and kissed the top of her head. 'Thanks for looking after her, Mum. Don't know what we'd have done without you.'

Jonathan said this often, more out of habit than anything, although he was vaguely aware that what he said was perfectly true.

He'd had to marry young, at just twenty, when the girl he'd been going steady with had fallen pregnant, and in truth, he'd never felt really happy about it – something that had always made him feel guilty. But there was no point in denying he'd felt trapped and a little resentful, and when his daughter had been born seven months later, he'd felt vaguely cheated. He'd expected – and wanted – a boy. Which had only increased his sense of guilt further.

But then, just three years after Marie was born, Jenny had been killed in a train crash, along with four others. She'd been on her way to Banbury to see about a part-time job, in the hopes they'd be able to afford to move out of his mother's house and find a place of their own.

Obviously, that had never happened. So, at the age of just

twenty-four, Jonathan McGillicuddy had become a very eligible young widower with a little girl to look after, and had quickly found that his unexpected freedom wasn't as wonderful as he might have imagined. He'd missed Jenny terribly. And far from being an unwanted child, his daughter had come to mean the world to him. Luckily, his mum, long since widowed herself, had been more than happy to step into the breach.

Now Marie called her 'mum' and seemed to have no memories of Jenny at all.

His mother set about buttering some toast for him and then made sandwiches for his packed lunch. Slightly plump, she still bustled about with energy, but she must, Jonathan mused, be beginning to feel her age a little bit. And once more, he felt a vague sense of guilt wash over him. Was it fair to keep on expecting her to look after his daughter and effectively 'keep house' for him? Perhaps it was time he thought about marrying again? But even as he thought it, he shied violently away from the idea.

He'd only had two serious relationships with women in his life, and both had ended in utter disaster. First Jenny and then . . . But no, he wouldn't think of *her*. He couldn't. It had taken years for the nightmares to stop, and sometimes they plagued him still, wrenching him out of sleep, sweating and shaking, with his heart pounding.

Sometimes, he wondered if he was actually cursed.

His own 'natural' father had died before he'd even got the chance to know him. Everyone, it seemed, left him. And what if something happened to his mum? Or to Marie?

He shuddered and, telling himself not to be so maudlin – or stupid – quickly ate his toast and threw on his mackintosh.

Everything would be fine. It had been for some time now. He mustn't think about that other time in his life, when it had seemed he must be going crazy. When the danger had been so sharp and acrid he could almost taste it. No, that part of his life was over, and it was never coming back. It couldn't. It was all dead and done and finished with.

Once again he absently kissed his mother on top of her head as she sat sipping her tea. 'Bye, Mum. See you about four,' he added cheerfully. 'It's no use trying to work in a garden after dark.' That was one of the few advantages of winter for a gardener – a shorter working day.

He was whistling slightly as he stepped out onto the wet path and closed the door behind him. And as he walked to the end of the street and the group of lock-up garages where he kept his old van, full of his gardening tools, he didn't notice the silent, watchful figure making careful note of his movements.

And it probably wouldn't have made much difference if he had.

Chapter Six

Trudy felt her jaw fall open as she looked at the house on the outskirts of Hampton Poyle, a pretty little village set deep in farming country. Large, built of Cotswold stone and uncompromisingly square in the Georgian manner, it stood in manicured grounds, looking effortlessly elegant and substantial.

'How the other half lives, eh?' Rodney Broadstairs said from the front passenger seat of the Panda car. Behind the wheel, Sergeant O'Grady smiled grimly.

'Better watch your Ps and Qs here, sonny,' he advised him flatly. 'Right, I dare say the son of the house is out on his bleeding horse, but he's promised his father he'll be back by ten. Rod, you stick with him like glue – especially come twelve o'clock. Trudy, I want you to make your way to the kitchen and talk to the staff. Pick up on any gossip you can about the family. We're not just interested in who wrote the letters – there has to be a reason Sir Marcus and this family were targeted, and we need to find out what that is. Got it?'

'Yes, Sarge,' Trudy said happily.

Finally, she was being allowed to get hands-on in a real case!

Jonathan McGillicuddy drove through the large village of Kidlington and parked his van under the bare branches of a large beech tree. The grounds he was currently working in belonged to a Victorian pile overlooking the Oxford canal, but the new owners were in Barbados, wintering in their villa there. Having only recently purchased the house, they had left him detailed plans for the changes they wanted made in the large garden, which included grubbing up the old orchard and creating a large pond there instead.

He began unloading the van, carrying a large pickaxe and several different types of saws through an overgrown herb garden towards the rear of the property and then into the orchard at the far perimeter. As he walked, he hummed the latest Ricky Valance song softly under his breath.

Having nobody living up at the house was a mixed blessing. On the one hand, he didn't have his clients looking over his shoulder every moment of the day to make sure he wasn't slacking, or to keep changing their minds about what they wanted done. But it also meant he couldn't just pop in to use their downstairs loo, or scrounge in the kitchen on a cold day for a warming cup of tea or bowl of soup.

He glanced at his watch as he unloaded the last of his gear by the first of several gnarled and mostly disease-ridden apple trees, so old even their topmost branches bent down far enough to almost touch the ground.

It was just gone nine.

The young lad he sometimes hired as casual labour to help

him out with the heavy work, Robby Dix, had another job on today, but Jonathan didn't really mind. He quite liked working alone.

As Jonathan set to work sawing off a tree limb, the figure that had noted his movements back in Cowley moved stealthily around the outskirts of the walled kitchen garden. And from the dark depths of the arched opening in one side of it, carefully peered out into the old orchard.

It was a damp day, the grass was long and wet, and the beginnings of a vague fog were forming. Although the house had neighbours on either side, the gardens were large and empty, and even the street outside was silent. No one was out and about on such a damp and dreary day – not even a dog walker.

Which was a definite bonus.

The figure withdrew and retreated to the even darker shadow cast by an old yew tree, which had been planted in one particularly obscure corner of the grounds. The patient voyeur now had less than three hours to wait. Not that he needed to actually wait until noon. It hardly mattered, after all, did it? He smiled grimly. *But if a thing was worth doing, it was worth doing well.*

Trudy ate her final morsel of Dundee cake and smiled at the cook. 'Lovely, Mrs Rogers, but I couldn't eat another bite.' She smiled, patting her flat stomach. She'd spent the last two hours, as Sergeant O'Grady had wanted, chatting to the staff and making friends with the housemaids, Milly and Phyllis ('call me Phil'). Both girls were only a year or so older than her, and far more interested in grilling her about what it was like to be a police officer than in gossiping about the family. Nevertheless, Trudy had persisted, and now thought she probably knew as much about Sir Marcus Deering and how his household was run as the man himself.

She knew, for instance, that Lady Deering had a bit of a gambling habit she was very careful to keep from her husband. She knew that the son, Anthony, was the apple of both his parents' eyes, and could do no wrong in their opinion; but both Milly and Phil said they had to keep an eye on him, otherwise he'd take advantage, if they let him. A good-looking man, apparently, but he tended to think his wealth and charm entitled him to take liberties.

Trudy had smiled and said she'd found most men to be the same.

This had led on to talk about Sir Marcus himself, who tended to be more pompous than promiscuous. 'He's so full of himself sometimes,' Milly had complained. 'I reckon it's because he's not a proper "Sir" at all. He only got his title for being one of them industrial barons, or whatever. He feels it, see. Not being a proper toff, I mean. It makes him on edge whenever they entertain. Always thinking the proper gentry are looking down on him, when half of them couldn't care tuppence.'

'But if they *are* miffed or like to look down on him, it's only because they're jealous he's got pots more money than they have,' Phil had agreed, displaying surprising insight into how the minds of the upper classes truly worked.

All of which had proved very interesting, of course, Trudy acknowledged as she checked through her notes, but she couldn't imagine what use all of this would be to the Sergeant.

Still, that wasn't for a humble WPC to say.

'That's the precious son and heir coming now,' Phyllis said, turning to crane her neck to peer out of the kitchen window, and earning a dark look from the much more circumspect Mrs Rogers. 'Well, I can hear his horse,' Phyllis insisted with a giggle.

Trudy, not wanting to miss the chance of being allowed to assess Sir Marcus's son with her own eyes, got quickly to her feet. 'Well, I think that'll be all for now,' she added politely. 'Thank you for your time.'

'I do hope you find that nasty poison pen soon,' the cook said anxiously.

Although the servants had already suspected that something was upsetting their employer – they'd all noticed he'd been particularly edgy of late – all of them had seemed genuinely shocked by the news that he'd been receiving death threats, directed at his son. Unfortunately, none of them had any idea of who could be behind it all. Likewise, they'd all professed ignorance about any possible dark misdeeds in Sir Marcus's past that might account for someone wanting revenge now.

It had all been rather discouraging, but Trudy's pace quickened with excitement as she stepped out of the kitchen and made her way outside.

It was half past eleven and, in the stable block situated at the back of the house, she watched as Rodney Broadstairs approached the young man dismounting from a lovely black hunter.

Trudy, a city girl through and through, knew nothing about horseflesh, but she instinctively recognised quality when she saw it. And it occurred to her, as Anthony Deering swept off his riding helmet and handed the reins to the stable girl who had stepped up to take them, that it wasn't only the horseflesh on display that was worth looking at.

As she got nearer, she saw that the son of the house was about the same height as she was, with thick brown hair and large, hazel-green eyes. Dressed in jodhpurs and a dark-green hacking jacket, he looked the epitome of an upper-class gent at play.

His eyes swept over her warmly, reminding her of Phyllis's warning. 'Let him near your bottom, and he'd as likely as not try to pinch it.'

Trudy smiled now as she contemplated how nice it would be to arrest this handsome young toff for assaulting a police officer if he was ever rash enough to try and pinch *her* derrière!

'Well, things are looking up, I must say,' Anthony Deering said, smiling into her eyes. 'And are you going to protect me from Dad's nasty letter writer too?'

'No, sir.' It was Rodney who spoke up first, his eyes shooting daggers at Trudy. 'WPC Loveday is just about to go inside and talk to your mother, sir.'

Trudy, taking the hint, nodded briskly and continued round to the back of the house, where she knew Sergeant O'Grady was with the Deerings in the large sunroom.

It was ten minutes before noon.

The sunroom was accessed by a pair of French doors with an aspect on the south-facing side of the house, and as she tapped on a glass pane and was bid to enter, she couldn't help but wonder what Anthony Deering must be thinking now.

And again, she glanced at her watch.

Just eight minutes to go.

Even though the young man's swagger and joking manner had suggested he really didn't take the threat seriously – as, indeed, most of them didn't – he must still, nevertheless, feel just a little trepidation, surely? Knowing that someone, somewhere, had vowed to kill you when the hands of the clock both stood straight up would be enough to make anyone feel a cold chill up their spine.

In some respects, the situation reminded her a little bit of the film *High Noon*. With herself, the Sergeant and Rodney keeping an anxious eye on the clock while waiting for something explosive to happen. Except that Anthony Deering was no Gary Cooper! And he certainly wasn't expected to face any gunmen alone.

Even so, she still maintained he wouldn't have been human if he didn't feel a little bit scared. And she knew for a fact that his parents definitely had the wind up for, inside the sunroom, Lady Deering, a tall, sparse woman with a rather long face, paced restlessly up and down, while her husband pretended to read the newspaper. Sergeant O'Grady glanced at her as she came in, smiled briefly, and continued to survey the expanse of fields outside the house.

Trudy glanced at her watch once again – she couldn't help it. Barely five minutes to go now.

Was it really possible that someone was outside, watching them, waiting to make their move? That, despite the police presence, they had figured out some fantastic way to end Anthony Deering's life right under their noses? Perhaps by setting up a booby trap of some kind? Or might they have simply decided that brute force was by far the easiest way, and would simply come in, guns blazing?

The thought of the possible carnage that would result if such an unlikely scenario came to pass made her feel sick, and she only hoped the women in the kitchen would have the good sense to stay hidden if anything bad did happen.

But, of course, nobody really believed it would. DI Jennings, the Sarge and even that plank, PC Broadstairs, were all sure it was nothing but a mare's nest. Which was reassuring, Trudy supposed. Even so, she knew her nerves weren't the only ones being stretched.

Outside the door, she heard Rodney Broadstairs' voice, and that of Anthony Deering answering him. In the next moment, both men stepped into the room.

Sir Marcus looked up from his paper and nodded. 'Sit next to me, Anthony, will you? I've saved you the crossword puzzle.' And he pulled out a section of the paper and handed it, along with a pen, to his son, who accepted both offerings, indulging him.

'Fine,' he said briskly, casting his father a wide smile. 'But at five past twelve I'm off to the kitchen for lunch, and then I'm going to Oxford, to catch a matinee at the cinema.'

Sir Marcus frowned. 'I wish you wouldn't, son.'

'Yes, why can't you stay here? At least for the rest of the day,' his mother insisted nervously.

Anthony sighed theatrically. He'd changed out of his riding clothes and now wore a tweed jacket with dark-grey flannel trousers. 'Oh, come on! This lunatic threatened to bump me off at twelve noon. Once we've got past that, I'll be fine. After all, why go to the trouble of specifying a time so precisely and then not stick to it? It doesn't make sense. Either something will happen at twelve o'clock, or it never will.'

'That's hardly guaranteed,' Sir Marcus muttered, unconvinced by such spurious logic.

'Nothing in life's guaranteed, as you well know,' his son shot back pithily. 'Come on, old fella, you can't expect me to hang around the old homestead forever,' he joshed his father. 'Buck up – we all know this is just some sad, silly person giving us the runaround. Nothing's going to happen!'

Sir Marcus sighed and glanced at the clock on the wall. Four minutes to noon.

Jonathan McGillicuddy paused, stretched, and put his palms in the middle of his aching back. Another hour and he'd take a break and go back to the van for his sandwiches and flask of tea.

He picked up a handsaw and bent down to tackle a particularly knotty and thick branch close to the ground. Despite the damp chill of the day, he'd managed to work up quite a sweat.

He didn't hear footsteps approaching him from behind, as the harsh scraping noise of the saw, and the soft, damp grass smothering the sound of booted feet, served to keep him in ignorance of the figure creeping up on him.

Away to his left, Jonathan McGillicuddy heard the mellow tones of the bell of the village church begin to strike twelve.

It was the last thing he ever heard.

Lady Deering began to laugh. Out in the hall, the grandfather clock chimed the last of the twelve strikes. The silence after the last one seemed profound.

Trudy felt like laughing too. Had she ever seriously imagined that some madman would burst in, spraying gunfire? Now she felt vaguely ashamed of her fears.

Anthony Deering looked up from his nearly completed crossword puzzle and grinned at his mother. 'Feeling better now?' he asked.

'Much, darling,' Martha agreed.

'See, Dad . . .' The young man turned to his father. 'I told you nothing would happen!'

It was six o'clock and fully dark before Mavis McGillicuddy began to really worry. It wasn't like Jonathan to work this late. It had been fully dark for nearly two hours. Where on earth could he be?

At nine o'clock she nipped next door and asked her neighbour if she wouldn't mind sitting with Marie for a while. The little girl had gone reluctantly to bed, but Mavis feared she might be naughty enough to get up, claiming she wanted a drink of water, and she didn't want her to find the house empty.

Marie, too, had expected her father to be home in time to read her their usual bedtime story, and Mavis wasn't sure her granddaughter had believed her lies about his arranging to meet with some friends and have a drink with them at the local pub.

The desk sergeant at the police station listened patiently to Mavis's report, then told her that her son, in all likelihood, probably really *was* currently drinking in some pub somewhere, just as she'd told his daughter, and that it was far too early to panic just yet. Only after Mavis had vehemently insisted it was something he'd never done before did he promise to check there had been no road-traffic accidents reported, involving Jonathan's van.

And more to get rid of her than anything else, he then rang around the local hospitals to see if anyone of Jonathan's description had been brought in.

No such reports had been made.

Eventually, knowing she had to get back home, since she couldn't expect her neighbour to sit in her house all night, Mavis forced the Sergeant to promise that, first thing in the morning, he'd send a constable round to the garden where her son was currently working. Just to check all was well there.

On nearing her house, her footsteps quickened with hope. Surely she'd find that Jonathan had come home while she'd been out? He'd be full of sheepish apologies on finding their neighbour in residence in the sitting room, and she would tell him off roundly.

But when she got there, there was still no sign of him.

Not surprisingly, Mavis didn't sleep a wink that night.

Mavis McGillicuddy was up with the dawn, and was sitting dry-eyed and hopeless in the kitchen, her hands feeling as cold as ice even though they were wrapped around a hot cup of tea, when she heard the knocking on her door.

She dragged herself to her feet and out into the hall. Through the frosted glass in the front door she could make out a large, ominous shape. When she opened it, it was to find a policeman looking back at her solemnly.

It was only then that she began to cry.

Sir Marcus Deering rose that morning with a cheerful whistle on his lips and ate a hearty breakfast. The whole mood in the house was jubilant now, and faintly shamefaced, as if acknowledging they had been silly ever to have worried.

Anthony was once more out on his beloved horse, since he was due back in London soon and was determined to make the most of a dry, if cold, day.

By nine-thirty Sir Marcus was seated behind the desk in his study, reading the morning post. There had been no green-inked missive to worry him, and if any more came, he would simply toss them, unread, into the bin. The poison pen had shot his arrow and missed by a mile. And never again would Sir Marcus be foolish enough to be conned into worrying about 'doing the right thing'.

When the telephone on his desk rang he reached for it absently. He heard his secretary telling him there was a woman on the line who insisted on speaking to him but wouldn't give her name.

'Oh?' Marcus frowned. 'That's odd.' His daytime calls were invariably with other businessmen or their secretaries – none of whom was unwilling to identify themselves. 'Well, put her through.'

'Yes, sir,' his secretary said. There was a short delay, a beep, and then he heard a tentative, tearful voice.

It took a moment for him to realise who it was on the other end of the line, and when he did so, his first instinct was to look furtively at the closed door of his study. 'I told you never to call me here,' he hissed angrily into the receiver, getting automatically to his feet. 'If my wife were to . . .'

But the voice frantically overrode him – something that had never happened before. And as he finally took in what was being said, all the anger washed out of him, along with the colour in his face, leaving him sitting white and shaken in his chair and fighting the urge to be sick.

Chapter Seven

At St Aldates police station, DI Jennings looked gravely at the faces turned towards him.

'Let me repeat, this is a murder investigation. Sometime yesterday, somebody brutally killed Jonathan McGillicuddy by bashing him over the head with his own spade.'

He went on to give details of the deceased, his work as a gardener in a house where the owners were absent, his failure to return home and the missing person's report filed on him by his mother as a result. He then went on to relate the discovery of his body in the morning by the PC sent from Kidlington, in response to the request from the desk sergeant on duty at Cowley police station.

'He subsequently found the victim dead in the orchard,' DI Jennings concluded heavily. 'He'd clearly been working clearing out the old trees, and our police surgeon reckons he'd been dead at least twelve hours – possibly fifteen. Probably longer, but he can't be sure. He's also given a preliminary cause of death as blunt-force trauma to the head – but again he won't sign off on it until after the autopsy.'

Trudy Loveday, along with the others, listened to all this dry-mouthed. It wasn't often that they had a murder case to deal with, and such a cold-blooded, savage attack was very unusual. Around her, everyone else was also tense and alert, and listening intently.

That poor man's mother, she thought, swallowing hard.

'The lad who sometimes worked with him as casual labour has been traced, but he confirmed he wasn't working that day with Mr McGillicuddy, but at a warehouse in Bicester instead. His alibi has since been confirmed. According to Mrs McGillicuddy, her son had no enemies, wasn't a drinker or troublemaker, and had always been a responsible, respectable lad. Widowed young, with a little girl to take care of, he'd lived with his mother all his life. And he's certainly not known to us,' the DI confirmed heavily. 'But it's early days yet. Somebody had a reason to kill this man. And that's where we need to start. Since the killer used the victim's own spade, one theory is that the murder was unpremeditated. Our MO confirms the initial and primary wound was to the back of the head, with several more blows as he lay prone on the ground. Now I want you to sort yourselves into teams and find out all you can about our victim. His mother says she knows of no female friends.' The DI paused and smiled at this. 'But that doesn't mean they didn't exist – only that her son played his romantic cards close to his chest.'

The DI shrugged. 'Then we need to find out all about his finances. He was basically a gardener for hire, so his over-heads should have been low and his income easily traceable.

Is it? Does he have debts? Maybe he's a bit of a gambler? Find out.

'Then there's the mother. Yes, I know, on the face of it she's an unlikely suspect. But families can be tricky things. We need to a do a house-to-house around the area where he was killed. Unfortunately, according to the PC who found the body, the house and grounds are large and relatively private. Plus, yesterday was a damp and cold day, and it's doubtful many people would have been out and about, but we need to find any that were. Did they notice the victim's van and, more importantly, were any other vehicles seen in the lane that day. If so, we need to trace the owners of those cars and speak to them. Did anyone hear loud or raised voices, or notice any strangers lurking about? We need to interview those who were in the vicinity – the postman, any tradesmen or callers. Was it rent week, or the day the man came around collecting the pools? We need to know anything and everything about that lane and what went on in it yesterday.'

'Sir . . .' A young PC shuffled up and handed him a message from the desk sergeant. He read it briefly, lips thinning slightly in irritation, then nodded at the Sergeant. 'O'Grady, carry on. I'll be back shortly.'

'Sir.'

But DI Jennings wasn't back for quite some time.

When he'd got the message that Sir Marcus Deering was in the station and was demanding to speak to him, DI Jennings had intended to deal with him quickly and shortly. While he was willing to pander to his superiors' insistence that the man be treated with respect when times were slow, he had no time to hold the entrepreneur's hand when he had a vicious murder inquiry just getting underway. Especially since the threats in the anonymous letters had proved to be so much nonsense.

But when he went into his office the businessman's first words floored him utterly.

Sir Marcus, sitting slumped in the chair in front of his desk, looked visibly haggard, and his hands were shaking uncontrollably.

'We were wrong, Inspector. They did kill my son, after all,' he said, his voice thick with emotion.

DI Jennings blinked and sat down heavily in his chair. Another murder inquiry, coming so fast on the heels of the McGillicuddy case? His first thought was that he'd need much more manpower.

'How did it happen?' he demanded at once. 'I was told nothing happened yesterday. When was Mr Deering attacked? Are you sure—'

'My son Anthony is fine.' Sir Marcus interrupted the barrage of questions flatly, leaving the Inspector slack-jawed and stupefied into silence. The older man stared down at his hands, unable to meet the DI's gaze. 'Fact is, er, Jennings, that in my younger days, well . . . I was rather fond of a young girl, a local girl, very pretty and perfectly respectable, but a bit . . . er . . . below us on the social scale, I suppose you'd say. A decent girl, and all that . . . but well, when she fell pregnant, my father . . . Well, let's just say my father and hers came to an arrangement . . .'

'I see, sir,' DI Jennings said briskly. Although he felt vaguely shocked and a little embarrassed by such revelations, it was not his place to judge. 'And this . . . er . . . local girl, I take it she had a baby boy?'

'Yes. He's . . . was . . . would have been thirty years old now.'

DI Jennings slowly felt a cold chill begin to creep up his spine. 'This girl, sir. Your son . . .?'

'His name is . . . *was* . . . Jonathan McGillicuddy,' Sir Marcus said flatly. 'His mother's name is Mavis. Naturally, he kept his mother's name. I believe her neighbours all think McGillicuddy is her married name. Er . . . less gossip that way.'

'I see,' DI Jennings said heavily. 'And did the lad, er, know who you were?' he asked delicately.

'Oh, no,' Sir Marcus said, sounding shocked. 'Mavis always told the lad his father died in an accident before they could get married. My father insisted on that.'

'I see,' Jennings said – and did too. No doubt Mavis McGillicuddy had received a small annuity to pay for the raising of her child only on the strict understanding that neither she nor the child would do or say anything to embarrass the Deering family.

'Mavis rang me this morning and told me . . . told me . . .' Sir Marcus began, but then couldn't get the words out.

'Yes, sir,' the DI said grimly. 'I know what she told you.'

'My . . . son. Jonathan.' The businessman finally raised his head from his inspection of his hands and looked the policeman squarely in the eye. 'He died at twelve noon yesterday, didn't he?' Sir Marcus asked bleakly.

'We don't know that, Sir Marcus,' Jennings admitted levelly. But he knew it would fit with the timeframe supplied by the police surgeon.

Sir Marcus gulped and raised his hands to his head, covering his eyes with his palms. 'When nothing happened yesterday, we were all so relieved. I thought the nightmare was over, but it's not. It's just beginning, isn't it?' he asked, his voice muffled by his fingers and despair. 'Whoever wrote that letter said they'd kill my son, and they did.'

DI Jennings opened his mouth, but didn't know quite what to say. That they had been protecting the wrong son at twelve noon yesterday was all too clear – and he could imagine the reaction of his superiors when this came to light. And, no doubt, if Sir Marcus had come clean right from the beginning about having a second son, he might not now be lying dead in the county morgue. But that cruel fact hardly needed saying out loud.

'You have to catch him,' Sir Marcus said finally. 'You have to stop him. Or Anthony . . .' He broke off and shrugged helplessly, not even daring to put the horrible thought into actual words. Not that he'd needed to, of course, for the DI had already reasoned it out for himself.

If the poison pen could kill once, they could kill again.

'Sir Marcus, I ask you again. Do you really have no idea what this person wants? What exactly is this "right thing" they want you to do?'

Sir Marcus shook his head. He was a pitiful sight now. Unshaven, pale and trembling, he was a far cry from the bustling, self-important businessman the DI had first met just a week ago. 'I don't know!' he wailed. 'Unless . . . there's only one thing I can think of, but it doesn't make sense. It truly doesn't.'

'I need to know anything that might be relevant, Sir Marcus,' Inspector Jennings insisted gravely.

And so the shattered man told him all about the fire.

Chapter Eight

Beatrice Fleet-Wright bit neatly into a thin slice of toast topped with a thin layer of Oxford marmalade, and reached for the copy of the local paper. Her husband was already reading *The Times*, while Rex, her son, ate without benefit of the written word, as was his custom.

Beatrice was just two years short of her fiftieth birthday, though if that landmark event loomed large in her life, you couldn't tell it by looking at her. Her short, dark hair was as well groomed as ever, and if hair dye played a major role in keeping the telltale grey at bay, it was too professionally done by one of the city's best hairdressing salons for anyone to be able to tell. Her green eyes still dominated an otherwise unremarkable face, but clever and discreet make-up had always served her well. As had her determination, over the years, to watch her weight.

Hers had been the generation that had grown up listening to the song 'Keep Young and Beautiful If You Want to Be Loved', and if she'd ever been inclined to forget, her mother had always been kind enough to remind her.

Outside, it was another dull and overcast day. She sighed, and to distract herself from the never-ending day ahead, glanced at the rather lurid STOP-PRESS headline that had clearly been rather hastily cobbled together. Obviously a major story had broken shortly before the morning papers went to press.

For a moment, she only took in the bare details – some poor soul, murder, and the horror of a discovery in a large Kidlington garden.

And then she saw the name.

McGillicuddy.

And her heart leapt into her throat, instantly cutting off her ability to breathe. It wasn't exactly a common name, after all.

For a moment, the room swam around her as, fearfully, her eyes scanned the small printed paragraphs for more details.

The name of the murdered man was Jonathan. It was *Jonathan*. The age was right. And he was a gardener . . . It had to be him.

For a moment, Beatrice thought she was actually going to be sick, right there at the breakfast table, staining the white damask cloth and making a total exhibition of herself, no doubt causing her husband and son much distasteful inconvenience.

But, of course, she didn't. Such behaviour was unthinkable. She was Beatrice Fleet-Wright, a Collingswood by birth. The daughter of a wealthy local brewery owner, she'd attended Cheltenham Ladies College, and later Somerville College. She had always attended her nearest church and had always done what was expected of her. Which included behaving like a lady at all times.

She had even made a good match – and one much approved

of by her parents – in marrying Reginald Fleet-Wright, whose father owned a large haulage firm that very nearly produced an annual income equal to that of her father's business.

She had produced two children and, if life had been fair, could then have expected to decline genteelly into middle age, with nothing more than the odd wrangle with the church-flower roster to blight her days.

Of course, that hadn't happened. Instead, she had faced tragedy, betrayal and loss. Not to mention scandal, and becoming the object of either pity or cutting censure. And now, just when it was beginning to look as if she had weathered all that, it seemed life was about to deliver her yet another vicious blow.

Although she had not loved Reginald when she married him, she had grown fond of him over the years. She'd always loved her children, naturally. But even here she had never worn blinkers, or been one of those mothers who insisted on seeing their offspring as veritable angels.

Which had been just as well.

Beatrice had always insisted on seeing life as it really was. And past bitter experience had taught her that, when faced with adversity, it was no use trying to bury your head in the sand. You had to face things head-on, and try to find a way to make the best of it.

So she quickly swallowed back the bile that had risen to her throat, and put down her toast with only a slight shaking of her hand. A quick glance told her that neither of the men at the table had noticed anything amiss.

This didn't surprise her either. To her husband, over the years, she had become more or less a fixture of the house – a vaguely valued one, like a really good chesterfield sofa, or a rather elegant painting that hung on the wall, quietly accruing value. And to her son . . . Beatrice sometimes wondered if Rex was actually aware she existed at all.

'I shall need to see that idiot over at Binsey Lumber again,' her husband was saying now. 'What on earth made him think he could just order twenty lorries at five minutes' notice and ex . . .'

Beatrice had no problem in tuning the droning words out, while giving every appearance of hanging on to his every word – and even offering a sympathetic murmur at just the right moment. She'd had years of patient practice with that particular skill, after all.

And if she thought she caught Rex eyeing her closely, she ignored that too. She was used to his silent antagonism. And understood it. Not that there was anything she could do about it.

Ostensibly Rex was a student, but he seemed to spend little time at college, and even less time studying.

But while she hadn't entirely given up on mending her broken relationship with her son, now wasn't the time to worry about that. She had a more immediate problem at hand.

Instead, her thoughts went back to the first time she'd seen Jonathan McGillicuddy, almost seven years ago now. A handsome, golden Adonis of a youth, she could remember that long-ago summer as if it were yesterday.

It had been the summer that her life, and that of her family, had turned to ashes.

And now he was dead too. And not only dead, but *murdered*.

She took a deep, shaky breath.

Surely this could have nothing to do with her, though? It couldn't affect her, or her family, could it? It had to be a coincidence. People died all the time. And she hadn't seen or spoken to him since . . .

Time passed in something of a fog. Her husband kissed her on the cheek, as he always did, before leaving for the office. Rex made some laconic comment about what he was going to do with the rest of his day, and sauntered off.

Beatrice was only vaguely aware of it all. Her tea went cold, her toast was left uneaten.

Jonathan McGillicuddy was dead. And somehow, Beatrice Fleet-Wright just knew this was going to spell disaster all over again. Disaster for herself and her family, just when she'd thought they'd finally managed to emerge from all the anguish and despair of the past, and those awful events.

She'd thought, then, that nothing could be worse than that.

And on the face of it, the death of someone from her past could hardly compare with the loss of a child and the scandal of the coroner's inquest. And all the long years of loneliness, guilt and fear she had endured since.

When you thought about it logically, what could possibly be worse than that?

And yet, as she forced herself to read the scant details about the death of a landscape gardener she had once, briefly and tragically, known, Beatrice could just feel in her bones that the worst was yet to come.

Chapter Nine

The coroner's inquest into the death of Jonathan Paul McGillicuddy was opened six days later, on a cold and grey windswept day in late January. All of those with business at either the court or the mortuary, which both shared a courtyard at the end of Floyds Row in the city of Oxford, were huddled up in their warmest clothes, and were glad to get in out of the elements.

Dr Clement Ryder watched his court filling up from a half-open doorway in the corridor connecting to his private rooms, and waited for the moment he would be called in by the usher.

He felt well today, his body free of aches and any damned tremors, and he was mentally reviewing the morning ahead and what needed to be done – which, at this early stage, would be very little. Experience had quickly taught him just how brief the inquest itself would be, unlike the general public, who'd come out in droves expecting to see some kind of spectacle. This rather ghoulish phenomenon was something the coroner was used to now, and he had little sympathy for the morbidly curious masses who would go away sadly disappointed.

He'd already spoken to the investigating officer on the McGillicuddy case, DI Harry Jennings, a sound enough police officer in his opinion, if rather lacking in imagination. They wanted an adjournment, of course, to give them time to gather more evidence, and naturally he'd ensure they got it.

It wasn't an unusual request in the early stages of a murder inquiry.

He heard his cue to enter and walked confidently into the court, feeling, as he always did, a certain sense of satisfaction in the sudden silence that fell over the room as he appeared. Taking his seat, he looked around the packed room. He noted, with a wry smile of distaste, the presence of the press. Then he glanced at the front seats, where members of the families concerned were usually to be found, and quickly picked out the victim's mother.

A small, shrunken lady, she looked pale and bewildered and lost.

He caught her eye, and nodded gently at her. He didn't smile. He never did smile while in court. He hadn't gone around grinning like a loon when he'd been in the operating theatre, and he didn't see why he should set about doing so now he was the public face of the judiciary system.

Mavis McGillicuddy, looking up at the silver-haired, smartly dressed and rather distinguished-looking man who seemed to rule over this baffling world of law and medicine like a demigod, swallowed hard and managed to nod back.

She understood nothing about what was about to happen, and a lot of the traditional pomp and circumstance surrounding the proceedings swept right over her head. But she instinctively felt that the man who was clearly in charge of everything would do right by her son.

But, in truth, she was finding it hard to care about the pursuit of truth and justice. The police had talked to her endlessly the past few days, asking questions about Jonathan and his life. At one point, they even seemed to suspect that she and her boy weren't close, and that all wasn't well at home, but she didn't care about that either. She'd been too tired to even get angry. Her neighbour had now all but taken over looking after Marie, but, so help her, she couldn't even seem to care about that either.

The only thing she knew or cared about was that her son was gone and she'd never see him again.

Clement firmly moved his gaze on from Mavis McGillicuddy's blank-eyed face as he called the court to order and proceeded along the well-worn and now-familiar path of opening a coroner's court proceeding. Once the initial preliminaries were over, the members of the jury had been instructed as to what was expected of them, and the clerks were happy with the state of their paperwork, DI Jennings was called to the stand.

As expected, the policeman made short work of stating the facts surrounding the case, giving away as little as possible about what the police were thinking, and asked for an adjournment in order for the police to gather more evidence.

Clement succinctly gave it.

He nodded to the clerk to make a proper record of this concession and, as he did so, eyed the journalists and reporters scribbling in their notebooks with a jaundiced eye. Early on, when he'd first been appointed, one or two of them had thought they might be able to take advantage of his inexperience and get a few morsels of information out of him regarding one of his more lurid cases. His response had since become legendary, and now no reporter, even the most ferociously ambitious or impertinent, would ever dream of approaching him.

It was while DI Jennings was leaving the witness stand, and his eyes were roving generally around the room, that Clement first noticed the woman sitting in the public gallery. At first he couldn't have said why she should have caught his attention. She was perhaps a shade better dressed than most of those in the packed room, but while she was handsome enough, she was hardly eye-catching. Perhaps it was the air of stillness that seemed to surround her, or the look of calm but razor-sharp focus in her gaze as she watched DI Jennings, that tweaked his inner radar.

Perhaps it was just instinct.

She certainly didn't have the look of the average bystander, or one of those repressed members of the public who came in hopes of hearing some titillating secret being unearthed, or else gruesome descriptions of death and injury.

He was so busy trying to figure out why she interested him that it actually took him a moment to realise he'd actually seen her before somewhere. Many years ago – in circumstances that, he rather thought, hadn't been particularly comfortable.

But before he could pursue the elusive memory, he lost sight of her as the room began to slowly empty, with spectators and court personnel filing out through the narrow doorway.

For a few minutes he remained in the empty room, sitting as still as a hunting heron on his chair, and thinking furiously. Just where had he seen those green eyes, set in that pale face and with that dark frame of hair, before?

He had a brief flashback – an impression of her stoic calm and dull voice – and was convinced she'd somehow known great pain and loss. And yet she hadn't been a participant in one of *his* courts, of that much at least he was sure. He had a clear and precise recall of all the cases he'd presided over – and there was nothing wrong with his memory.

Unless this damned disease had begun to rob him of some of his mental faculties? Angrily, he shook his head, stubbornly refusing to give credence to such a disaster.

And yet . . . Yes – it was coming back to him now. And he *had* seen her in a coroner's court before – just not one he'd been presiding over!

When he'd first decided to become a coroner, he'd started haunting the courts, sitting in the public gallery and watching as case after case was heard, listening and distilling the essence of what was happening. And one particular case . . .

Suddenly he snapped his fingers and, reaching forward, picked up his copy of the McGillicuddy folder and stared intently at the victim's name.

And suddenly he had it.

McGillicuddy.

Of course, *that's* where he'd seen her before.

Slowly, he leaned back in his chair, a small smile playing on his lips. Now he understood what had brought Beatrice Fleet-Wright to this inquest.

And he wondered.

He wondered quite a lot.

He'd thought there had been something very wrong about the Fleet-Wright case. But at the time he'd been in no position to question the residing coroner's verdict. He hadn't even started his training then. But that hadn't stopped it from grating on him. He'd been convinced then that a number of the witnesses in that case had lied. Lied and lied again. And that one of the worst of these offenders had been Mrs Beatrice Fleet-Wright.

He hadn't liked the evidence of the PC either – the first responder at the scene. He hadn't trusted him one inch.

And Clement had had no doubt that the verdict handed down had been wrong – very wrong.

Naturally, he'd known it would be pointless to interfere. The coroner, one of his now-retired but very esteemed predecessors, wouldn't have listened to the opinions of a man – no matter how eminent in his own field – who hadn't even had the benefit of any legal education.

Besides, Clement had got the distinct impression that, behind the scenes, some very delicate wrangling was going on. Not that he'd ever have been able to prove it.

So, he'd had to just let it slide – much as it went against the grain. And it was one of the many reasons why, when he'd taken office, he'd sworn to himself there would never be anything iffy about any of *his* cases. Everything would be out in the open and above board, able to withstand any amount of public scrutiny.

He knew his way of doing things had made him a lot of enemies, but everyone, from the police and the Town Hall, to Oxford's wealthiest and most prominent people, knew he couldn't be bought, cajoled, fooled or lied to. He simply wouldn't tolerate it.

And now, finally – perhaps he just might be in a position to do something about that earlier case as well? If he was very careful and rather clever?

Chapter Ten

DI Jennings returned to his office with the satisfied air of a man who had just completed one hurdle and now faced several more. Not that he'd expected any trouble at the inquest, of course, but with Dr Clement Ryder presiding, there was always that chance.

The coroner was notorious for his unpredictability, a fact Jennings and the rest of the city police knew only too well. Oh, he was a very clever man, the Inspector willingly conceded, and without doubt knew his stuff – both legal and medical. Everybody knew he'd once been a surgeon, and many was the time he'd tripped up the police surgeons or other professional medical witnesses when they'd been giving evidence, catching them out on some minor point or honing in on something they'd been trying to fudge over. Which hardly endeared the coroner to them, naturally. Medicos were used to getting their own way, and it definitely didn't please them when the man they were giving evidence to clearly knew more about medicine than they did!

Not that the police got off lightly either. Many a PC – and

occasional sergeant, or even DI – had felt the cutting, sardonic lash of Dr Clement Ryder when they'd tried to pull a fast one in his court.

But the man was scrupulously fair and, to give him due credit, had a legal mind every bit as sharp as his medical one, allied to an uncanny instinct and nose for the truth, which allowed him to spot the lies witnesses slipped past the jury. And he would have none of it. Once the coroner's inquest was called into session, there was no doubt at all who was in charge. To be fair again, he had a real passion for seeing justice done.

Perhaps, Jennings thought wryly, therein lay the problem. Sometimes Dr Clement bloody Ryder thought he knew better than the police did. Four times in the past, he'd strongly called into question the line the police were trying to take in a case. More annoyingly still, in all four cases he'd eventually been proved right – to the intense embarrassment of the police team investigating the cases. And while he and his colleagues knew that a coroner's jury, made up of ordinary members of the public, could be steered, very gently and carefully, into giving the verdict the police favoured, you didn't try that on when Dr Ryder was overseeing the case.

Still, so far, Harry Jennings had never fallen foul of the egotistical, astute coroner, and would take pains to make sure he never did. The last thing he wanted to do was lock horns with the likes of Dr Ryder. The man might be a menace, but he also had friends in high places.

So now, as he sat down behind his desk, he breathed a gentle sigh of relief that the McGillicuddy inquest had gone so smoothly and, pulling open a file, began rereading the latest findings on the Deering case.

When Sir Marcus had finally come clean about what might have been behind the chilling anonymous letters, he'd had his team investigate the fire at once. At first it had seemed such an obvious and overwhelming lead; but the more they'd gone into it, the less likely it seemed. As Sir Marcus had insisted, it was hard to see how anyone could blame him for what had happened.

The facts were simple. When Sir Marcus had left university, nearly thirty years ago now, he'd taken a position as personnel manager at a large retail warehouse in Birmingham. The warehouse had been the repository for a wide range of merchandise that quickly found its way to shops in the area, including everything from bed linens and ceramics, to gas tanks for domestic use, to wooden furniture and cleaning agents. In other words, several items that were highly flammable.

One autumn day, when there had been a brisk wind blowing, a forklift operator, taking a break and smoking a cigarette, had accidentally started a fire that had quickly swept through the large building, killing three and badly burning five more people, including the forklift operator. The blaze had been made worse by the high winds, which had helped sweep it to all areas, creating a veritable inferno.

The company had admitted responsibility, and their insurance had made payments to the next of kin of those who had died, and had also made some reparation to the injured – although, at the time, the victims hadn't been overly impressed with the generosity of the payments.

The fire had naturally been thoroughly investigated, and been adjudicated an accident. The forklift driver had been spared prison on account of his serious burns, but had died barely a year later – some said of guilt, while others insisted he'd drunk himself to death.

But as Sir Marcus had pointed out, no reasonable person could ever have said or believed that *he* was in any way personally to blame for the tragedy. He wasn't the employee in charge of health and safety, he wasn't a fire marshal, and hadn't even been at work on the day of the accident. In fact, the only way he could be said to have any connection to it at all was that, as the personnel officer, he had been responsible for the hiring of the forklift driver. But even then, the man had had a spotless record and, before the accident, had certainly not been known to be a heavy drinker. So how could anyone hold him responsible? And why now, after all this time, would they be seeking retribution?

While Jennings was inclined to agree with Sir Marcus that no reasonable person would blame him, it was also a fact that no reasonable person would write threatening letters and then make good on those threats by actually murdering a totally innocent man.

So he'd had his team checking out the current whereabouts and status of the victims of the fire who had survived, the families of those who had died, as well as all those who had worked at the warehouse at the time and been particularly vociferous about the company's fire precautions and paltry compensation paid out to the injured. Anyone, in fact, who might feel they had a grievance. It was always possible – if a shade unlikely – that, in the intervening years, someone might have developed a mental fixation that had allowed them to view Sir Marcus Deering as the man to blame for all their ills.

Perhaps some poor sod who had escaped injury from the

flames and avoided the worst effects of smoke inhalation had gone on to have nightmares. Nightmares that had lasted for years, resulting in his becoming too tired to do a job of work and hence becoming long-term unemployed. Which, in a poisonous domino effect, might have led him to lose his family as the wife left and took the kids with her.

And perhaps this mythical someone had simply woken up, some twenty years after the event, seen the ruination of their lives and just snapped, deciding to take revenge? It was easier to blame someone else for all your woes, wasn't it? Especially if that same someone had then gone on to make a vast success of their life, ending up owning their own business empire, and living on a beautiful country estate.

But the list of possible suspects was a long one and covered a lot of people who, in the intervening years, had become dispersed throughout the country. And it took time, not to mention the cooperation of a lot of other police forces, to track them all down and investigate their current status.

So far they hadn't found anyone who looked good for it. But DI Jennings hadn't given up on that line of inquiry just yet. Because, barring any other evidence coming to light, it was hard to see why anyone would have taken such a murderous dislike to Sir Marcus Deering. And yet clearly someone had, and if they didn't find out who, and soon, they might well have another death on their hands. And this time, the blame for not preventing it would rest squarely on their shoulders.

Chapter Eleven

The day after the inquest on Jonathan McGillicuddy had been held and quickly closed, Trudy found herself blushing deeply as she walked into the station with the topcoat of her uniform wrapped firmly around a naked man's waist.

As expected, she was instantly greeted with hoots of derision and a few catcalls from her colleagues – the loudest wolf-whistle coming from that clown Rodney Broadstairs. The desk sergeant on duty, an old-timer called Phil Monroe, who'd seen it all, merely gave her a weary smile as she trooped dejectedly past.

'So, you caught the flasher then,' Walter Swinburne said as she frogmarched her defiant captive into the open office area and tried to steer him towards a free desk. The oldest PC in the station looked over her specimen without much enthusiasm.

A sorry-looking, fifty-two-year-old named Charles Frobisher, he was skinny as a rake (save for a surprisingly rounded pot belly), balding on top, and so pale and – given the cold weather – goose-pimpled that he reminded Trudy of nothing so much as a plucked chicken.

Exactly why he thought the good housewives of Oxford would be interested in seeing him in all his naked glory, she couldn't imagine. Nevertheless, for the past few weeks, he'd taken to jumping out of the evergreen bushes in their local parks and then streaking off down the paths to the bemusement of the local dog-walkers.

She knew DI Jennings had only given her the job of patrolling the local parks to keep her busy, and probably hadn't ever expected her to be in the right place at the right time, so she felt absolutely chuffed to prove him wrong. Not that this particular episode was likely to cover her in glory. Even now, she could see how amused her colleagues were.

And when the sorry-looking specimen went before the judge, he'd probably only be bound over to some sort of mental-health facility to see if the psychiatrists there could cure his exhibitionism.

Which would hardly cause her star to shine any brighter with her superiors!

As Charles Frobisher strutted around the office like a cock bantam, his nether regions safely cocooned in her overcoat, she sharply ordered him to sit down in the chair opposite her desk and began the painstaking task of typing up the paperwork.

Not that it should take her all that long to type out her report. After all, she'd simply been standing under a large, bare horse chestnut tree, trying to keep out of the worst of the cold January wind, when she'd heard a startled shriek. Turning around, she'd observed an indignant, middle-aged lady, who'd been walking a little West Highland terrier, trying to hit a naked man with her handbag.

The little dog had started nipping valiantly at the man's bare ankles as he'd tried to dance away from the gnashing canine teeth. And since he was barefoot, when he'd taken off on seeing Trudy's approach, she'd been able to catch him easily. Needless to say, he hadn't put up any struggle, much to her relief. (She'd not been quite sure which bit of his unprepossessing body to grab first. Some things just weren't covered in police training.)

Now, as she typed furiously, her cheeks still burning, she wasn't sure whether she should be admiring the exhibitionist's stamina and fortitude in going naked in the middle of January, or cursing him for making her the butt of station jokes for the next month (at least) to come.

'Can I have a cup of tea then, lovely lady?' Charles Frobisher asked her politely. A single man, who lived with his mother on what he called 'a private income', he'd listed his occupation as 'poet'.

'No. Sit down and keep quiet,' Trudy hissed, casting a quick look over at the DI's door.

'Don't worry – he's not interested in what the cat dragged in. He's got the vulture in with him,' PC Swinburne reassured her amiably.

Trudy blinked at him. 'Who?'

'Our beloved coroner, Dr Clement Ryder,' the old PC told her. 'You're new, so you haven't had a chance to come across him yet, but you will. We all have to run that particular gauntlet sooner or later. One day you'll have to testify at one of his inquests and when you do, my girl, just you make sure you refer to your notes and don't slip up. The old sod will have you, if you do.'

From the way he spoke, Trudy guessed the old constable was talking from bitter experience.

'Oh,' she said nervously. 'He sounds a bit of a nightmare.'

Walter grunted. 'He was one of those bigwig fancy heart surgeons up in London before he quit. And you know what *they're* like,' he added grimly. 'Think they're closely related to God Almighty, most of them. Having the power of life and death in their hands, and all that rot. Now he's coroner, he thinks he's bleeding Perry Mason and Dick Tracy all rolled into one. Trouble is, he's well respected in this city – invited to dine at a lot of High Tables and all that. Like this with the mayor,' he said, crossing his fingers in demonstration. 'So we have to indulge the big-headed old coot. Even if he does like to stick his nose in where it isn't wanted.'

Trudy blinked. 'Sorry?'

Walter Swinburne sniffed angrily. 'Thinks he can tell the police what's what. That's probably what he's doing now, I shouldn't wonder. Trying to tell the boss how he should be handling the McGillicuddy case or something. Not that *that's* any business of his, mind, but you can't tell *him* that. None of the other coroners give us half as much trouble as the old vulture does. The boss won't like it,' he predicted with savage satisfaction, pursing his lips. 'Nope, the boss won't like it all.'

As it turned out, the old constable was only half right. DI Jennings *didn't* much like having Dr Ryder breathing down his neck, but the coroner wasn't there to tell him how he should be running his latest murder investigation.

Instead, he seemed to have some sort of bee in his bonnet about an old case.

When the coroner had called in that morning, just expecting

Jennings to drop everything and make time for him (which, of course, Jennings had, damn him!), the DI had sensed trouble ahead. After he'd listened to what Ryder actually wanted, he'd become even more displeased. Because the damned man only wanted him to reopen and investigate an old case, a death by misadventure, dating from nearly five years ago.

'Like I've been trying to tell you, Dr Ryder,' Jennings said now, his patience wearing thin, 'I simply don't have the authority to reopen a case just on your say-so, especially one that seems to have brought in a perfectly adequate verdict. And before you carry on . . .' He held out a hand as if to physically ward him off. ' . . . I don't believe my immediate superiors would allow it, even if I were to ask them,' he said shortly.

He paused as he heard a sudden laughing roar outside, and glanced through the internal window that screened him from the rest of the office, just in time to see the pretty new probationary WPC come in with a naked man.

He drew his breath in sharply. Bloody hell, she'd actually caught the flasher, he thought blankly. Then he scowled as he watched her steer a skinny old man, covered by her overcoat, to a chair. There was something distinctly seedy and vaguely nauseating about the scene, and he only hoped nothing untoward would come of it. It would only take one silly matron on some influential committee with the ear of City Hall to complain about how wrong it was to expect respectable young women to catch dirty-minded perverts to cause one hell of a big stink. She'd complain to her civil-servant husband, who had the ear of the Chief Constable, and before you knew it, his immediate superior would be hauling DI Harry Jennings over the coals for . . .

'I only want someone to help me do a little discreet digging.' The caustic and precise tones of the coroner brought his mind snapping back to the problem at hand.

'I believe the Fleet-Wright case was seriously flawed. And given the connection to your latest murder victim, I can't understand why you're deliberately dragging your heels, man,' Clement Ryder put in cannily.

Harry Jennings sat back down behind his deck with a sigh. 'The fact that our murder victim, McGillicuddy, once knew someone who died in what you insist on calling mysterious circumstances hardly makes for much of a connection, Dr Ryder,' he pointed out wearily.

Clement drew in a long, slow, patient breath, and the policeman felt his spirits sink ever further. Clearly the older man wasn't going to give up on this, and the last thing he needed was Dr Clement bloody Ryder running loose on some sort of a crusade.

'I'm not asking you to officially reopen the case yet. I'm not even asking you to assign a team to it,' the coroner said magnanimously.

Harry Jennings smiled grimly. 'Kind of you, I'm sure, sir,' he muttered sardonically.

'In fact, I'm perfectly willing to devote my own spare time to it,' Clement said, hiding a satisfied smile as the DI's eyes grew rounder and wider than those of an owl, and the younger man nearly rocketed out of his chair in alarm. 'But naturally, I can't do that,' Clement carried on mildly before the DI had a chance to protest, 'without some sort of official status or help from the city police.'

Jennings, who'd slumped back in his chair in relief, quickly shot up out of it again. 'That's impossible, man,' he snapped, finally at the end of his tether. 'My team are all busy with the McGillicuddy murder case. Surely you must realise that?'

As he spoke, he wandered back to the internal office window and looked through, relieved to see his team busily working. 'And as you can imagine, my superiors would prefer we solve it sooner rather than later.'

'I understand that, naturally. But surely you can spare me one person? Just a body in uniform is all I need to give me a bit of official status when I re-question some witnesses,' Clement cajoled. 'And who knows, it's possible the Fleet-Wright case just *might* connect back to your McGillicuddy case. And think how stupid you'd look if that turned out be the case and you hadn't followed up on it – especially since I'd even offered to do it for you! Just think of it as killing two birds with one stone, man. What have you got to lose?'

'You have no authority to go around questioning anyone,' Jennings snapped, pushed beyond endurance.

'Exactly,' Clement Ryder said smugly. 'Which is why I need an actual police officer. Someone to work closely with me and follow my lead. Surely you have someone unimportant you can spare me?'

Instantly, as he said this, Harry Jennings thought of PC Swinburne. The old man was just putting in time until his retirement anyway. And by now, he was willing to do almost anything in order to get the old vulture off his back. But when he looked back into the outer office at his team, the first person he saw was WPC Trudy Loveday.

Who'd just caught the flasher.

And would need to be reassigned to some other case where she couldn't come to any harm or get in his way.

And suddenly he began to smile.

'You know, Dr Ryder,' he said, turning back to smile through gritted teeth at the trouble-making coroner. 'I think I have just the person for you . . .'

When Trudy returned from depositing her prisoner in the cells (Frobisher having been clothed by a kindly Salvation Army colonel who'd come in with some donated items), she was surprised to be called into the DI's office. She could almost count on the fingers of one hand the number of times her superior had actually wanted to see her, and secretly suspected he wished he hadn't been assigned any female staff at all. It was almost as if he didn't know what to do with her, and so he usually left it to the Sergeant to assign her details.

And when she stepped inside his office, she was even more surprised to see that the DI's visitor – a rather distinguished-looking man – hadn't yet left. Dressed in a smart charcoal-grey suit, with an imperious thick sweep of silver hair, he regarded her from beneath bushy eyebrows with obvious curiosity. Although his grey eyes looked somewhat watery, the expression in them was razor-sharp as they observed her.

Under their influence, Trudy could feel her spine begin to stiffen, and she became instantly alert.

'WPC Loveday, this is Dr Clement Ryder, one of the city's coroners,' Harry Jennings said dryly.

'Sir,' Trudy said. But whether to her superior office, or to the man lounging in the chair watching her, nobody in the room could tell – including Trudy.

'Dr Ryder has rather an interesting proposition that he wants to put to you,' DI Jennings said, slightly mischievously. Because, of course, he knew it was actually up to him to give the police constable her orders and that she really had no say in the matter.

He just didn't want to make it easy for the old vulture.

And as the coroner shot him a chastising look, Trudy, with Walter Swinburne's words of warning about this man still echoing in her ears, said cautiously, 'Oh?'

Chapter Twelve

Mavis McGillicuddy stood at her sink, listlessly washing up the breakfast things. Marie had gone back to school. The poor mite now only had her grandmother to look after her, and Mavis felt the responsibility keenly.

She stared out of her kitchen window vaguely as she automatically began to dry the teacups. Her neighbours and friends had been wonderful, rallying round, but they couldn't be with her every minute of the day. And the house now felt so empty and quiet and nothing felt normal.

Even the people passing by out on the street paused to look at her house now. As if expecting to see something . . . What? Interesting? Frightening? Mavis didn't quite know. But at the least the reporters had stopped bothering her for the moment and she was being left in peace.

But no sooner had she thought this than Mavis noticed the woman at the bottom of the short garden path. She seemed to be walking up to the gate, as if trying to make up her mind to open it, but then she'd veer off, as if losing her nerve.

Slowly, Mavis McGillicuddy's hands stilled on her tea towel. The woman was a stranger, she was sure. Nicely dressed, by the cut of her tailored coat and . . . yes, her nice leather gloves.

Although, since Jonathan's death, she'd become used to casual 'gawpers', as she thought of them, this woman didn't strike her at all as one of the usual, run-of-the-mill curiosity-seekers.

Almost curious now, Mavis watched the woman thoughtfully. And frowned. Did her appearance ring a faint bell?

She looked to be nearly two decades younger than herself, and was still attractive. And now, again, she had marched back to the gate with a determined step, her back ramrod-straight, as if steeling herself for something unpleasant. And this time, her elegantly gloved hand even got as far as reaching for the gate latch. But then, at the last minute, she turned away again. This time there was the slope of defeat in her shoulders as she turned and walked away.

And didn't come back.

With a shrug, Mavis reached for another plate and slipped it into her washing-up bowl, not realising she'd washed and dried it once already.

'So, have you got all that clear?' DI Jennings asked Trudy, who was standing straight and alert in front of his desk.

The coroner, Dr Clement Ryder, had just left and her superior was watching her closely.

'Yes, sir,' Trudy said, feeling both excited and vaguely puzzled. 'You want me to read the inquest file Dr Ryder has left, give you a summary, and then work closely with Dr Ryder as he pursues his inquiries. And at the end of each day I'm to give you a written report of our activities.'

DI Jennings nodded. The girl had a quick mind and good grasp of things, he'd give her that.

'And I'm to report to you at once if I believe Dr Ryder has overstepped the mark in any way.' Here, Trudy began to feel a shade uneasy, since she wasn't quite sure what the DI had meant by this. What would her boss consider overstepping the mark to be, exactly? 'And when we interview any witnesses, I must be the one to do the questioning.' She parroted his instructions back at him.

'Exactly. Dr Ryder is a civilian, despite his role as coroner, and has no authority to make an arrest, question witnesses outside of his court, or otherwise play the role of a police officer. Is that clear?'

'Yes, sir,' Trudy said smartly. What wasn't clear to her – not by a long shot – was why the Inspector was indulging the old vulture in this way.

After having briefly met the man, she could see now why Walter Swinburne and the rest of the station thought of him as a vulture. It wasn't just the fact that the man dealt with death in the course of his job – for others did that too. Nor was it his beak-like nose that tended to give him the appearance of an imperious bird of prey. It was those cold, watchful eyes that gave you the shivers.

Jennings now sighed heavily. 'Dr Ryder is a very clever man, with powerful friends, Constable Loveday – always remember that. He also has an annoying habit of being right. So if he thinks there was something off about this old case . . .' He indicated the buff folder that lay on his desk. 'Then, like as not, there probably was. And since there's a tenuous link to our murder victim, McGillicuddy . . .' Here Trudy's eyes widened in real interest. ' . . . We need to check it out. Within reason.'

Now Trudy wanted to turn cartwheels across the floor. She'd never thought, as a humble probationary WPC, that she'd be allowed to get within a mile of a real murder case. And although it was clear the Inspector didn't think there was anything in it, to be able to work on even the periphery of an ongoing case, even in such odd circumstances as these, was far more than she could ever have wished for.

She'd be a fool not to make the most of it. 'I see, sir,' she said eagerly. 'When do I start?'

'Tomorrow will be soon enough. I don't want the old vul— er . . . Dr Clement to think we'll jump to his tune whenever he snaps his fingers.' Even if he just had! 'So study the case.' He picked up the file, glanced at the name on it. 'It's one Gisela Fleet-Wright, death by misadventure, I think. When you're sure you have a good grasp of it, call on Dr Ryder first thing in the morning. He's said he'll be in his office. You'll then help him investigate whatever it is that needs investigating.'

'Yes, sir. And I'm to, er, follow his instructions?' She wanted this point clarified.

'Yes, but as I've already said, only within reason,' he added cautiously. 'Just jolly him along, and if you can actually get to the bottom of whatever it is that's bothering him, and get him off our backs altogether, so much the better.'

Trudy nodded, trying to bite back a growing grin of excitement. Even if the old case wasn't that interesting, it had to be better than catching bag-snatchers and flashers, surely?

'Yes, sir. I'll do my best, sir.'

DI Jennings waved her out of his office, his mind already on other things. It had turned out that there just might be a lead from the fire incident in Sir Marcus's dim and distant past, after all, and he was keen to follow up on it.

Chapter Thirteen

It didn't take Trudy long to read quickly through the file and get a basic grasp of the Fleet-Wright case. But it took several long hours of sitting at her desk and taking painstaking notes before she was confident she knew the case inside and out.

Once she did, she had to admit to feeling a slight sense of disappointment. When DI Jennings had told her that the wily coroner had been unhappy with this particular verdict, she'd expected something a little more . . . well, spectacular. Instead, the case she'd just read, while very sad, hadn't struck her as being at all out of the ordinary.

The facts seemed simple and straightforward enough – but, as far as she could tell, though tragic, they didn't seem particularly suspicious. Worse still, the connection to their murder victim was fleeting at best.

In the summer of 1955, twenty-one-year-old Gisela Fleet-Wright, daughter of Beatrice and Reginald Fleet-Wright, had been found dead in her bedroom. It had been a lovely sunny day, and her mother, who had found her, had tried to revive her without success. She had then rung up the family doctor, the GP arriving at the house some ten minutes later. He'd conducted a brief examination and declared the poor girl dead.

He had then called in the police.

This was, perhaps, the first sign that all was not quite right, since it immediately told Trudy the doctor was concerned about the circumstances of the death, and hadn't been any too keen to write out a death certificate.

But given that Gisela had been only twenty-one, and supposedly in reasonable health, that wasn't all that surprising.

There were no signs of violence on the body and it transpired that, although Gisela had a history of depression and 'mood swings', she had no underlying heart problems or any other medical conditions that might account for her sudden and unexpected death.

Naturally, the police had asked for an autopsy. The family, Roman Catholics, hadn't particularly liked this idea, but, of course, had been unable to prevent it. Again, to the lay mind, this might have seemed suspicious, but Trudy knew most families instinctively shied away from the idea of their loved ones 'being cut about' and that this objection by the Fleet-Wrights didn't necessarily indicate they had something to hide.

The results of the autopsy showed Gisela had higher than normal levels of the various antidepressant medicines she had been prescribed in her bloodstream: enough to cause the heart failure listed as the cause of death.

And this is where, Trudy supposed, Dr Clement Ryder's first interest in the case had been piqued.

Although he hadn't yet been a coroner when the inquest was heard, he'd told DI Jennings that he'd sat through the entire proceedings, wanting to learn more about his newly chosen profession and get a feel for what the job entailed. He had thus paid very close attention to every aspect of the evidence being given, and of the witnesses' testimony.

And he had obviously convinced the DI that there was – at the very least – a possibility that something might have been amiss with the coroner's verdict, since they were now reviewing it.

But for the life of her, and no matter how often she reread the witness statements, she couldn't see where the problem might lie.

As Trudy had learned at police training college, a coroner's inquest is not a trial. A coroner investigates deaths that appear to be due to violence, have a sudden or unknown cause, occur while in legal custody, or are otherwise deemed unnatural. And even then, a coroner's inquest is only there to establish who the deceased was, and how and when they died.

In the Fleet-Wright case, there was no confusion or uncertainty over the victim's identity, or when or where the victim had died. What was more, the coroner's jury had been told by the medical witnesses that death had been caused by the victim ingesting too many of her prescribed pills. So, on this matter at least, they had no trouble bringing in the cause of death – they merely had to agree with the pathologist's findings. The trouble and confusion lay in deciding how the overdose had come about.

Here, Trudy paused to lean back in her chair and stretch her arms luxuriously over her head, to give her eyes a little rest from reading. Her mind, however, remained as busy as ever.

Clearly, she mused, there were only a few ways in which

Gisela Fleet-Wright could have taken too many pills. First, she could have taken them on purpose – in which case any jury would find that the victim had taken her own life, perhaps while the balance of her mind was affected. This, Trudy knew, was a kind way of saying a suicide victim wasn't really responsible for their actions, and was often brought in by kind-hearted juries to make things easier on those left behind. Especially when the family concerned was Roman Catholic.

Second, the overdose could have been accidental – in some way, the poor girl had taken more pills than she intended. In which case, accidental death or the verdict that had eventually been reached – death by misadventure – would have been the correct conclusion.

And lastly, and most unlikely by far – somehow, someone had forced her to take the pills, resulting in her death.

In other words, murder.

In the rare cases where no cause of death could be agreed upon, the coroner was able to record an open verdict. This was never popular, however, or satisfying, as it was an admission that the court simply didn't know what had happened. But it left the case 'open' for further investigation at some point in the future.

Once again, she turned back to the file and reread the evidence for a third time, determined not to miss anything. In spite of everyone commiserating with her on her new assignment working with 'the old vulture', Trudy knew this could be her big chance to prove to the Sarge and DI Jennings that she could do more than the menial tasks nobody else wanted.

It was her chance to show she had brains as well as ambition, and she was determined not to blow it. So, despite her eyes feeling as dry as those of a member of the temperance society, she forced her attention back to the papers in front of her.

The police report, as well as the findings of the subsequent forensics report, made it clear there had been no signs of forced entry at the Fleet-Wrights' house – a large, detached villa in north Oxford, surrounded by large gardens. On the day in question, both the victim's mother, younger brother and two gardeners had been in and around the house at various times, and none had reported seeing any strangers. Neither had anyone heard the victim scream. The pathologist's report also made it clear there had been no signs of bruising on the girl's body, no skin scrapings under her fingernails to indicate she might have fought off and scratched an attacker, and no signs of any 'interference' with the body.

The first police officer at the scene, a PC who walked that beat and had been asked to attend the scene and report back, also stated that he'd found the victim lying peacefully and fully clothed on her bed, and that the bedclothes underneath her were barely rumpled. Her bedroom had likewise shown no signs of a struggle. Furthermore, since it was a fine, sunny day, her window was open, and if she had cried out, one of the gardeners working below would surely have heard her.

Clearly, then, murder had seemed extremely unlikely.

Next, suicide had to be considered. But here again, there was no evidence for this. The victim had left no note – which wasn't totally unheard of – but it seemed to be the consensus of opinion that young women, on the whole, *did* tend to leave a note behind, if only to say sorry or to try and explain or justify their actions. Furthermore, her family and friends all testified that Gisela wasn't the kind of girl who'd just give up on life, despite her bouts of depression. What's more, she had showed no signs that she might be thinking of taking her own life.

Naturally, Trudy had thought when she'd first read this, you'd expect them to say that. Nobody, after all, liked to think they might have missed the signs, and thus feel culpable for letting down a loved one.

However, against that, Gisela *had* been treated for depression for years before her death, and several of her friends testified that she could be 'difficult', describing her as 'being up one minute and down the next'. There had been some hints, too, that she could be 'highly strung' at times.

It was also noted that the victim had recently broken up with her boyfriend of six months or so, one Mr Jonathan McGillicuddy. Although their courtship had been over for several months, many of her friends reported that it had affected her badly, leaving her 'wild with anger' or, alternatively, 'weepy and distraught'.

But all her friends agreed that Gisela herself had been adamant they would eventually get back together. It was also agreed among her friends that the breakup of her courtship with McGillicuddy, a young widower with a small child, had made her, if anything, angry rather than suicidal. One friend had even testified that Gisela was so determined to win him back that she was making plans for an engagement party.

Which perhaps indicated the thinking of someone unstable enough to swallow a whole bunch of pills?

But there had been nothing concrete for the jury to latch on to, and it wasn't really surprising that they might have been reluctant to bring in a verdict of suicide on such skimpy and mostly hearsay evidence.

Not that, in the event, this had proved to be a problem for them, because everything had changed with the mother's testimony. Indeed, it had been Beatrice Fleet-Wright who had been instrumental in their bringing in the verdict they did – death by misadventure.

Gisela, like a lot of people suffering with depression and a vague, unspecified, so-called 'mental illness', hated taking the drugs prescribed for her by doctor. Often she complained that they left her feeling tired or sluggish, and as if she was 'watching the world through a pane of glass that had been smeared with grease'. Not surprisingly then, she often tried to get out of taking them, swearing she'd swallowed the prescribed dose when, in actuality, she hadn't. And the fact that her family could tell when this was the case proved just how much she needed them to keep her depression and mood swings at bay.

So her mother, and sometimes her father, had taken to standing over her and making sure she took them in the morning, at noon and in the early evening, as prescribed.

Unfortunately, Beatrice Fleet-Wright (often described in the court transcripts as 'weeping' or 'clearly distraught') had once or twice caught her daughter being sick in the bathroom, and suspected she was deliberately making herself ill shortly after taking the pills in order to prevent them taking effect.

This could lead to some confusion, she had testified – a number of times, she'd had to make sure her daughter took some more pills and then kept them down. And very often, she further testified, her daughter would take a short nap after taking the pills, as they made her drowsy, and, on waking, could be 'somewhat confused' and 'wildly unpredictable' for a short while, until she seemed to 'balance herself out'. During these bouts, she could become forgetful, playful, morose or angry, depending on her state of mind at the time, and thus could forget she'd already taken the prescribed dose, leading her to take them again.

As her evidence went on, it became clear that Beatrice Fleet-Wright was convinced the overdose had been accidental.

She'd testified that, on the morning in question, her daughter, a third-year student at a local non-affiliated college, studying for a BA in English literature, had promised her she'd taken her pills, but that she, her mother, hadn't believed her. She'd said that, when her daughter had promised her this, she'd shot a guilty look at the bathroom, causing Beatrice to suspect she'd brought them back up again.

So she had given her daughter a second dose, just to be sure. This, of course, wouldn't have been anything like enough to kill her, even if she'd been mistaken and Gisela had, in fact, taken the dose she'd said she had.

When she'd left Gisela alone in her bedroom, her daughter had been taking a nap, sleeping peacefully, as was usual.

But what, Beatrice had speculated, if Gisela had then woken up in a confused state and, not realising she'd already taken her pills, decided to take some more? Sometimes, on waking, she could be in a slightly tearful and contrite state, and would apologise to her mother, or father, or anyone else present, vowing she would 'try to be good' and take her pills. And, sometimes, she had seemed childishly keen to do so.

What if that had happened this time?

If Gisela hadn't, in fact, regurgitated her first set of pills, she would have had two doses inside her, making her even more confused. If she'd then woken up in a 'contrite' state of mind, she might have taken yet a third dose. And, since it might have been close to lunchtime when she woke up, might she then have taken her 'second' dose of the day, which would in effect have been a fourth or fifth?

At this point in her testimony, Mrs Fleet-Wright had become 'inconsolable' as she admitted she must be responsible for her daughter's death, telling the court she blamed herself for not being right there, in her daughter's bedroom, at the fatal moment. For even though she'd been due to attend a meeting that afternoon, discussing an up-coming charity event with her fellow WI members, she'd cancelled it at the last moment and had remained in the house, but doing odd little jobs of housekeeping throughout her home instead.

The coroner had told her she mustn't 'speculate' about what had happened and 'stick only to the facts', but nothing he said could convince the witness she wasn't responsible for her daughter's overdose.

Distraught, and still blaming herself, Mrs Fleet-Wright had been led from the witness stand.

After that, things had moved along fairly crisply, with both the jury and coroner in agreement. It was found that Gisela Fleet-Wright had died after accidentally taking too much of her medication, and a verdict of death by misadventure had been duly entered into the records.

Now, nearly five years later, as Trudy tidied up her desk and got ready to call it a day, she felt her heart ache for that poor girl's mother. To lose a daughter at all was surely tragic enough – but to have to live the rest of your life feeling and believing you were to blame (and who knew, perhaps she actually *was*?) must be awful.

As she walked down St Ebbes, she paused to look in the brightly lit shop window of Coopers, one of her mother's favourite stores, but found little in the window display to attract her attention.

Just what was it about the Fleet-Wright case that had got Dr Clement Ryder so worked up? She was fairly sure, at least, that the fact of their murder victim knowing the dead girl could have no possible bearing on his murder all these years later. Clearly the old vulture was merely using the coincidence to get his own way in re-examining the dead girl's case!

Chapter Fourteen

The next morning found Sir Marcus Deering sitting in his study, in his usual chair, staring in numb disbelief at the envelope in his hand. His secretary, after delivering it, had backed out quickly as he barked at her to telephone the police at once.

He sat for several frozen seconds, simply staring at the familiar, green-inked block capitals, then found his hand was shaking so much that he couldn't actually physically manage to open it. His fingers felt like so many numb sausages. In the end he stopped trying and simply dropped the thing onto the top of his desk.

He told himself he should probably leave it alone anyway. The police should be the ones to open it, obviously, in case of fingerprints or clues, or something.

Swallowing back a sudden rush of nausea, he turned in his swivel chair and surveyed the garden through the window. But in January there was little out there to distract his eye, and inevitably, as they so often did now, his thoughts turned to Jonathan. The son he'd never acknowledged. Had never, in fact, even met. And whose dead body now lay in the city morgue.

When Mavis had told him she was pregnant, he'd been relieved to let his father take care of it all, hushing up any scandal and paying her an allowance that would allow her to bring up his grandson in a reasonable manner.

Mavis had been unhappy, of course, as was her family, but in the end they came to see it was for the best. Marcus hadn't even started university, and it was clear he was too young to take on the responsibilities of fatherhood.

As the years went by, although Mavis had offered him plenty of chances to get to know his son, he'd never felt the urge to take her up on them. And once he'd made such a good marriage, and Martha had presented him, first, with Anthony and then, a couple of years later, with Hermione, it had become even more unthinkable that he would play any part in the boy's life. After all, Martha knew nothing about his past indiscretion, and for Anthony and Hermione to suddenly be presented with an older sibling – a cuckoo in the nest – was out of the question.

Besides, the boy was loved and cared for. Mavis had kept him informed of his progress – his marriage, the birth of his daughter, the loss of his wife, and the setting up of his own gardening business.

And if, in the back of his mind, he'd sometimes fantasised about meeting the boy, or perhaps just watching him walk down the street, well . . .

Well, that could never happen now, could it?

Wordlessly, Sir Marcus Deering began to weep; big, fat, desolate tears that rolled down his cheeks unnoticed.

He was dry-eyed and in control of himself, however, when Sergeant O'Grady arrived a short while later and, wearing gloves, carefully opened the letter, preserving the evidence in a plastic bag.

The message had been short, clear and unequivocal.

Unless Marcus Deering did the right thing, his other son would also die.

And it was then that the businessman finally had to acknowledge that the nightmare wasn't over yet – not by a long chalk.

'Well, come in and sit down,' Clement Ryder said flatly. 'I don't bite.'

'Good job you don't, sir,' Trudy said smartly. 'That would constitute assaulting a police officer and I'd be obliged to handcuff and arrest you.'

For a second, the coroner stared at her. Then, unbelievably, he shot her a quick flash of his teeth – which she took to be a smile – and nodded.

'Good. At least you've got some gumption,' he congratulated her. 'I was worried Jennings had fobbed me off with the office idiot.' He paused and looked at her closely. 'Do you have any A-levels? How old are you?'

Trudy flushed. 'I'm nineteen, sir,' she said flatly. 'And I have eight O-levels and two A-levels.'

'Science?'

'English and history.'

'Oh, well. That's better than nothing, I suppose,' he muttered.

Trudy flashed her own teeth at him. He could take it for a smile or not, as he pleased.

The old man grunted, but from the flash of his eyes and slight twist of his lip, Trudy guessed, with some relief, that he'd been rather pleased with her responses.

Which was just as well, for, when contemplating the task that lay ahead of her, it had occurred to her that perhaps appeasement wasn't the way to go when dealing with a strong-minded character such as Dr Ryder. And although he was certainly an important man who expected obedience and respect, the sooner he acknowledged she wasn't going to be ridden roughshod over, the better.

'So, you've had a chance to read the Fleet-Wright file?' he said briskly. 'What do you make of it? And sit down, girl – you're beginning to give me a crick in the neck.'

Trudy, who had been unknowingly standing at attention, quickly hooked a large, comfortable-looking, black-leather chair and sat down.

She was dressed in her crisp, neat uniform, complete with hard-peaked cap, and in the leather satchel thrown over her shoulder she had her full set of accoutrements. From this satchel she now drew out her own notebook, where she'd jotted down the salient points, and the copy of the file.

As she handed the latter document back, she cast a quick look around his office, which was definitely one up on the offices back at the station, that was for sure! Huge landscape paintings hung on walls that had been painted soft beige, and a fire roared away in the fireplace. On top of the grand mantelpiece were ranged a number of brass, art deco-style ornaments. The coroner's leather-topped desk dominated the room, and a number of bookshelves, crammed with law, medicine and history tomes, gave the room the feeling of a library in an exclusive gentlemen's club.

'Be glad when they get some damned central heating in this place,' Clement grumbled, glancing behind him at the large windows giving a view out onto what looked to be an old, cobbled courtyard. And even Trudy, who was seated further away from the panes of old glass, could feel a distinct chill coming from them. It didn't help that, once again, the weather outside was cold, wet and windy.

Trudy took a deep breath. 'Well, sir,' she began firmly, trying not to sound as nervous as she felt, 'it seems to me that, given the evidence, both the jury and coroner arrived at the only verdict possible. Death by misadventure.'

She looked up from her notebook, waiting for him to lambaste her. Reminding herself of her promise not to let herself be cowed, she watched him steadfastly.

When old Walter had heard she'd been seconded to work with Ryder, he'd filled her in rather gleefully on yet more tales of how the old vulture had tripped up many a copper on the witness stand. And had once made such a pest of himself that the Chief Constable had even contemplated taking early retirement.

Even the Sergeant had warned her that the old man, though 'sharp as a tack', could be a bit irascible, and that she was to take no nonsense from him. So, considering the man had such a reputation for not suffering fools gladly, she half-expected to feel the knife-edge of his temper right away.

Instead of berating her for not agreeing with his contention that there was something wrong about the case, however, she found him watching her thoughtfully instead, and even nodding slightly.

'Yes. From the evidence presented, the jury couldn't really come up with anything else, could they?' he said mildly, instantly making her doubt she'd heard him properly.

'You're agreeing with me?' she heard herself say stupidly.

Then felt herself flush. 'I'm sorry, Dr Clement, but I'm rather confused. I understood . . . that is, DI Jennings told me you weren't happy with the verdict. That, in fact, I'm supposed to help you re-examine the case?'

'You are.'

Trudy blinked.

The coroner was dressed in his trademark dark suit, with a tie that she suspected either represented his specific Oxford college, or maybe some equally high-up medical establishment. His abundant silver hair was neatly brushed, and his watery-looking grey eyes were as sharp as ever. He didn't look like somebody who was either losing his marbles or liked to indulge in word games.

Nevertheless, she definitely felt as if he was messing her about, and her own gaze hardened. 'Perhaps it would simply save us some time and effort, sir, if you were to tell me exactly what it is you'd like us to do?'

Clement Ryder smiled faintly. 'A decisive woman of action. Very well, WPC Loveday,' he said briskly. 'I want us to question the witnesses who testified at Gisela Fleet-Wright's inquest, and re-examine the evidence in the cold light of day nearly five years later. And to perhaps start with your newest murder victim, Jonathan McGillicuddy.'

'But why, sir? Mr McGillicuddy, according to the transcripts, gave only a very short witness statement. He simply said, in effect, that he and Gisela had been "going steady" for a while, but that they had broken it off. And that he hadn't been in contact with her for weeks before she died.'

'That's what he said, yes,' Clement Ryder agreed mildly.

'And you think he was lying?'

'He certainly wasn't telling the whole truth.'

Trudy slowly leaned back in her chair. 'Do you have any evidence of this, sir?'

'Of course I don't,' Clement said testily. 'If I did, I wouldn't need you to find it for me, would I?' But as Trudy flushed – either in anger or embarrassment – he swept on before she had a chance to protest. 'But he's not the only one who lied. And since the man is dead, we can't actually ask him why he did, can we? So we'll need to start with a living witness who might know, and his mother is the obvious starting point for that.'

Trudy took another long, deep breath. Instinct was telling her she needed to keep her wits about her with this man, and that once she'd let him bamboozle her, it would set the pattern forever. So she'd damned well better make sure it didn't happen.

'Not quite so fast, sir, if you please,' she said smartly, but with a brief smile. 'Who else do you believe lied on the witness stand?'

Clement Ryder gave a brief, ironic grunt. 'Who lied? It would be easier to say who didn't!' He leaned back in his chair and sighed. 'Apart from the expert witnesses – and, I think, the two gardeners who were called to testify that they hadn't seen any strangers hanging around – they all had something to hide. At the very least, some of them were fudging it. And the more brazen of them were telling downright lies in an attempt to pervert the course of justice.'

Trudy felt her jaw starting to drop at this arrogant, sweeping statement, and quickly clamped her teeth together. She noticed that the older man was watching her with some amusement now, probably well aware she was only holding on to her temper with a bit of an effort, and again she felt a telltale flush of repressed temper cross her cheeks.

She really wished she could get out of this childish habit of colouring up whenever she felt angry or disconcerted.

'*All* of them, sir?' she said mildly, but allowing her tone to sound downright sceptical. 'You're saying they were *all* lying? The girl's father?'

'Him, certainly.'

'Her mother?'

'Her especially.'

'And, as you say, our murder victim. What about her friends who testified as to her temperament and state of mind?' she asked sardonically. 'Did the conspiracy of lies extend to them as well?'

Totally ignoring her sarcasm, Dr Ryder shook his head. 'No, not them so much,' he admitted airily. 'I think they tried to be as honest as they could, given the circumstances. Of course, they were all rather reluctant to speak ill of the dead, but that's a common enough phenomenon. The point is, I don't think any of *them* was trying to be deliberately obstructive. And they certainly painted a clear and honest picture of the victim, who had been a rather brittle and self-destructive character.'

Trudy, for the moment, was willing to let the old vulture's rather outlandish statements stand, because now he'd come to something that had struck her too. On reading through the file for the fourth and final time last night, what had made the most lasting impression of all on her was the character of the dead girl.

Although the medical witnesses had talked of her depression and mood swings in medical lingo, and her parents, naturally, had talked of her as a loving daughter with distressing mental issues, what had come across to Trudy was the sheer instability of the girl.

One moment Gisela had been up, the next down. One minute contrite, the next manipulative. One moment she was sure she was going to win back her former boyfriend, the next she was roundly ranting about him and blaming him for all her woes. But underneath it all, she'd sensed that Gisela Fleet-Wright had been a volatile, perhaps spoilt girl; one who was used to getting her own way, and didn't like it when she didn't. A bright girl – her university place had shown that – and, from the photographs of her, a very beautiful one too. And beautiful girls, as Trudy had often observed, were very good at getting what they wanted.

And Gisela, like a child who probably hadn't grown up, had thrown tantrums when thwarted.

Another thing that had stood out, in Trudy's mind at least, was Gisela's obvious obsession with their latest murder victim. Whether Jonathan had been the one to end the relationship, as most people believed, or whether Gisela had in fact ended it (as she had insisted to all her friends she had), everyone was in agreement that the dead girl had been totally besotted with Jonathan McGillicuddy. Either with winning him back, or paying him back, depending on her mood of the moment.

Trudy quickly flipped through the file and picked out a photograph of the dead girl, taken barely a month before she died. About five-feet-eight or so, she'd had lovely long dark hair and vivid green eyes in a heart-shaped face. Almost too slender, she had an elfin rather than voluptuous beauty, and even if she hadn't already been aware of the girl's ultimate fate, Trudy would have said she had a fragile look about her. The sort of girl who could pose for a pre-Raphaelite painting of some tragic maiden, doomed to die of love.

'You think she was a bit of a madam?' was what Trudy found herself actually saying. And again, saw the coroner give her a swift and approving look.

Which, in turn, made her feel rather pleased with herself.

'I think that's a pretty good description, yes,' he agreed wryly.

Instantly forcing the warm, fuzzy feeling his approbation had given her to one side, she looked across at him flatly. 'And do you think her personality had anything to do with what happened to her?'

'Our personalities always affect our lives,' Clement said, and there was some echo of sadness in his voice that puzzled her. 'How can it not?'

Clearly, this man had known pain and regret, she thought fleetingly.

Then his eyes sharpened on her once again, and any desire to feel pity for the man instantly fled. It would be a poor fool indeed, Trudy thought in that moment, who offered tea and unwanted sympathy to Dr Clement Ryder.

'What I intend to find out is how and why that young woman died,' he said crisply. 'Because I'm damned certain that what we heard at the inquest was a carefully edited version at best, and a damned travesty of the truth at worst.'

It was clear the older man was angry now – but more than that. He felt indignant, as if in some way, even though he'd never even known Gisela, or been the one to preside over her case, it was a personal insult that the right verdict hadn't been handed down.

And with a flash of insight, Trudy understood that, to this man, truth and justice weren't just lofty ideals to be aimed for, but real necessities.

Feeling somewhat humbled – and rather young and callow – Trudy swallowed hard. 'Yes, sir,' she said. Then, more cautiously, 'But I still don't understand why you think it didn't happen the way her mother said.'

It was one thing to feel uplifted by the man's passion, Trudy mused, but another altogether to just assume he was right.

'That Gisela took too many pills by accident? That between Mrs Beatrice Fleet-Wright's actions and those of her daughter, she accidentally ingested too many pills?'

'Yes.' She nodded.

'Because if that was the case, why did so many of the witnesses lie?'

Trudy coughed nervously. She wasn't sure how she could say what she wanted to say now in any tactful way, so she just girded her loins and said it out loud. 'Well, sir, we don't know for a fact that they *did* lie, do we? After all, although you may have felt sure in yourself that they were lying . . .'

'I could have been wrong?' Clement finished the sentence for her flatly.

Trudy again felt herself flush, and took a swift, angry breath. 'Is that so unthinkable, sir?' she managed.

She waited for the storm to break over her head.

But, again, it never happened.

Instead, as a grandfather clock ticked ponderously in one corner behind her and, outside, the wind and rain lashed against the ill-fitting windowpanes, the silence felt more amiable than hostile.

'Of course it's *possible*,' Clement Ryder acknowledged a shade impatiently. 'But I maintain that it's highly *unlikely*. I've knocked about this world a bit, WPC Loveday,' he carried on, his precise, educated voice becoming almost hypnotic now. 'I've worked all my life in stressful environments, where you need to keep your wits about you. And more than that – get to know and fully understand human nature in all its glory and ignominy.'

For a moment he paused. Then shrugged. 'I've had patients who've ignored their symptoms for years, and convinced themselves they were as right as rain when any idiot could have told them they were sick. And during my years on the coroner's bench, I've had people stand up and tell truths that would break your heart. I've seen courage and cowardice, greed and selflessness, petty self-absorption and vanity like you wouldn't believe. I've listened to tales of devotion and madness and the full gamut of emotions in between.'

It was only when Trudy finally let out a long breath that she realised she'd been holding it in.

'So when I tell you that I just know when people are lying, either to themselves or to others, I suppose I'm asking you to take that on trust. Not that I think you'll need to do that for very long,' he added crisply, once more spearing her with those iron-grey eyes. 'You strike me as an intelligent enough sort. And I think once we start picking this case apart as it *should* have been picked apart four and a half years ago, it won't take you long to be as convinced as I am that there's something rotten in the state of Denmark. Or, in this case, at the heart of the Fleet-Wright family.'

Trudy, at that moment, wouldn't have taken any bets that the old vulture would be proved wrong.

Chapter Fifteen

When Mavis McGillicuddy opened the door to find two strangers on her doorstep, she didn't look particularly surprised. Perhaps it was because one of them, a pretty young girl dressed – to her eyes – rather incongruously in a policewoman's uniform, wasn't a totally unexpected sight.

She'd seen many police officers, in all sorts of shapes and sizes, since Jonathan had died. Even the older man looked familiar to her somehow.

'Please, come in,' she said vaguely, leading them into the rather chilly front room, which she hardly ever entered herself except to dust and straighten the antimacassars on the backs of the chairs. Returning a few minutes later with a tea tray, she deposited it on the oak coffee table that was one of the few bits of furniture she'd inherited from her parents.

It was only when she was seated and wondering if she should have brought in some cake that she remembered where she'd seen the man before.

'You were in court. My Jonathan's court. I mean, when his case . . . Would you like a biscuit?'

Clement, who had in fact introduced himself on the doorstep and given his name and occupation, now smiled gently. 'No, thank you, Mrs McGillicuddy. Shall I be mother and pour the tea?' Without waiting for an answer, he reached out and poured from the large, heavy teapot.

Trudy felt her heart squeezing tightly in her chest. The poor old lady looked so vague and so tired that she doubted she'd have had the strength to lift the teapot. Although she'd agreed with Dr Ryder that they probably should start their investigation with Mrs McGillicuddy, she now found herself wishing they'd chosen someone else. Someone who looked as if they could stand up to questioning much better than this dazed, grieving old lady.

She shot a quick, troubled glance at the coroner, but, in the event, needn't have worried. Although he might not suffer fools gladly, and at first acquaintance could indeed come across as a cold, calculating man – and maybe even an arrogant one – her earlier assessment of him had been spot-on. He was clearly no bully.

Instead, as he began to talk very gently to the old lady, Trudy found the tension slowly easing out of her. The more she listened and learned, the more she realised just how skilfully Dr Ryder was getting Mrs McGillicuddy to talk about her son in a way that was actually beneficial to her. Instead of trying to gloss over or ignore the circumstances of Jonathan's loss, as probably most of her friends and family members did, Clement let her talk it all out. After all, why wouldn't she want to talk about him, and the horror and anger she felt about it all?

From time to time, Trudy marvelled at the easy way he slipped in questions that would help their investigation, and she could see that Mavis herself had no idea she was being questioned at all. Instead, she was being encouraged to speak about her boy – his early marriage, the shock of losing his wife at such a young age. Her pride in him when he'd started up his own business; and then, finally, the shock of his death.

But Clement didn't dwell on that, and very quickly took her back to happier times. A now more animated Mavis, one with a little more colour in her cheeks and looking less vague as this obviously important man took such an interest in her boy, began to talk freely, even eagerly, about him.

However, rather frustratingly, and as time went on, it became more and more clear to Trudy that she didn't seem to know all that much about her son. Or rather, to be more specific, that much about his relationships with women. Which was perhaps not that surprising. Most young men, Trudy knew, tried to keep such matters a secret from their mothers. She knew her own brother was just the same.

'But after he'd had time to mourn the loss of Jenny, things must have become harder and harder for him,' Clement was saying now. 'A young man, and such a good-looking one too.' He smiled over at the photograph of her son that Mavis had willingly shown them. 'He must have started to feel lonely?'

'Oh, yes. But he had Marie to think of, and his business to see to. He wanted to build that up, see. He had ambition, my Jonathan,' the old woman said proudly.

'But he must have started courting, Mrs McGillicuddy,' Trudy put in gently, deciding it was time she earned her keep, and hoping the other woman would feel more comfortable discussing her son's private life with her, rather than with another man. 'You wouldn't have wanted him to be lonely all his life, would you?' she prompted. 'After all, he was young enough to marry again.'

'Well, no, of course I didn't want him to be unhappy,' Mavis said at once. 'And I expect he did see girls, from time to time. But he never brought any of them home,' she added with a sigh. 'He always seemed to be working all hours of the day . . .' She trailed off with a weary, listless shrug.

But before she could descend back into gloom, Clement was determined to come to the crux of the matter.

'Do you remember much about that inquest he had to attend – oh, must be nearly five years or so ago now?' he asked gently.

'Inquest?' Mavis looked puzzled.

'A young girl who accidentally died. Gisela Fleet-Wright?' he said gently.

'Oh. Oh, yes. I think . . . yes, she was the daughter of one of his clients, wasn't she?'

Trudy glanced at Dr Ryder significantly.

'He worked for a lady in a big house up near Five Mile Drive somewhere,' Mavis went on. 'And her daughter was found dead in bed. Is that who you mean?'

'Yes.'

Mavis nodded. 'Yes, he had to testify to . . . oh, what was it now – something about the state of her mind? I remember, there was some talk that she might have killed herself. But she hadn't. I think it was some tragic mistake over her medicine.' Mavis sighed. 'Her poor mother. She must have been devastated.'

Again Trudy and Clement eyed one another warily.

'Didn't she and Jonathan . . . Weren't they rather close at one time?' Clement asked gently.

But Mavis only frowned slightly. 'No, I don't think so.'

'Ah,' Clement said. Clearly, Jonathan had kept quiet about his relationship with Gisela. And given the girl's obvious mental-health issues, perhaps that wasn't so surprising.

And although they stayed a little longer, it was clear that, as a source of information about what might have happened between the dead girl and her son, Mavis McGillicuddy was a total dud.

After a decent interval, they extricated themselves gently from the grieving mother and stepped outside, walking briskly in the wind and rain to the coroner's car – a Rover 75-110 P4, more commonly known by the popular nickname of 'Aunty Rover'.

Now, as he reached forward and turned the ignition, she sighed softly. 'His mother had no idea he'd been seeing Gisela, had she?'

'No,' he said. 'Which is a little surprising, don't you think? The Fleet-Wright case *must* have made the local papers – and if it didn't, you can be sure all the local gossips would have been talking about it.'

Trudy, seeing where he was going with this, nodded slowly. 'Yes. Her neighbours would have picked up on it. Even if her closest friends were too polite to mention it, somebody would have told her.' Trudy's lips twisted into a grim smile. 'If only because they thought she "ought to know". People can be so generous like that, can't they?' she added sardonically.

Clement smiled grimly. 'News travels fast, bad news travels faster, and scandalous gossip travels at the speed of light.'

'So you think . . . what? That Mrs McGillicuddy was lying to us?' Trudy asked, beginning to wonder if the coroner saw lies and conspiracies everywhere.

But again he surprised her. 'No, not necessarily. I just think Mrs McGillicuddy is very good at keeping her head down and only seeing and hearing what she wants to see and hear.'

'Hmmm. She lives in her own little world, you mean, and doesn't really venture out into reality much,' Trudy mused. Yes, she could understand how that could happen. There were some women in her neighbourhood like that as well. Their families and homes were their entire world, and as long as the front doorstep was scrubbed, and tea was on the table at six, all was as it should be.

But Trudy was determined not to let her world shrink to such an extent. Although she wanted a home and family of her own one day, right now she was far more interested in forging a satisfying career for herself. After all, men did it all the time. Who was to say a woman couldn't do the same?

'And don't forget, she's lived all her life clinging on desperately to respectability, and keeping the family secret,' Clement Ryder added.

She knew DI Jennings had already put him in the picture about Jonathan being illegitimate, and that the reason for his murder lay in Sir Marcus Deering's household, rather than that of the McGillicuddys.

'Right,' Trudy agreed. 'She'd have been conditioned into keeping things about her son close to her chest for fear of her unmarried state getting about. No doubt that would have rubbed off on Jonathan too. Apparently, Mrs McGillicuddy had spun him some tale about his father dying in some sort of accident before he was born. And I daresay, whenever he asked her about him, she brushed him off, or made it clear it wasn't to be discussed.'

'So he learned at an early age to keep anything private or in the least "not quite nice" to himself. Yes, I agree,' Clement mused grimly. 'The mother, careful to keep up the front of respectable "widow" at all costs and ignoring the wider world around her. And her son, the "celibate", hard-working man, pretending that only his child and business mattered. Neither of them actually talking to the other about anything important.'

'That's so sad,' Trudy said faintly.

Clement merely grunted and Trudy felt glad when he turned into the traffic and drove them away from the neat, unhappy little terraced house in Cowley.

Chapter Sixteen

Anthony Deering sailed across a low hawthorn fence on his favourite hunter, a handsome black horse called Darjeeling, and heard the horse snort with the effort as it landed in the ploughed field. Together, horse and man made their way around the edge of the field, both of them feeling rather pleased with themselves.

Although he had been due back at work in London, Anthony had taken a week's leave. Like his father, he was keen to see this bloody and nasty business come to some sort of conclusion as soon as possible. And until it did, he felt unable to move on with his normal life.

How could he go back to London with all this hanging over their heads?

Clearly this maniac who was stalking his father meant business. It had come as quite a shock to him, naturally, to learn he'd had a half-brother knocking about the world all this time. And even more of a shock to learn he'd been murdered.

Although his mother had begged him to go back to London,

Anthony had managed to dissuade her. After all, there was nothing to stop the killer from simply following him back to the capital and then taking a pop at him there. And in the hubbub of town, the killer could quickly be swallowed up and lost in a crowd, whereas here a stranger would stand out. Furthermore, out here, he knew the lay of the land and felt he had the home advantage.

Darjeeling suddenly snorted and gave a quick sideways trot, almost unseating him. Anthony, his heart rate accelerating rapidly, swiftly got the horse under control and looked sharply around.

They were still in the ploughed field, near a small copse of hazelnut and ash trees. Was someone there in the woods, watching him?

Then a pheasant rocketed out of a clump of dead grass, giving its usual raucous cry, and Darjeeling tossed his head again. Anthony laughed and, stretching forward, patted the horse on its glossy neck. 'Easy, boy. My nerves are stretched tight enough as it is. I don't need you getting the skitters too.'

But as he turned his mount away from the copse and headed for the open sheep pastures on the other side of the hedge, he couldn't help but wonder if some human agency had caused the pheasant to flee. And whether, even now, malign eyes were boring into his back as he turned and rode away.

'Where to now?' Trudy asked as they drove away from the McGillicuddy house and headed towards North Hinksey.

'I thought we'd talk to Julie Wye. Now Mrs Ferris,' Clement said.

Trudy immediately recognised the name. Julie Wye had been

one of Gisela's closest friends. She'd been with Gisela the day before she died, and had testified at the inquest as to her state of mind. She and Gisela had grown up together in north Oxford, attending the same local primary school and then local girls' grammar.

Now living with her husband and infant son in a large, spacious flat on the ground floor of a Victorian house, she seemed surprised to find the police at her door.

When Trudy explained she wanted to talk about Gisela, though, she immediately – if somewhat erroneously – made the connection.

'Oh, this is about Jonathan McGillicuddy, isn't it?' she said as she led them through to a rather cluttered living room, scattered with children's toys, but well lit by the natural light streaming in through large, double-height sash windows.

Neither Clement nor Trudy bothered to correct her. They could always steer the conversation around to Gisela and the events of five and a half years ago when they were ready to.

'Just let me put Charlie down, and I'll put the kettle on,' Julie said. She was a rather large-boned woman, with a mass of red-brown hair and a smattering of freckles across her nose.

Within minutes they were seated in comfortable chairs before a large fire, surrounded by a wire-mesh guard to stop sparks from popping out and setting fire to the liver-and-white King Charles spaniel lying in front of the grate, snoozing contentedly.

'When I read about his murder in the papers, I couldn't believe it,' Julie said, pouring out the tea. This time, Trudy noticed with a brief smile, the coroner didn't offer to 'be mother'.

'Poor Jonathan. First Gisela, now him. It seems neither one of them had much luck, did they?' Julie said. She had rather deep-set, almost black eyes, reminding Trudy of a teddy bear. 'I sometimes think that was what attracted Gisela to him in the first place.'

'Sorry?' Trudy said, not quite following. And Julie gave herself a little shake and laughed in apology.

'No, I'm sorry. I often think of things in my head, and then say something out loud about it, and, of course, nobody else knows what I'm talking about. It drove my mother wild when I was a kid, and now my husband! Sorry, I was just thinking about that summer they met.'

'Yes, tell us about that,' Trudy said encouragingly.

'Well, it was typical of Gisela. In the first place, Jonathan was working as a gardener, little more than a common labourer. Of course, neither of her parents approved of them getting together, which was part of the attraction for Gisela. Cocking a snook at her parents' old-fashioned ideas and all that. And it didn't hurt that Jonathan was so good-looking. And a bit older than her.'

Julie sighed.

'And then, of course, he had such a tragic back story, which was like catnip to a girl like Gisela!'

'His wife dying young, you mean?' Trudy prompted.

'Yes, and him having a young daughter to look after.' Julie nodded, beaming at her in approval for catching on so quickly. 'I'm sure Gisela saw him as if he were a character in one of those Gothic novels she loved so much.'

'The tragic hero?' Clement put in.

'Exactly!' Julie smiled. 'Mind you, that was Gisela all over. I sometimes think she saw herself as the tragic heroine too – Jane Eyre, or Tess of the D'Urbervilles. Her whole life revolved around drama.'

'You never went to university, Mrs Wye?' Trudy asked.

'Me? Good grief, no. Didn't have the brains for it,' she said, self-deprecatingly.

'But Gisela did?'

'Oh, yes. Gisela was always clever. Smart as a whip, even when we were little.' Julie beamed.

'But a troubled girl too,' Trudy carried on, sensing that Clement was happy to leave most of the questioning to her.

Julie sighed. 'Yes. Yes, I suppose that's fair.'

'From what I've learned about her, she seemed, as far as Jonathan was concerned, to be rather . . . well, I suppose obsessed is the word?' she probed delicately.

Julie sighed, then shrugged. 'Oh, well . . . I suppose it doesn't hurt to say it now. But yes, you're right. She was really fixated on him. The trouble was, you see,' she said seriously, fixing Trudy with an earnest, steadfast gaze, 'that Jonathan was the *first* real love of her life. Now, for most of us, our first love is always special, isn't it?'

Trudy nodded, but in fact didn't know if that was true or not. She herself had yet to find herself a 'proper' boyfriend. Much to her mother's chagrin.

'And for most of us,' Julie swept on, snapping Trudy's mind back to the matter at hand, 'we fall for someone, and then we break up and get our heart broken, and we cry, but then we get over it and find someone else. Pretty normal and run-of-the-mill, I daresay.' She laughed lightly. 'But for Gisela it was different.'

Trudy nodded. 'She felt things more keenly, perhaps?' she prompted.

'And how!' Julie sighed, shaking her head. 'To her, Jonathan was the be-all and end-all of her existence, and she couldn't possibly live without him.' She smiled wryly. 'Looking back on it now, it all seems so impossibly naive and . . . well . . . *stupid*! From the moment he broke it off it was as if Gisela's whole world fell apart. At first, you know, she couldn't accept the fact that *anyone*, let alone her Jonathan, would throw her over. It, well, it *amazed* her. She had a rather healthy ego, I'm afraid! And then, after the shock wore off, she got so angry.'

Julie paused and, looking down at the teacup in her hand before setting it aside, gave a little shudder. 'I don't mind telling you, she scared me sometimes with the sheer depth of her passion and rage. And despair. It was like she had no filter on her emotions. No protection from life's knocks. So their breakup and the aftermath just tore her apart.'

For a moment Julie stared blankly out of the window. 'I didn't know how to help her. None of us did,' she said forlornly.

'She was already on medication then? For her depression and anxiety issues?' Trudy slipped in gently.

'Oh, yes. Gisela was always highly strung, even when we were little. She could throw some really massive tantrums, I can tell you.'

'Do you think that was why Jonathan eventually stopped seeing her?'

Julie nodded. 'At first he was starstruck by her, like everyone was when they first met her. She was so pretty and delicate and quick and witty. Sophisticated, but fragile – like a delicate, dazzling butterfly. But after a while she became so demanding.

Always wanting to know where he was and what he was doing. And if she saw him even talking to another girl, even someone nowhere near as pretty as her . . . woooh! Fireworks, I can tell you. And then she'd be all contrite and sorry. And needy!' She rolled her eyes expressively. 'If Jonathan didn't keep telling her how much he loved and adored her, she'd get scared. And yet, at the same time, it was as if she thought she owned him. Like he was her property – like a piece of expensive jewellery she could show off.'

'And no man likes to be made to feel uncomfortable,' Clement put in thoughtfully.

Julie Wye shot him a quick, assessing look. 'No. You're right. We all noticed how jittery Jonathan would get if Gisela started in with one of her drama-queen scenes.'

'So you weren't surprised when he broke up with her?' Trudy said.

'No. We could all see it coming.'

'Except for Gisela.'

'No. But then, I don't think she ever really admitted it had happened. For weeks afterwards, she'd make like she'd be seeing him again sometime. She'd make plans for a picnic and tell us he'd be coming. Of course, he never did. And then she rewrote the story in her head, so that *she* was the one who dumped *him*!'

'And so became even more obsessed with him?'

'Yes. Sometimes, she'd turn up in the gardens where he was working. More than once, she'd got him fired from a job for making a nuisance of herself.' Julie sighed. 'But it was as if she had to know every single thing about him. It drove her wild, for instance, that he never really knew who his father was. His mother told him he'd died in some sort of farming accident before he was born, but that was it.'

She failed to notice the quick, knowing look her two visitors exchanged at this. 'He said his mother never wanted to talk about it. But that was Jonathan all over – he never seemed to have much curiosity about things. But Gisela simply had to know everything!'

'It helped feed her obsession,' Clement said quietly. 'The more she knew, the more she could "own" the object of her desire.'

'I suppose so,' Julie said, but it was clear from her slight frown that such philosophical musings were beyond her.

'It must have been a terrible shock to you when she died,' Trudy said sympathetically.

'Oh, it was . . . Gisela had been a presence in my life . . . well, since forever. She made you feel so *alive*. Do you understand?'

Clement nodded.

'You testified to her state of mind at the inquest,' he said mildly. 'As I remember, you said that, the day before, she'd seemed much the same, and not particularly depressed?'

'No. I thought she seemed more upbeat if anything. A little excited maybe. As if she had something pleasant on her mind, or at least something that pleased her.'

'Another scheme to win Jonathan back, perhaps?' Clement asked.

'Perhaps,' Julie said, a shade doubtfully. 'It was almost as if she'd finally decided to give up on him. I felt relieved, I can tell you. But then . . . well, there was that mix-up with the pills. Her poor mother. I always liked Mrs Fleet-Wright.'

Clement nodded. 'She said at the inquest that Gisela didn't like taking her pills and often lied about having taken them when, in fact, she hadn't?'

'Oh, yes, that was quite true,' Julie confirmed at once. 'We'd all seen her do that. They numbed her feelings, you see, and Gisela did love to feel things. She said people who felt nothing weren't really alive.'

So her mother hadn't lied about that at least, Trudy thought, glancing across at the coroner thoughtfully.

'And Mrs Fleet-Wright also said that sometimes Gisela would make herself sick after taking the pills?' he mused casually.

Julie sighed. 'I wouldn't be surprised. It was the sort of thing Gisela would do and think she was being clever. She could be awfully sly, you see. When she didn't get her own way.'

Trudy nodded. It was just as she'd thought. Gisela had been the kind of girl who brought nothing but chaos to herself and everyone around her. The question was – had her legacy somehow reached out and engulfed Jonathan McGillicuddy, nearly five years after her death?

And with the best will in the world – and notwithstanding her growing respect for Dr Clement Ryder and his opinions – she just couldn't see how it could have.

It was getting dark by the time they'd talked to another of Gisela's friends from that time, Mandy Gibson, a woman who'd since gone on to work for the BBC in London. And she'd done little more than confirm Julie Wye's own assessment of the dead girl.

Clement had surprised Trudy by asking Mandy if she had kept any keepsakes of their friendship, such as a letter from the dead girl, or a birthday card perhaps. Mandy had looked nonplussed for a moment, but then remembered she'd kept a postcard Gisela had sent her from a holiday she'd once taken with her family in Italy.

Promising he'd get it back to her in due course, Clement had pocketed it. Trudy had meant to ask him why he'd wanted it on the drive back to Oxford, but somehow it had slipped her mind.

Now, as the coroner brought his Aunty Rover to a stop outside St Aldates station, Trudy picked up her cap from the back seat and set it firmly on her head. But before opening the door and going inside to write up her first day's report for DI Jennings, she hesitated and turned towards the older man.

'You think she killed herself, don't you? Gisela?' she challenged him flatly. 'And that her mother covered it up?'

'It's a possibility, don't you think?' Clement asked mildly.

'It certainly makes sense.' Trudy decided to press him. 'That's what you've been angling for all along, isn't it? With the family being Catholic, suicide is an even bigger social and religious no-no for them, which gives them even more of a motive to try and hush it all up. They'd not only have had to go through the scandal of having a child take her own life, but also have had to face the trauma of not being allowed to bury her in consecrated ground.'

'So you don't think it was death by misadventure any more then?' Clement challenged her right back, his voice sounding amused now. 'And after only one day too?' He smiled in the pale light from one of the streetlamps. 'And here was I, thinking it might take you a week or so to come around to my way of thinking.'

Trudy gave a small, irritated grunt and got out of the car. 'I'll see you tomorrow, Dr Ryder,' she said stiffly.

'Looking forward to it, Constable Loveday.' His laconic voice followed her out into the darkening street, and Trudy slammed the car door shut behind her much harder than was probably necessary.

With a slight and annoying flush rising to her cheeks, Trudy marched firmly into the station.

Chapter Seventeen

Anthony Deering didn't realise anything was wrong for quite some time.

He'd slept in late that morning, rising at just gone half past nine when normally he'd have been up and about for two hours or more. But lately he'd had trouble sleeping – which didn't surprise him much.

When his father had first told him about the letters threatening his life, he'd been inclined to laugh them off. Clearly they were the work of some feeble-minded individual who got his jollies putting the wind up people. And you simply couldn't go around giving credence to people like that – they'd just make your life a misery if you let them. Besides, he was a fit and able young chap and had even done a bit of boxing back in his schooldays. So if anyone tried anything with him, he was pretty confident he'd be able to give a good account of himself.

But then Jonathan McGillicuddy had died – the brother he'd never known he had – and suddenly it was no joke. He no longer felt quite so confident. It was an eerie feeling, knowing that someone, who had already killed once, now had you in their sights as their next victim.

Life felt distinctly tenuous whenever he thought of his half-brother, another fit and healthy young man like himself, lying dead in a morgue somewhere. Going around with a perpetual cold itch down your back, imagining you could feel someone watching you all the time, was bound to wear you down. As was jumping at every sudden sound, and checking all the time that doors and windows were shut and locked.

Reluctant though he was to admit it, his nerves were definitely beginning to fray, as were those of his parents. So much so that it had now got to the point where the atmosphere at the house was becoming unbearable.

So, that morning, once he'd had breakfast, he'd decided he simply had to get out, if only for an hour or so. Using the excuse that he needed to go into Oxford in search of a new pair of wellingtons to replace his old pair, which were starting to let in water, he left the house with a determined step.

Though it wasn't possible for the police to keep a man permanently stationed at the house, Sergeant O'Grady, a sound and practical man, had given them all tips on how to keep the house secure, and measures they could take to maximise their personal safety. As Anthony left the house, he was sure to check there was no one around.

His car, a Vauxhall PA Velox, was parked around the back, near the stable block. He'd liked the look of the car the moment he'd first set eyes on it. With its acres of chrome, tailfin and 'wraparound' front screen painted a cherry red with white trim, it appealed to something flamboyant in his nature that he was usually at pains to keep hidden.

A lot of his friends scoffed at it in public, but he suspected that, in private, they secretly wished they'd had the guts to buy something like it for themselves.

Mindful of O'Grady's advice (and feeling slightly foolish), Anthony quickly bent down and checked underneath the car, but could see nothing suspicious taped to the undercarriage, after which he took a quick look under the bonnet. Not that he could really bring himself to believe someone would plant a bomb under his car!

As he slipped inside, the big, comfortable bench seat enveloped him in familiar comfort and he gave a small sigh of satisfaction. The dashboard of the car was as flashy as a jukebox and, when he turned the key in the ignition, he smiled contently as the six-cylinder engine roared in response.

Taking the car out on the open road was always a joy. What did he care if his friends all said it made him look as if he belonged to the ranks of salesmen who liked to thrash up and down the roads?

Today, something glitzy, vulgar and fun was just what he needed to lift his spirits and remind him that life was for the living! He was damned if he was going to go around like a whipped dog, shaking like a jelly!

He tuned the radio to the nearest station and heard Connie Francis, one of his favourites, singing her big hit from last year, 'Where the Boys Are', and began to sing softly along as he drove down the gravelled drive. At the end, he turned off onto the narrow country lane and headed for the B-road that would take him towards Kidlington.

For the first part of the short drive towards Oxford, everything seemed fine. Connie Francis had been replaced by Emile Ford and the Checkmates, and even the sky looked as if it might brighten up. And then, as he approached a curve in the road and put his foot down on the brake, suddenly everything wasn't fine at all.

The brake pedal went down, but nothing much happened. Quickly he took his foot off it and stomped down again. And again nothing happened. The car didn't even start to slow down. Abruptly he broke out in a cold sweat as he felt his heart rate start to soar.

He was travelling at over fifty miles an hour, and in a moment of total, almost calm, clarity, knew he wasn't going to make the sharp bend that was just coming up.

Praying that nothing was coming his way on the other side of the road, he began to feverishly go through the motions he remembered from the days when he'd taken driving lessons, on how to slow a car down in case of brake failure.

Go down the gears. Turn off the engine. Put on the handbrake. But now he had to turn into the curve, and almost at once he could feel the big, heavy car start to fishtail out of control on the wet and greasy road. And then the world became a kaleidoscope of green and brown as a hawthorn hedge rose up in front of the windscreen, blocking out his view of the sky. His world darkened in a shattered kaleidoscope of glass and sound.

DI Jennings walked into the interview room of St Aldates police station and nodded amiably at the man seated at the table.

Clive Greaves had declined to bring a solicitor along with

him when he'd been asked to come down 'for an informal chat' and Jennings intended to make the most of that while it lasted.

With a brief smile he sat down and asked the fifty-two-year-old gamekeeper if he'd like a cup of tea. Balding and built like a former rugby player, the man watched Jennings cautiously. He had deep-set, rather bear-like eyes that glared out at the world from the startling ruin of his scarred face.

'Sure. Milk, two sugars, please,' he finally muttered.

Jennings nodded to the young PC who'd been standing in one corner and the lad left without a word.

'So, Mr Greaves, I have just a few questions I'd like to put to you, if you don't mind?' the DI began casually, reaching into his jacket pocket and producing a pack of Player's cigarettes. 'Fag?'

'I prefer Piccadilly.'

Jennings shrugged, produced a lighter and set about enjoying his fourth cigarette of the day. 'Suit yourself,' he said mildly through the slight haze of smoke.

'So what's this all about then?' Clive Greaves finally asked flatly, glancing at his watch. 'I need to get back. I've got pheasants to feed.'

Jennings nodded. He knew from the papers his team had put together that Greaves had worked as a gamekeeper on an estate near the village of Aynho for nearly eight years now. Unmarried, he lived in a tied cottage, and was known to be a bit of a drinker. The station house over at Deddington knew of him, and had sent over some details. Five times they'd had to pull him out of pubs for causing an affray. Once, he'd been on the point of being charged with causing bodily harm after getting into a rather messy brawl in which someone's nose had been broken, but, after sobering up, the plaintiff had decided not to go ahead with a court case.

But it wasn't Clive Greaves's temper while under the influence of alcohol that was of interest to Jennings.

'We won't keep you long, Mr Greaves,' he said now, smoothly. 'Like I said, we just need to clear a few things up. You are Mr Clive Randolf Greaves, aged fifty-two, formerly a resident of Perry Common in Birmingham?'

Clive's eyes suddenly narrowed, which had the effect of making his features look even more misshapen and disfigured. And Jennings was already finding it hard to look at his suspect properly, since his eyes couldn't quite make up their mind where they should alight. The gamekeeper's whole face had the tight, shiny, red-and-white lines of a man who had been severely burned. Staring straight into his small, almost black, eyes made him feel uncomfortable – but letting his eyes stray to the other parts of his ruined features was even worse.

'Yeah, but that's going back a bit,' Greaves said, giving a brief shrug. 'I ain't lived in Brum for years.'

'And you're unmarried, Mr Greaves?'

Clive Greaves snorted bitterly. 'Whaddya think?' he said, pointing one callused finger to his face. 'Not exactly Errol bleeding Flynn, am I? What woman in her right mind would wanna put up with waking up next to this every mornin'?'

Which gave Jennings just the opening he was looking for. 'Fire, wasn't it?' he said, trying to keep his voice casual. He made a show of checking his notes. 'Nearly thirty years ago now. You were working in a warehouse when the goods caught fire?'

'S'right.'

'Says here you were hospitalised for nearly ten weeks.'

''Ere, what's this got to do with anything?' Clive suddenly demanded aggressively. 'I thought you pulled me in to have a word about last Saturday night.'

Jennings smiled grimly. 'No, sir. I'm not interested in the altercation you had at the Wheel and Wagon.'

'So that jumped-up pipsqueak ain't made a complaint against me then?'

'No, sir.'

'So why am I here?'

'I want to talk to you about Sir Marcus Deering,' Jennings said softly.

And had the satisfaction of seeing his man stiffen.

Chapter Eighteen

'Trudy, love, don't forget to call Brian,' Barbara Loveday said as she neatly folded a large brown headscarf into a triangle and tied it under her chin. It was one of her favourites, with a pattern of gold, red and russet autumn leaves scattered over a cream background.

She checked her appearance in the hall mirror and glanced at her watch. With a bit of luck, she might just collect enough Green Shield stamps from her shopping today to get that toaster she had her eye on.

Trudy, who wasn't due to meet Clement Ryder until one thirty, and had popped back home for lunch since the house was almost on her morning beat, swallowed the last of her Marmite on toast and frowned. What on earth was her mother on about now?

She stepped out into the tiny hall just as Barbara reached for the front door.

'Brian?' she echoed blankly.

'See! I knew you weren't listening to me, our Trudy! I told

you this morning, Brian Bayliss called around yesterday teatime. He was dead sorry not to catch you in, but I told him you was working late. All them different shifts you have to do, our Trudy. I wish you didn't! Anyway, he said he wanted to invite you out to the pictures. He said to tell you that that film was on that you wanted to see.'

Trudy sighed. She'd known Brian Bayliss all her life, since he lived only three doors down, was the same age as she was, and they'd gone to the same local schools. A raw, big-boned lad, he worked as a mechanic at the same bus depot where her father went each morning to pick up his beloved bus. Perhaps because of this close and constant interaction between their families, her parents (and Brian's too, probably) had somehow got it into their heads that the two of them were a couple. Or were destined to get together, or some such nonsense.

Worse, she was beginning to think Brian thought the same.

It didn't help that most of her friends thought he was quite a catch, since he was six-feet-three, with a fine head of sandy-red hair and unusual golden-brown eyes that had been described by one of them as 'dreamy'. He also had a good job with a good wage. And to top it all off, he also played rugby for the local team, which made a bit of a hero out of him, apparently.

A nice enough lad, but Trudy had no intention of marrying him, or anyone else for that matter, for some time yet.

And although she'd said, over and over again, that earning her sergeant's stripes was the only goal she had in mind, nobody ever seemed to take that in. Or take her ambitions seriously. Not her parents, or her brother, or her friends, or even Brian himself. It was as if she was one of those little dolls that, when you pulled the string, said something sweet and cute and totally unmemorable. She half-expected everyone to pat her on the head whenever she expressed her determination to succeed at her chosen career, and say how quaint she was, before going on to talk about which local girl had just got engaged. Oh, and had she thought about baby names yet for when she had little 'uns of her own?

Now, with a sigh, Trudy put on her cap and followed her mother out into the street. It was pointless arguing with her. 'I'll maybe call him later. If I pass a telephone box,' she muttered instead.

'That'll be nice, dear. It's Peter Sellers,' Barbara Loveday said.

'Huh?' Trudy blinked.

'In the film – the one you wanted to see. Brian said something about him being in prison and planning to steal a diamond or something,' her mother said vaguely.

'Oh. Right . . . er . . . I think it's called *Two-Way Stretch*', Trudy said, remembering saying once, while out with a group of friends, that she'd quite like to see the film when it came round to Oxford. Had Brian been out with them that night?

'Well, that'll be nice. Perhaps you can have a bite to eat afterwards. Dad says Brian earns a good screw down at the depot so he can afford to treat you.'

Trudy sighed. 'Yes, Mum,' she said wearily.

But as she walked into the station house, all thoughts about her social life disappeared, as it quickly became evident that something was up. There was an air of tense excitement about the place that you could have cut with a knife.

It was Rodney Broadstairs – naturally – who was the first to tell her what it was. Rodney always liked rubbing it in that he was 'one of the boys' and she wasn't. 'Our nutter's only gone and taken a run at Anthony Deering! He's in the hospital. Someone fiddled with his brakes,' he told her, as he shrugged into his uniform jacket and plonked his helmet on his head. 'The boss wants us to get out there and take witness statements.'

Trudy, trying not to grind her teeth at being left out of all the excitement, watched as Rodney set off, whistling cheerfully. Then – after a quick glance at her watch – she realised she needed to get herself down to Floyds Row pretty sharpish. She couldn't see the old vulture taking any excuse for her being late!

She sighed heavily. Although the Fleet-Wright case had its interesting points (and was definitely better than walking the beat), it lacked the excitement and immediate drama of the Deering/McGillicuddy case.

'I wouldn't be at all surprised if that little brother of hers hasn't turned out to be as batty as Gisela, poor thing.'

They were seated in a rather cramped little den, in a rather cramped little cottage, just the other side of Middleton Cheney, where Mary Allcroft was now living. Along with Mandy Gibson, Mary had been considered a contender for the role of Gisela's 'best friend'. Although one of the first things Mary had said to them, when they'd tracked her down and asked if it was all right if they had a chat, was that being a friend of Gisela's was often something that could be open to interpretation.

Mary currently worked in the market town of Banbury, as a secretary in the offices of a narrowboat yard, so they'd been lucky to find her in on her afternoon off.

They'd been sipping strong, hot tea from slightly grubby

mugs as Mary, after comfortably tucking her hair neatly behind one ear and settling down into an overstuffed armchair, happily answered any questions they put to her.

Which had started with her expanding on her remark about what being 'friends' with the dead girl actually entailed. Which was, apparently, to worship at her altar and put up with her moods.

'Gisela was a funny thing,' she'd explained. 'One moment you were flavour of the month, and the next – for no fathomable reason – you were out in the cold.'

Both Trudy and Clement had agreed she sounded like hard work, but Mary had remained touchingly loyal to her dead friend. A short, round sort of girl, with an unruly cap of curly yellow hair and big blue eyes, she'd simply shrugged and told them she'd always felt sorry for her, and had been willing to put up with her 'eccentricities'.

'She was so clearly unhappy, you see, most of the time,' Mary told them simply.

This had led to a general discussion about Gisela's constant battle with depression and mood swings, which, in turn, had led to Mary's latest comment about her little brother, Rex, being just the same way. It was almost as if she saw unhappiness like a physical trait you could inherit in your genes, along with the colour of your eyes or hair.

'The little brother,' Clement said now with a slight frown. 'I don't remember him being called at the inquest.'

'Oh, he wouldn't have been,' Mary said promptly. 'He was only a kid when Gisela died.'

'What – five or six?' Trudy asked. She, too, had seen no mention of the younger Fleet-Wright sibling in the records.

'Oh, no. A bit older than that,' Mary said. 'Thirteen or fourteen maybe?'

Clement nodded. As a general rule, the court preferred not to call minors to the stand to testify, unless it was absolutely necessary.

'How did they get on?' Trudy asked, genuinely curious now. 'I get the impression, from all I've been learning about her, that Gisela liked to be the centre of attention.'

'Oh, Gisela didn't mind him,' Mary surprised her by saying airily. 'Of course, she was always daddy's little princess, and Mr Fleet-Wright doted on her. She could always twist him round her little finger.' Mary laughed. 'And it didn't hurt that Rex adored his big sister either.'

Ah, Trudy thought with a wry smile. *That would explain it.*

'He used to follow her around like a little puppy dog sometimes, which amused her and pandered to her ego.' Mary paused and frowned slightly. 'To tell you the truth, I found it a bit creepy sometimes.'

'How so?' Clement asked sharply.

'Well – with boys, it's usually all "mummy" this and "mummy" that, isn't it?' Mary said comfortably. 'But with Rex, it was as if the sun and moon shone out of Gisela, not out of Beatrice. Maybe Rex picked up early on the fact that Gisela was the real focus of the family dynamic, making his mother more or less irrelevant.'

'And Gisela's health problems . . .' Trudy chose her words very carefully. 'Those would naturally have concerned her parents greatly, taking up all their time and anxiety.'

'Yes, quite,' Mary said. 'Everyone worried about Gisela, which only played to her dramatic side.' Mary paused and shrugged.

'Even Rex fretted over her constantly, making sure she was warm enough, or ate her dinner. Of course, it didn't help that Gisela used to play up to him either. I remember once, me and Mandy were round their place one summer, and Mrs Fleet-Wright had told Rex he couldn't have a sherbet dip because it would ruin his appetite for tea. And Gisela immediately sneaked off to the local shop and bought him one and gave it to him. I wouldn't have paid any attention to it if I'd thought she was simply being kind. But Gisela deliberately engineered things to make sure Rex was caught eating it. Naturally, that put her mother in a bind. If she took it off him, it would make Mrs Fleet-Wright the villain. And if she didn't, it would just undermine her authority all the more.'

At this point, Trudy glanced thoughtfully at the coroner. Clearly, the Fleet-Wright family had its issues.

'So, what happened?' Clement asked, careful to keep his voice calm and neutral.

'Oh, Mrs Fleet-Wright simply shook her head and said that if he didn't eat all his tea there'd be trouble. In the event, Rex ate all the sherbet dip and seemed to adore Gisela all the more.' Mary shook her own head now as she thought back. 'The trouble was, Gisela was as inconsistent with Rex as she was with everyone else. One moment she'd make a proper pet of him; the next she'd be scornfully telling him to go away, that he was being a pest, and that nobody in their right mind would want him around. Rex would be heartbroken and wander off like a whipped puppy, and Gisela would just laugh.'

'That sounds rather cruel,' Trudy felt compelled to say.

'Oh, it was. But then, in a way, it wasn't,' Mary said, rather enigmatically. 'I mean, I don't think Gisela did it to be deliberately cruel – I think she just didn't understand it *was* cruel. Do you see the difference?'

Trudy smiled. 'She didn't set out to hurt her brother, it was just that she didn't care if she did.'

But again, Mary was inclined to remain loyal to her dead friend. 'Not quite. With Gisela, the only thing that mattered was how *she* felt. How *her* life was going. How she could *entertain* herself. Oh, I'm not explaining this very well!' Mary said, cross with herself. 'Gisela was the sort of girl who always had to be *feeling* things. To her, life wasn't really being lived unless something was *happening*. She loved rows and arguments because she could become heated and indulge in clever language, and fire things up. She loved melancholy, and feeling sad, because at least then she knew she was alive. That's why she kept that diary of hers. She was always writing in it, dramatising herself and what was happening to her. She'd spend hours writing in it, as if she expected somebody to publish it one day! She never let us read it, of course, but I suspect it was pretty sensational.'

Trudy nodded. 'Gisela saw herself as a heroine in a novel?' But as she spoke, she wondered: where was this diary of Gisela's now? She was sure she'd seen no mention of it in the case files.

'Yes. Exactly.' Mary beamed. 'And most of all, of course, Gisela loved being in love. And that was why that thing with Jonathan McGillicuddy really threw her for a loop, because, for the first time, I think it was the real thing. And not just one of her fantasies or self-indulgences.'

'Ah,' Clement said, nodding his head. 'Gisela actually fell in love, instead of just playing at it.'

'Yes. With Jonathan it was different. That's why it really

broke her up – and for real, I mean, not pretend. It shocked her to the core when he left her,' Mary said sadly. 'I don't think it had ever occurred to her that any man *could* leave her.'

Trudy made a brief note in her notebook. Here again was independent confirmation that Jonathan had been the one to break off the relationship, not Gisela, as the dead girl had tried to insist.

'Did you know Jonathan well?' Trudy asked. Mindful as she was that the coroner's interest lay in getting to the truth about the Fleet-Wright case, she knew DI Jennings expected her to keep the McGillicuddy murder and Deering case at the forefront of her investigations.

And she was determined to prove to her boss that she was reliable.

'Not really. I knew him because he was Gisela's boyfriend, but we didn't get to meet him that often. Her friends, I mean. Gisela kept him guarded as if he was treasure. She wanted to make sure none of us stole him from her.'

'She was possessive then?'

'Very!' Mary confirmed wryly.

'What did you make of Jonathan?' she asked next.

'Oh, he was a bit of a catch, I suppose. Even though he was only her parents' gardener, he was really good-looking and just that bit older than us, which made him intriguing! And the fact that he was a widower with a young daughter just made him even more glamorous.'

'Did he seem to have any enemies?'

'No,' Mary said, her normally cheerful and open face looking openly dismayed now. 'I read about his murder in the paper. It's terrible! I hope you catch who did it.'

'We will,' Trudy said grimly, earning her a sharp, not entirely approving look from her companion. While she knew the police didn't always solve their cases, and that she shouldn't really throw out promises so rashly, she didn't care. Let the old vulture be cynical – she could just feel it in her bones that they were going to catch the poison-pen killer of Jonathan McGillicuddy. 'So, when you knew him, you weren't aware of any problems he might have had?' she pressed on.

'Problems?'

'Drinking, gambling, running around with a bad crowd?'

'Oh, no. Nothing like that,' Mary said.

Trudy sighed but nodded. It was as she'd always thought. Jonathan had died because he'd been Marcus Deering's son, and some madman had a grudge against Deering. And with Jonathan being the illegitimate, secret, *unprotected* and unsuspecting son, he had presented a far easier initial target than the much more cosseted – and beloved – Anthony.

Still, she'd had to ask.

Ten minutes later they left the little cottage and headed back to Oxford. 'It's looking more and more likely that it was suicide, isn't it?' Trudy said, as Clement tried – and failed – to overtake a trundling tractor that was blocking two-thirds of the narrow country road ahead of them.

But it was as if the older man hadn't heard her. 'I want you to go and talk to former PC Richard Gordon,' he said out of the blue, then gave his horn an impatient blast.

Ahead, the tractor made no obvious signs of moving over to accommodate him.

Trudy instantly recognised the name. 'The PC who was first

on the scene when the doctor called in the police? Why?' she demanded. 'As the local beat officer he'd have been asked to make an initial assessment and then report back, but it would have been the officer who then took over the case – DI Harnsworth – who'd have the best handle on it.' Unfortunately, they wouldn't be able to talk to Harnsworth, as he'd died shortly after retiring from the force last year.

'Humph!' Clement grunted then blasted on the horn again. In front, the tractor trundled placidly on down the middle of the road.

'I tried to talk to Gordon right after the inquest,' Clement admitted reluctantly. 'He wasn't helpful. He seemed to think I was questioning his competence. Clearly, members of your profession have fragile egos,' he stated flatly.

Which, coming from the old vulture, Trudy thought with a catch in her breath, was truly an example of the pot calling the kettle black!

'Which is why I want *you* to talk to former PC Gordon on your own and without me. Perhaps he'll be less prickly with one of his own.'

But Trudy (apart from being much entertained by thoughts of how the ego-laden coroner had been put in his place by a lowly constable) wasn't so sanguine about this. As a young probationary WPC, she doubted very much that the retired Richard Gordon would think of her so much as 'one of his own' as someone who had no right to be wearing the uniform in the first place.

Which was what everyone else at the station thought as well, with the possible exception of Sergeant O'Grady and maybe the old desk sergeant, who seemed to like her.

Not that she'd let any of that stop her!

Her chin came up as she said evenly, 'I'd be happy to talk to Mr Gordon.'

Clement Ryder turned his angry eyes away from the stubborn tractor driver in front to give her a thoughtful look. And noting the determined thrust of her chin, his lips twitched.

'Thank you, Constable Loveday,' he said mildly.

Chapter Nineteen

The editor of the *Oxford Mail* was intrigued and a little puzzled by the piece submitted by Sir Marcus Deering for inclusion in the next issue of the paper. But, like the good newspaperman he was, he scented a story in it somewhere, which was one of the reasons he'd agreed to include it. It was hardly breaking news, but Sir Marcus was a rich and powerful man, and his department store in the city centre paid well to be a regular feature in their advertising section – which was always something to keep in mind.

That, and the fact that Sir Marcus regularly dined with the newspaper's owner.

There was also that little matter of his son's recent minor car accident, which had barely merited a line or two on the bottom of page nine. Now he wondered about that. Could there be a connection?

And so the piece, outlining the great man's humble beginnings in business, and his angst, regret and horror over a warehouse fire that had happened when he'd been employed in one of his first positions, ran on page five, with a nice little publicity shot of the entrepreneur himself. Along with the mention that he'd just donated five hundred pounds to a local orphanage.

And, apart from a mental note to himself to 'watch this space', the editor thought no more about it.

Trudy found the Gordon family residence easily enough. Situated in Kidlington, on the leafy outskirts, where the Oxford canal ran close to the railway line, the now-retired PC Richard Gordon lived with his wife, Glenda, and the youngest of his five children, who had yet to marry and move away.

But there was no sign of either the remaining chick or his wife when her erstwhile colleague opened the door, made a show of checking her credentials, and somewhat reluctantly led her through to a small living area.

Off on one side, she could just see through the window a glassed-in extension that his wife would probably call an orangery, where several rather sick-looking plants struggled against the cold of the January day and the minimal hours of daylight.

'You're lucky to catch me in. I work three nights a week as a night watchman, so I'm often in bed this time of day. So, what's all this about?' Gordon asked her flatly.

At sixty-one, he was a heavy man, rapidly going bald, and had a pair of rather boiled-gooseberry blue eyes. A large nose did little to enhance his looks, and red-veined cheeks told Trudy he was probably partial to the booze too. Nicotine-stained fingers plucked aside one of the curtains as he peered outside, perhaps to see what his neighbours thought of this visit by a uniformed police officer.

Which was odd, surely, Trudy thought, for a man who'd once worn the uniform himself? What did he have to be ashamed of?

But when Trudy looked out into the lane beyond, she noted that, like the Gordon residence itself, the houses here were all rather nice. Modestly detached, with several showing the recent additions of garages, extensions and the odd conservatory or two, there wasn't a council house in sight.

'Well, Constable?' Richard Gordon barked, and Trudy knew she was blushing again, having been caught letting her mind drift.

'Sorry, sir, I haven't been on the job that long,' she said smartly, trying to play the little-lost-lamb card. She'd found it amazing how much she could learn, from middle-aged men especially, if she acted like a poor, helpless female in need of male help. 'I expect, in your day, a man with your experience would have got down to the nitty-gritty already,' she added, figuring it wouldn't hurt to stroke his ego a little either. Another lesson she'd long since learned was that it was almost impossible to flatter a man too much. 'It's about an old case of yours, sir,' she added.

Of course, that was stretching it a bit. The Fleet-Wright case had never been 'his'. As a lowly beat constable, his sole role had been to respond to the original call, assess it, and report back as to what the situation warranted. Once he'd left the Fleet-Wright residence after that, he'd played no further part in the case – except to give evidence at the inquest.

'Well, sit down then,' Richard said a shade impatiently, indicating the armchair of a rather nice three-piece suite in beige rayon. Instantly, she wondered how much it had cost, and quickly darted her eyes around the room, taking in the rather swanky lampshade in one corner, and the sheepskin rug in front of the gas fireplace.

'Thank you, sir.' She beamed at him, hoping she wasn't overdoing it. 'You may have read in the papers about the murder of a man called Jonathan McGillicuddy?'

Richard shot her a sharp look. 'You're not on that are you, Constable? You look young enough to still be in your probationary period!'

'Oh no, sir. I'm not on the murder case, I mean,' Trudy said hastily. 'I wish! No, sir, I've been seconded to the coroner's office to help the current coroner with an old case. Gisela Fleet-Wright?'

Instantly, she saw the older man stiffen, and his expression, which had ranged from condescending to vaguely amused as she chattered and gushed, now went curiously blank. A moment later, however, he was frowning and making a good show of a man trying to cast his mind back. But Trudy wasn't deceived. She would willingly have bet a month's wages that this man remembered the case perfectly well.

And again, she felt a growing sense of excitement. Was it possible that the old vulture really was on to something significant and important, after all?

'Not sure I recall the name,' the former PC said vaguely.

'A young girl, sir. Found dead in bed. The coroner's verdict returned death by misadventure. She'd accidentally taken too many pills?'

'Oh, yes. Yes, of course, now I remember. Shame. A pretty girl. Young too. Yes, her mother called the doctor, and the doctor called us in.'

'That's right,' Trudy said brightly. 'What can you remember about that case, sir?'

Richard, who had sat down on the sofa, now laid his arms across the back of it and shrugged. 'Not much.' On the coffee table in front of him lay an issue of that morning's *Oxford Mail*, opened at the crossword puzzle. Trudy knew it also carried the piece Marcus Deering had had put in, after DI Jennings had sanctioned it.

The thinking on that was clear enough, she supposed. Obviously the killer was looking for some kind of sign of remorse on the part of the businessman, and the piece in the paper was meant to appease him. She truly hoped it would work, but somehow didn't think it would.

Anthony Deering was recovering in hospital, having only sustained some minor wounds in the car crash. Luckily, he'd managed to slow down the big car he'd been driving sufficiently enough to prevent real injuries. But it hadn't taken the police mechanics long to ascertain the man's brakes had been interfered with in a deliberate act of sabotage.

'It was a sunny day when you found her, I believe, sir?' Trudy prompted, since it was clear that former PC Gordon was in no mood to be helpful and wasn't about to volunteer information.

'Yes, that's right. She was lying on the bed looking as if she was asleep. The windows were open, I remember. And the gardens were lovely. I remember thinking that when I first answered the call.'

Of course, McGillicuddy would have worked on those gardens too, in the early days of his courtship with the daughter of the household. Trudy felt a pang of sadness as she acknowledged he'd never be able to plant another flower or shrub again. Briefly, she thought of his poor mother, sitting alone in her quiet house.

'You were on the beat?' She forced herself to keep her mind on the job at hand. Both Sergeant O'Grady and Rodney Broadstairs had told her off in the past for empathising too much with the victims and not concentrating on her police work.

Grimly she told herself to damn well toughen up.

'Yes. I'd just checked in, actually. That's why the desk sergeant, who knew where I was, asked me to look into it. I wasn't more than five hundred yards away when the attending doctor called it in.'

Trudy nodded. Sometimes you just happened to be in the right place at the right time.

'So what's this got to do with the McGillicuddy case?' Richard suddenly demanded, and for a moment Trudy looked at him blankly as he scowled back at her. 'When I first asked you what this was all about, you mentioned the recent murder,' he reminded her.

Trudy flushed again, this time genuinely feeling stupid for having forgotten that. 'Oh, yes, sir. Well, Mr McGillicuddy was a former boyfriend of Gisela Fleet-Wright. There was some speculation that her recent breakup with him might have led to her death.'

'But it didn't, did it?' Richard snorted impatiently. 'Didn't the mother put her hands up for it? Something about her daughter not taking her medication, so she accidentally gave her too much or something?'

'Yes, sir. You followed the case then?' Trudy said blandly.

''Course I did. I found the poor girl, didn't I?' The older man bristled. 'Something sad, like that. You take an interest.'

Trudy nodded. She supposed that could be true enough, so why didn't she believe him?

She was aware she'd taken an instant dislike to her former colleague, but she wasn't letting that affect her judgement. No, it was something else that was bothering her about all this. She was sure the man was prevaricating, if not downright lying to her.

At that moment, however, the front door opened and a woman's voice called through. 'Hello, Dickie, I'm home. I got some steak and kidney for . . . Oh, sorry, I didn't realise . . .'

Glenda Gordon was a few years younger than her husband, and probably several stones heavier, with a round, pleasant face, a mass of dyed-brown curls and big hazel eyes. She looked at Trudy uncertainly, taking in her uniform and shooting her husband a quick, questioning and – yes, Trudy was sure of it – distinctly anxious look.

'This is WPC Loveday, Glen,' Richard said, very casually. 'She's just asking me for some help with an old case of mine. Nothing to worry about. Why don't you pop the kettle on.' He got up. 'The constable was just leaving anyway.'

Was I? Trudy thought grimly. But a quick glance at the shuttered, unhelpful face of the older man told her it would be pointless pressing him any further now. She knew that look, having seen it on perpetrators' faces before, and it told her he would only dig his heels in and become even more stubbornly unhelpful if she pushed him.

'Yes, thank you, sir.' Trudy forced herself to smile. But as she passed Glenda, she saw that the woman was biting her lip – a sure sign she was worried about something.

The house behind her remained eerily quiet as she made

her way through the small hall and out to the front door, and she knew the married couple were waiting for her to leave before they started talking to one another.

How she wished she could be a fly on the wall when they did!

All the way back to the station, as Trudy sat swaying on the bus, she tried to figure out what it was that was bothering her about the whole interview. It was more than just the fact that former PC Richard Gordon had been less than honest. She simply couldn't shake the feeling that something obvious was staring her in the face that she'd yet to see.

She knew she still had a lot to learn, and sometimes her inexperience annoyed and worried her. Worse, it could some-times make her second-guess herself.

It wasn't until she was walking down St Ebbes that it finally struck her. How did a constable with five kids end up retiring early and living in a nice little detached house in upmarket Kidlington?

The killer of Jonathan McGillicuddy read that morning's article in the *Oxford Mail* by Sir Marcus Deering with a great deal of interest.

And a thin, rather sardonic little smile.

Chapter Twenty

'The boss wants to see you,' Phil Monroe, the desk sergeant, said the moment she stepped into the station house, and Trudy gave a tight little nod.

Was she in trouble? It wasn't often the DI actually deigned to notice her, let alone actively seek her out, and her first instinct was to cast her mind around for some misdemeanour she might have committed.

'Don't worry,' said Phil, grinning at her, reading her mind easily. 'He didn't sound like he was out after blood.' Two years off retirement, he had a granddaughter Trudy's age and often gave her encouragement where he could.

'That's a relief!' Trudy gave a brief smile. She half-turned to go, but Monroe was anxious to get the gen on the latest station-house gossip. Which, as everyone knew and accepted, was one of the main prerogatives of a desk sergeant.

'I hear the DI has thrown you to the wolves then? Or, in this case, the vultures?' he said slyly.

Trudy gave a wry grin. 'If you mean our esteemed coroner, then yes. I'm helping him out with an old case.'

'Bit of a tartar, our Dr Ryder,' the desk sergeant said. 'Bloody brilliant chap, mind you. Nothing gets past him.'

'No. I think that's why DI Jennings consented to let me help him. He's worried he might be on to something,' Trudy admitted. 'And you know something?' She leaned forward a little and lowered her voice. 'I wouldn't be surprised if he isn't.'

'Ah,' Phil said appreciatively, nodding eagerly. Here was juicy gossip indeed. 'What you working on then? An unsolved murder?'

'I wish!' Trudy said, frowning. 'The original coroner's verdict was death by misadventure. A young girl took too many pills. I think the old vult—I mean, Dr Ryder, suspects it was really suicide.'

The desk sergeant nodded, looking a little impressed now. 'Nasty, that. Suicides – especially when it's a youngster.'

Trudy nodded. 'I agree. And I don't really see why, even if the wrong verdict was given, we should pursue it,' she muttered. For some time now, she'd felt a pang of conscience over this issue. And since everyone else confided in the desk sergeant – indeed, it was almost a prerequisite that they did – she thought now was as good a time as any to get it off her chest and seek his wisdom.

'Say Gisela Fleet-Wright *did* kill herself, and her parents covered it up. Is that so terrible?' she demanded. 'I mean, I don't see what good can come of raking it all up again. It's not as if her parents haven't suffered enough, is it? I just don't see the point.'

'Hmmm. Fleet-Wright? That name rings a bell,' the desk sergeant said thoughtfully.

'Mrs Fleet-Wright confessed at the inquest that she might have been responsible for giving her daughter too many pills. Nothing came of it – I mean, no formal charges were brought against her.'

'No. That's not it.' The desk sergeant shook his head. 'I remember that case vaguely. But this was something else . . . something that came across my desk . . . something minor but . . . Fleet-Wright . . .' He sighed and shook his head. 'No, can't think what it was.' He tapped his temple ruefully. 'Old memory's not what it was. But I'll remember it sooner or later,' he promised her. 'Like as not when I'm lying in bed at three o'clock in the morning. Don't worry, though. When I do, I'll let you know.'

Trudy thanked him and scuttled off to the DI's office to see what he wanted. And as she did so, she wondered why she hadn't, as yet, quite come up with the gumption to ask Dr Clement Ryder outright why he seemed so hellbent on proving Gisela had killed herself.

It wasn't as if she thought he was a particularly vindictive man.

DI Jennings informed the station house's only WPC that she would have to do some extra shifts, along with all the other PCs, now they had acquired a prime suspect in the Marcus Deering/McGillicuddy case.

This was the first Trudy had heard of it, and she listened intently as her senior office briefly filled her in.

Apparently, a victim of the warehouse fire had settled locally, finding work as a gamekeeper. When pulled in for questioning, he hadn't satisfied Jennings at all on the issue of whether or not he held Deering, or the company he'd once worked for, responsible for his injuries.

'He had motive, and clearly, living in the area, opportunity. As for means – anyone could have picked up that spade and bashed Jonathan over the head. And most men have some basic working knowledge of cars – certainly enough to half-file through a brake line. So we're going to be keeping a close watch on him from now on. And if he goes anywhere near the Deering estate, we'll nab him. Which means round-the-clock surveillance. That means extra shifts and all hands on deck. Including you, WPC Loveday.'

'Yes, sir,' Trudy said happily. She'd never been detailed to observation duty before, and was looking forward to it. And adding another skill to her repertoire never hurt. Although the DI then proceeded to warn her that surveillance involved long, boring hours watching a suspect or a suspect's residence, often while sitting in a cold car or some other equally cold spot, Trudy didn't care.

'You'll still work with Dr Ryder, naturally, but just let him know you won't be exclusively at his beck and call,' Jennings concluded. 'And talking of our Dr Ryder, you might as well give me a verbal report now on your progress so far. It'll save you writing one up for me later. Where have you been today?'

Trudy could tell the DI didn't like it when she mentioned she'd been talking to an ex-cop, but when she'd finished her report, he merely sighed.

'All right. Carry on then.'

It wasn't until she'd got to the door, however, that he stopped her. 'WPC Loveday?'

'Sir?'

'What's your opinion of the case? Do you think Dr Ryder is on to something?'

Trudy hesitated for a moment, knowing that, for the first time, her superior officer was actually asking her opinion on something. And it was important she get it right. But exactly what was he asking her? Did she agree that the witnesses at the inquest had lied? Yes, she did. Did she think pursuing a grieving family in order to force them to admit their daughter had killed herself was 'being on to something'? She wasn't quite so sure.

But something, some tiny niggle of instinct, told her she shouldn't lose faith in the old vulture just yet.

'Yes, sir,' she finally said. 'I think there's probably something . . . suspect . . . about the Fleet-Wright case. But it's too early, yet, to say what exactly.'

She didn't think it would be politic, at that point, to tell the DI about her suspicions concerning former PC Gordon's affluent retirement either. With her boss under pressure from Sir Marcus, the Chief Constable and the press to solve the McGillicuddy case, the last thing she wanted to drop into his lap was the possibility of police corruption.

With a heavy sigh, Jennings nodded, and indicated she could leave.

It took Trudy a little while, but eventually she found PC Richard Gordon's personnel file. However, after studying it she had to admit that, if he'd had rather an undistinguished career, there was certainly nothing about it that set off alarm bells.

Trudy was not naive, and she knew some coppers were 'on

the take'. For most of them, it amounted to little more than getting good deals on meat at the local butcher's, or never paying for a drink in a pub.

Occasionally, though, something more serious happened.

But she could find no evidence that, during his thirty years on the beat, PC Gordon had ever seriously overstepped the mark. No raids on fences in his beat area that hadn't panned out, or robberies in premises included on his patrol where a blind eye had been turned. And although he'd had a few complaints lodged against him, what copper didn't? And most of the complaints against PC Gordon had been made by inebriated members of the public who had objected to being manhandled into the cells.

So, as far as she could tell, PC Richard Gordon had walked his beat, made his reports, done his fair share of football-hooligan duty at the local matches, and had generally had a routine, if dull, career.

But feeling dissatisfied, she carried on digging. Because even with his full pension, and given that his wife might have had a job as well, she couldn't see how they could have afforded that house, or that nice furniture.

But it wasn't until she'd almost given up that she finally hit pay dirt.

She remembered just in time the former PC's claim that he did a part-time job as a night watchman. And although she couldn't see how this would add much to the Gordon family finances, she'd nevertheless doggedly followed up on it.

One good thing about being forced to do paperwork and boring filing duties, Trudy realised now, was that it taught you how to work the system. And with a little help from an unhappy clerk at the tax office, she eventually discovered that Richard Gordon now worked at a site on the outskirts of Headington, guarding the fleet of lorries owned by one Reginald Fleet-Wright.

Chapter Twenty-One

'So I have to ask myself,' Trudy said excitedly, half an hour later, 'why did PC Gordon get a job, and at such a good salary, too, for a mere night watchman, at Fleet-Wright's lorry yard?'

Opposite her, and watching her with a mixture of amusement and approbation, Clement smiled gently. She was so full of enthusiasm! So eager, he could almost see her nose twitching, like a dog that had picked up the scent.

When DI Jennings had agreed he could have the services of a PC to help him with the Fleet-Wright inquiry, Clement – who was nobody's fool – had always expected to be fobbed off with the dregs of the station house. After all, Jennings had no incentive to offer him anyone decent. Which hadn't worried him at all, since all he needed was a body in a uniform to lend him the bona fides he needed to make it all legal and by the book. He didn't actually *require* his police liaison to have any brains, let alone enthusiasm.

So when he'd first been introduced to probationary WPC Trudy Loveday, he hadn't been fazed – either by her youth or total inexperience. Furthermore, it had soon become clear to him that Jennings, the fool, hadn't known what to do with the girl. No doubt he'd been obliged to take a WPC onto his team, but he was the kind of man who lacked imagination.

So Clement hadn't been surprised to learn, from inserting the odd, deft question here and there into their conversations, that Trudy's career so far had included little more than office work. With the odd foray onto the street in pursuit of purse-snatchers, or into the park to nab flashers!

But it hadn't taken long before he began to suspect that the girl not only had ambition and gumption, but intelligence too. Clearly, she was still wet behind the ears, and as green as they came, but Clement didn't mind that. In his days as a surgeon, he'd been used to guiding young medical students, and trying to teach them what was really needed to do the job properly. Admittedly, they'd all been older than WPC Loveday. But as his old professor had told him – if you could get 'em young, and before they'd acquired too many bad habits, you could mould them into something worthwhile.

Now he waited to see just how much his protégée had picked up on during her visit to the Gordon residence.

'What put you on to that in the first place?' he asked mildly. As he did so, he reached for the cup of tea his secretary had not long since placed on his desk. As he picked it up, however, his hand had a spasm and he hastily put it down again.

'The house,' Trudy said promptly. Her eyes went to the rattling cup, and noted that the old vulture had spilt some tea onto his paperwork. Thinking nothing more of it, she quickly explained the sort of house the Gordons were living in, and the quality of their beige-rayon three-piece suite.

'And it didn't occur to you, perhaps, that, during his career, PC Gordon might have . . . ah . . . acquired some savings?' he asked delicately, carefully pulling his hand back across the table and letting it drop out of sight into his lap.

Trudy scowled at him angrily. 'Of course it did,' she snapped. 'His personnel file was the first thing I checked. But there was nothing . . . er . . . worrying about it.'

She certainly wasn't about to discuss one of her former colleagues with the old vulture in any detail. DI Jennings would have a fit.

'Quite,' Clement said mildly. 'So you cast around for something else that would explain it?'

He glanced down and noticed that his hand was fluttering like a bloody butterfly trapped in a glass jar. Slowly he eased it down, pressing it between his thigh and the armrest of his seat.

'Yes. And that's when I found out he worked for Gisela's father,' Trudy said, leaning forward in her chair in an unconscious gesture of excitement. 'That's got to mean something, hasn't it?' she demanded.

'When did PC Gordon retire, exactly?'

And his growing faith in her abilities and competence grew as she checked her notebook. Clearly, she'd had the foresight to check that out.

'Thirty years after first joining the force,' she confirmed. 'Still shy of his state-pension age – but a lot of coppers do that,' she added, determined to be fair. 'It's one of the perks of being in the force. You can put in your thirty years, collect your pension, and still get another job, or part-time job, to help see you out.'

Clement nodded. 'And how long after the inquest would this have been?'

'About five months,' Trudy said.

'So, getting a part-time job with the Fleet-Wright company *could* have been a coincidence?' he asked blandly, rather enjoying playing devil's advocate. Especially when his companion rose to the bait so delightfully.

'At almost double the salary as other night watchman jobs?' she snorted. 'I don't think so! He's earning almost as much doing those three nights a week as my dad earns driving the buses!'

'So, from that you conclude . . . what?'

By his side he could feel his hand trembling. Damn it, the spasms were getting longer with every month that passed.

Trudy flushed. 'I'm not prepared to say, just yet. We don't know enough,' she said cautiously.

Clement nodded. 'Very wise. But it is interesting, isn't it? That not long after the inquest, the first copper on the scene takes early retirement and lands a job – a rather suspiciously well-paying job, with the father of the dead girl?'

'Yes. What's more, I've done some more digging.'

'Have you?'

'Yes!' Trudy shot him a fulminating look. Did the man think she was a complete idiot? 'At the time of Gisela's death, the Gordons – all seven of them – were living in a three-bedroom council house in east Oxford. Then they bought the house in Kidlington, outright mind, just before Gordon handed in his papers.'

'Outright?'

'Yes – for nearly three hundred and twenty-five pounds. No

mortgage, nothing. I couldn't actually trace how he paid it,' Trudy was forced to admit, 'as the banks aren't obliged to give us information like that without the proper paperwork.'

'Pity,' Clement said. 'But it would be interesting to see if Mr Reginald Fleet-Wright's bank balance was depleted by that same amount, at the same time, wouldn't it?'

Trudy nodded. 'So what do we do now?' she asked, unable to mask her excitement. All her earlier doubts about the justification for following up on the case were being eroded as she discovered she didn't like it when the authorities were being lied to any more than Dr Ryder did.

'Oh, by the way, I have to do some surveillance duty, so I might not be available tomorrow,' she remembered to inform him.

She didn't mention they now had a prime suspect in the Marcus Deering/McGillicuddy case. It wasn't, after all, any of the coroner's business. Besides, Dr Ryder had now all but given up even pretending that the tenuous link between Jonathan McGillicuddy's death and that of Gisela Fleet-Wright was likely to go anywhere. Now he'd got his way, and the old case that had always been his main focus of attention was being properly re-examined to his satisfaction, he clearly didn't feel the need to dangle that particular carrot in front of her DI's nose.

For him (and now for her too) this was all about getting to the truth surrounding the death of an unhappy, unlucky and mentally unbalanced young girl.

'So, what do you think we should do now?' she asked eagerly.

'Well, I think we've learned all we can about the background of the case, don't you?' Clement raised one bushy, silvery eyebrow. 'Now I think it's time we spoke to the main character in our little drama.'

Trudy blinked for a moment, and then swallowed hard. 'You mean Gisela's mother?'

'I mean Gisela's mother,' he agreed.

Chapter Twenty-Two

Trudy didn't quite know what to expect from Mrs Beatrice Fleet-Wright. She knew from reading the files that the woman had been born into an affluent family (her father's company brewed half the beer sold in the county) and that she had gone on to marry an equally affluent man. A fellow Roman Catholic, Reginald Fleet-Wright had inherited his father's haulage company, whose lorries had probably helped deliver her family's beer, among other things.

Before her marriage, Beatrice had lived in a large house in Woodstock with the rest of her family. After her marriage, she had moved into a large house off Woodstock Road in Oxford.

She had produced two children, which was perhaps a smaller amount than most Catholic families. She did a lot of charity work, and she had admitted in open court that she might have been responsible for the death of her daughter.

Who wouldn't want to meet such a woman and try to unlock her secrets?

All of these thoughts and more flooded her mind, making

her almost tremble with nervousness and excitement, as Clement Ryder pulled into the driveway of the white-painted north Oxford mansion and cut the engine.

And even in the depths of a bleak and grey winter, Trudy could see that the gardens, in spring and summer, would be wonderful. Neatly clipped box hedging bordered rose bushes that, at the moment, looked cropped back and almost ugly. Several silver birches, though, still managed to look magnificent, with their lace-like branches and silver bark.

Could Jonathan McGillicuddy, when he'd worked in these lovely gardens so many years ago as a young man, ever possibly have imagined that one day in the future people would walk through all this lush beauty in order to ask questions about his murder?

As her eyes swept over the six – or was it seven? – bedroomed house, with its double-glazed windows and impressive front porch, Trudy found herself wondering what her mum would make of a house like this. Would Barbara Loveday ever have dreamed of living in a place like this? Trudy smiled to herself and shook her head. Of course she wouldn't. Houses such as this were for the likes of women who dressed in clothes that had been cut to fit, and wore silk gloves in church, and pearls at their necks and in their ears.

Not for the likes of them!

The maid who answered the door looked surprised to see Trudy in her uniform, but relaxed a little as the distinguished gentleman with the thick silver hair and lovely educated voice introduced himself and asked if the mistress of the house was at home.

She was.

Trudy was now so agog to actually meet one of the main characters in the case that she had to prevent herself from breaking out into a run as they crossed the small but immaculate front hall. Absently, she noted the old-fashioned William Morris tiles on the floor, and thrush-and-strawberry-patterned wallpaper on the walls. The whole space was redolent of the scent of lavender furniture polish, and as she passed a grandfather clock, ticking ponderously in one corner, its mahogany exterior glowed with the evidence of centuries of care.

'If you'd like to wait in here, I'll tell madam you're here,' the maid said. She was about Barbara Loveday's age and, as she left, Trudy, trying not to appear curious, wondered if her mother had ever considered domestic work. And if so, would she have liked to work in a place such as this?

She'd have to ask her when she went home for her tea.

She watched the coroner walk slowly around the room – clearly a little-used sitting room – and made a note of the lush, mustard-coloured velvet curtains, an accent colour that was mirrored in the autumn-coloured patterned carpet, and the chintz covers on the chairs. A low coffee table, mahogany like the rest of the furniture, bore a single coffee-table book, featuring arty black-and-white photographs of Oxford. And just when, Trudy wondered with a somewhat bitter smile, had anyone in this house actually bothered to look at them?

'Hello. Maud tells me you want to see me?'

The voice that came from just over her left shoulder was soft, well educated and utterly lacking in curiosity. Trudy turned and straightened her spine as she looked at the woman closing the door behind her.

At around five-feet-eight, she was a couple of inches shorter than Trudy, and had immaculately cut and styled short brown hair. No doubt Mrs Fleet-Wright was a regular visitor at some fancy hair salon in Summertown. Her green eyes watched them, seemingly without curiosity as well, as Dr Ryder strode forward, his hand held out in greeting as he introduced them.

But although the woman smiled at him and shook his hand, Trudy noticed that she was far more interested in her. Not that she made it obvious. Perhaps it was the police uniform? Perhaps it brought back old, bad, sad memories of when people had questioned her before, dressed as Trudy was now.

'Please, sit down,' their hostess said. 'Tea?' she offered politely.

'No, thank you, Mrs Fleet-Wright,' Clement answered for both of them. 'We're sorry to bother you, but we're talking to everybody who knew Mr Jonathan McGillicuddy,' he began.

Trudy wasn't taken by surprise at this opening gambit. They'd discussed beforehand, and at some length, just how to approach this interview, and both had agreed that telling Beatrice they were once more looking into her daughter's case would almost certainly be counterproductive. If she'd lied once and under oath (and now Trudy was as convinced as the coroner that she had), they could hardly expect her to be more truthful now.

So they'd agreed that the oblique approach might be the way to go if they were to have any chance of learning something new. And making her believe this was all about Jonathan, and the recent murder case, was the obvious way of doing that.

'Oh, yes, I see.' Beatrice sat down in a large armchair that seemed to dwarf her. Both Trudy and Clement had opted to sit at opposite ends of the sofa, facing the chair. 'I read in the papers about . . . Well, It's all so shocking.'

The older woman turned to Trudy, her body language now screaming tension. Her back was ramrod-straight and she was sitting perched on the very edge of her seat, her neat legs tucked ladylike together and leaning slightly to her left. Her hands, inter-clasped on her lap, twisted restlessly. 'Do you have any idea who might have done it? He was such a nice young man.'

Nice? Trudy blinked. According to all the evidence she had, Gisela had been put through hell by Jonathan McGillicuddy, especially when he threw her over. Odds were that she'd even killed herself over her love for him, and the trauma of his desertion.

'Surely, Mrs Fleet-Wright, you couldn't have approved of the way Mr McGillicuddy treated your daughter?' Trudy said flatly.

For a moment, Beatrice Fleet-Wright looked totally flustered. She went white, then red, then white again. She opened her mouth, seemed about to speak, then closed it again. Eventually, she took a long, slow breath and forced herself to sit back in the chair. Her hands, though, remained clutching the ends of the armrests on the chair. Indeed, her fingers were digging in so deeply, she looked afraid she might fall off, or maybe just float away into space, if she didn't hold on tight and anchor herself down.

Behind her artificially calm face, Beatrice told herself frantically that she needed to calm down. She was already behaving foolishly. And it wasn't as if she hadn't known, right from the first second she'd read of Jonathan's death, that this moment would surely come to pass at some point.

But she'd thought she was better prepared than this. And

yet, with the very first question, the pretty young girl with the dark hair and big brown eyes had totally stumped her. She simply hadn't expected such an immediate attack.

But she mustn't panic.

It wasn't as if these people actually *knew*.

'Jon—Mr McGillicuddy's relationship with my daughter was . . . was very difficult,' she heard herself say calmly. *Good. That was better.* 'Gisela could be difficult. She had mood swings, you see, that weren't always easy to cope with. It wasn't . . . Mr McGillicuddy was a young widower with a little girl. He had other priorities . . . He was our gardener, as you probably know, and my husband never approved. It was never going to work out between them . . . I, we, could all see that, so in some ways we were relieved when it came to nothing. But . . .'

She let her voice trail off and gave a soft sigh. 'This is very hard to explain, I know. But I never blamed J—Mr McGillicuddy for what happened – that wouldn't have been fair. Gisela could be very possessive. Clinging. And . . . well, manic sometimes. But that wasn't her fault,' Beatrice said, with a sudden flash of spirit. 'She was ill, you see. It was the same as if she'd had influenza or diabetes, except it was mental . . . Oh, what's the use!' She threw up one hand, then let it fall back to the armrest, where she resumed digging her fingers into the upholstery. 'Gisela fell so hard for him, and so completely. She always expected far too much from life! She thought it would end in wedding bells and children. And, who knows, perhaps Mr McGillicuddy thought so too, at some point.'

Beatrice paused to take a long, rather shaky breath, and glanced briefly out of the window, her face flickering with remembered pain. 'But I always knew my daughter would wreck it. It always seemed to me that it was Gisela's fate to always make herself unhappy.'

For a moment the ineffably sad words hung in the staid, stale air of that beautiful but arid room, and Trudy felt herself swallow hard. Beside her, she could feel Clement sitting totally still, as if afraid to break the mood by even breathing.

Beatrice then sighed sadly, and she carried on talking quietly. 'My daughter became increasingly more and more possessive and jealous as their relationship progressed. Always asking where he'd been, and whether he'd been speaking to other girls. Then she'd swing the other way and apologise, and beg him to forgive her. She would buy him gifts . . .' Beatrice flushed a little at this. 'Inappropriate and expensive gifts. A gold cigarette lighter and case. An onyx signet ring. Things like that. I could tell that Jon—Mr McGillicuddy . . . was embarrassed by them. I mean, he was just a jobbing gardener then – it wasn't as if he could wear fancy jewellery to work! And in his social circles . . . well, bringing out a gold cigarette case at his local pub . . .' Beatrice shrugged. 'It annoyed my husband too. More than once he stopped her allowance so she couldn't spend money on him.'

Beatrice paused and looked down at her hands. With some effort she seemed to lever them off the armrests and force them into her lap. 'He gave them back, you know. After she . . . died. He gave them back to me – the cigarette case and ring. I have them still, in a drawer upstairs. Well . . .' She shrugged hopelessly. 'I didn't know what else to do with them.'

She glanced across at them both and smiled. The young girl looked sad, and she could tell that nearly all of her earlier antagonism had died away. The older man, though, the man who had introduced himself as a coroner – she couldn't tell what he was thinking.

'Do you have any idea who might have killed him?' Beatrice asked pensively. 'I feel so sorry for his mother! I know, you see, what it's like to lose a child. And if you were close to making an arrest, it would help her, I think.'

Trudy put on a professional smile and ignored the blatant fishing for information. 'Inquiries are ongoing, Mrs Fleet-Wright. I can assure you we're following up all available leads.' The policewoman in her recited the trite phrases primly.

Beatrice nodded dutifully, hiding an inner sigh. 'Yes, of course,' she murmured. Clearly, they weren't going to tell her anything useful.

'Mr McGillicuddy first met your daughter when you hired him to work on your garden?' Trudy asked her softly.

'Yes. At that point he was working for a gardening firm I'd been using for years. It was only a little while later that he struck out on his own,' Beatrice confirmed.

'And he and Gisela quickly became an item?'

'Yes.'

'You said your husband wasn't happy about it,' Trudy reminded her gently. 'But how did *you* feel about it?'

'Oh, I was worried too, but not for the same reasons as Reginald,' Beatrice responded. 'I knew Gisela would become even more emotional and intense. I was worried it would make her mood swings worse, and bring back the awful bouts of depression. And I was right. When they broke up, her depression became almost uncontrollable. Her medication was increased so much . . . I worried for her.'

Sometimes, Beatrice had worried for her daughter's very

sanity, but of course she couldn't say that. Not out loud. Not now and not to these people. She'd not even spoken the words out loud to her own husband.

'But you must have blamed Mr McGillicuddy to some extent for all this?' Trudy persisted firmly.

'No, not really,' Beatrice said helplessly.

In discussing their strategy at length, Clement had made it clear Trudy's job was to push the witness as far as she could. He would then watch and listen as Beatrice was put under pressure and try to spot any telltale signs she was lying. And although Trudy didn't particularly like the idea of doing it, she had seen the sense in that.

And so now, in spite of the fact that her more tender instincts were telling her she shouldn't be badgering this woman, a mother who must, even nearly five years after the event, still be grieving the loss of her child, Trudy tensed to do her duty.

If she was ever to make anything of herself in this job, she knew she had to get used to questioning witnesses, and sometimes, if the occasion warranted it, even be ruthless about it. And if that meant growing a slightly thicker skin, then so be it.

Even so, as she formed her next question, she felt a little bit sick inside. 'I'm sorry, Mrs Fleet-Wright, but I simply don't understand how you can say that. It's all right, you know, to admit that you didn't *like* the victim. I know Mr McGillicuddy's just been murdered, and that you may not feel comfortable speaking ill of the dead, but I assure you . . . we'd rather you spoke the truth. Don't you feel even a little bit of satisfaction that the man who caused your family so much grief is now dead himself?'

There! She'd done it!

But Beatrice Fleet-Wright didn't look angry or defiant – or even guilty. She looked, in fact, shocked. Genuinely shocked.

'No! Oh, no, how can you say that?' Beatrice said, appalled. 'Of course I'm not glad he's dead!' Her voice had risen a full octave, and as the sound of her suddenly strident voice echoed back at her in that sterile room, she suddenly seemed to become aware of it.

Beatrice caught a breath, and got a rein on her scattered wits. *No, you mustn't lose control*, she told herself. *Keep calm*. Don't let them provoke you. *Don't give yourself away*.

'All right, Mrs Fleet-Wright,' Clement now interposed smoothly. Clearly, despite a valiant effort, his young companion had failed to pierce the woman's armour. So now a different approach was needed. 'Can you tell us what you remember most about Jonathan? He worked for you for some time, after all. And then he was your daughter's young man. Did you like him – as a person, I mean, as opposed to the individual your daughter was seeing?'

Trudy, now that Dr Ryder had stepped in and taken over, took the opportunity to take stock and do some observing of her own. Leaning slowly back against the sofa and letting some of the tension ease out of her painfully tight shoulders, she watched the older woman carefully.

Beatrice had turned to the coroner and looked instantly more at ease. Was that because he was a man, and she was used to appeasing men? Or was it because the interview had now veered away from the topic of her daughter and her tragic death?

'Well, I always felt sorry for him, of course, losing his wife so young and being left with a child to raise,' Beatrice admitted. 'And I admired his hard work and ambition in wanting to start his own company.'

Clement sighed inwardly. That was all very polite and noncommittal but he couldn't let her continue with such nonsense.

'He was a good-looking young chap too, I think.' Clement smiled. And then wondered. A middle-aged woman, still attractive and trapped in a dry, unsatisfying marriage; perhaps she'd had her head turned by a young, attractive, available man? It wasn't exactly unheard of.

But if she suspected the way her visitor's thoughts were going, Beatrice made no sign of it and instead laughed lightly. 'Yes, that too,' she admitted simply. 'But he was also kind, uncomplicated and sometimes he could be very funny. I wasn't surprised Gisela loved him so.'

'Did he ever mention any enemies he might have had?' Clement went on perfunctorily. Like Trudy, he doubted that McGillicuddy had died through any fault of his own; he had simply been unlucky enough to be fathered by Sir Marcus Deering, who had acquired a very deadly enemy indeed. But to keep up the pretence that it was Jonathan's murder they were investigating, and not the circumstances surrounding the death of her daughter, it was necessary he ask questions like these.

'Oh, no. I'm sure he didn't. Either have an enemy, or tell me about having crossed someone, I mean, he wasn't that kind of man. He was just . . . ordinary.' Beatrice shrugged helplessly.

Clement glanced at Trudy. And it was a measure of how

well they were beginning to work together that she was able to interpret the message in that casual glance so easily.

Time for her to take over again.

'Naturally, Mrs Fleet-Wright, we, the police, are anxious to explore all elements of Mr McGillicuddy's life, to see if we can find a motive for his murder,' Trudy took up the baton smoothly. 'And, if I may say so, the only things of significance that happened to him, that we can ascertain, were the death of his wife, and the death of your daughter. It strikes me that he was very unlucky in love, wasn't he?'

Beatrice nodded wordlessly, refusing to be drawn.

'Can you tell me where your husband was on the day Mr McGillicuddy died?' Trudy asked flatly.

Again, this strategy had been decided between them beforehand. It was all part and parcel of putting the pressure on her.

'Reginald?' Beatrice looked astonished. 'He was at work, of course, where he always is. And Rex was at college. And I was here, at home,' she offered, before she could be asked. 'I can assure you that none of my family had anything to do with Jonathan's murder. It's ridiculous to even think so! It's been almost five years since Gisela died!'

Again her voice was rising, and again, she forced herself to calm down. It was becoming more and more clear to her now that these people had no clue as to what had happened all those years ago. Or anything else about Gisela and Jonathan, or that awful, awful day. And all she had to do to keep it that way was to keep her wits about her, watch what she said and, above all, hold on to her self-control. If she could do that, all would be well.

It would all be over soon anyway, Beatrice told herself. It had to be. They'd find out who had killed Jonathan, and it would turn out to be nothing to do with her, or her family, and everything would go back to normal.

Dull, safe, dead, normal.

'I see,' Trudy said flatly. 'And you have nothing else you'd like to tell us?' she asked gently. 'Nothing about your daughter, and what really happened the day she died?'

It was to be their last shot, that final question, and posed at the end of the interview, when Mrs Fleet-Wright was at her most upset and vulnerable.

Clement had been adamant that the woman be given the opportunity to confess, or at least amend her previous testimony. The human instinct to unburden itself, he'd told her, was a very strong one indeed. And it might just turn out that all Beatrice needed to take that final step would be to have a pair of sympathetic ears ready to listen to her.

Now, Trudy felt herself tense as the older woman fixed her with startled, suddenly terrified, green eyes. 'What do you mean?' Beatrice managed to whisper. 'You already know what happened that day. Gisela took too many pills. By accident. It was my fault . . .'

Her voice trailed off as Trudy gently shook her head.

'But that's not true, is it?' the young policewoman said softly.

Beatrice felt the blood drain from her face. She felt, suddenly, cold. Desperately cold. Was it possible that she was wrong? That far from not having a clue, these people really already knew *everything*?

'Gisela didn't forget to take her pills, did she?' Trudy

persisted. 'You weren't confused about whether or not she'd taken the right dose. You didn't accidentally give her more.' Trudy, despite trembling with tension, kept her voice soft and gentle and coaxing. 'You lied at the inquest, didn't you? You can tell us the truth, Mrs Fleet-Wright,' she encouraged gently.

And for a moment, for just one magical, split second, she could feel something in the room shift – something change. Beatrice's lips fell apart. Her eyes went huge and round.

'Lie?' Beatrice said desperately, her voice so thin it hardly sounded human. 'No . . . no . . .'

'Yes, you did,' Trudy all but whispered back. She could feel that the coroner, on the other end of the sofa, was as tense and expectant as she was. 'You can tell us,' Trudy urged, trying not to sound as desperate as she felt. 'You'll feel better if you do,' she promised.

Would I? Beatrice Fleet-Wright thought, and for one, insane moment her heart lifted at the thought. After so many years of misery and guilt, was that possible?

'Your daughter killed herself, didn't she?' Trudy finally spoke the words.

And Beatrice Fleet-Wright blinked.

'And you covered it up, didn't you?' Trudy added softly.

And then something totally shockingly happened.

Beatrice Fleet-Wright began to laugh.

She laughed, and laughed, and laughed, and laughed.

Chapter Twenty-Three

Upstairs, in his large bedroom – part of which had been given over to a model railway – Rex Fleet-Wright stood at the window and watched as the woman police constable and the tall man with white hair left the house.

He wondered, vaguely, what lies his mother had been telling them now.

His mother, as Rex well knew, was very good at telling lies.

He sighed and, after their car had driven away, turned and went back to his bed, throwing himself down on it so heavily he actually bounced.

Or perhaps his mother hadn't lied, but had managed to distract them in some other way instead. She was good at that too.

He turned on his side and gazed at the large photograph resting on his bedside table. It was of his sister, of course. Gisela, when she was nineteen, her long dark hair covering one green eye, her mouth wide open and laughing.

It was funny, Rex thought, how, even after nearly five years of being dead, his sister still seemed the most alive person left in the house.

'So, what do you think?' Trudy asked ten minutes later, as they sat in Clement's car in the courtyard at Floyds Row. 'It was hysteria, wasn't it? All that insane laughing at the end? She was in shock?'

'Yes,' Clement agreed thoughtfully.

After her initial burst of spontaneous laughter, Mrs Fleet-Wright had seemed unable to stop. She'd apologised, or tried to, around her guffaws.

'I'm so s-s-sorry,' she'd gasped, mopping her streaming eyes with a handkerchief. 'It's just so . . . so . . . s-s-silly of me.' But even then, she'd simply carried on laughing helplessly.

Eventually, she'd managed to get a grip on herself, but after that it was impossible to continue the interview. Apart from the fact that the lady of the house had simply risen to her feet and offered to show them out, it was clear they would get nothing more from her after such a shocking lapse of self-control. Because of the shame of her breakdown, she had rapidly built a frigidly cold wall of politeness around herself that would take a battering ram to knock down.

And, if she was honest, Trudy was feeling so emotionally spent herself by that point that she just wanted to get out in the fresh air and try and clear her own head.

'So, what do you think?' she demanded again now.

'I think,' Clement Ryder said slowly, 'that Mrs Fleet-Wright is a lady with a lot of secrets.'

Trudy sighed heavily. A fat lot of help that was! Sometimes the old vulture could be so annoyingly enigmatic. But she knew the sense of anger she felt wasn't really directed at him.

'I made a right mess of it, didn't I?' she said miserably.

Clement smiled. 'No, you didn't,' he said honestly. 'And I doubt anyone else could have done better. So cheer up – next time, things might be different.'

Trudy nodded. They would, of course, have to question Mrs Fleet-Wright again. But it wasn't, if she was honest, something she was particularly looking forward to. 'So, what now?'

'Don't you have surveillance duty to do?'

'Yes,' Trudy said with a heavy sigh. She'd spent six hours yesterday watching Clive Greaves's lodgings in the company of PC Rodney Broadstairs, who'd bored her silly, talking about football all the time.

Just as DI Jennings had warned her, it was cold, tedious work indeed. And, she was honest enough to acknowledge wryly, her enthusiasm at learning a new skill hadn't taken very long to wane.

'But I'm free tomorrow afternoon,' she added brightly. 'What do you want me to do?'

'What do you think you should do?' he asked curiously, interested to see how logically the girl could think.

Trudy, blissfully unaware she was being tested, merely thought about it for a moment, then nodded. 'I think I should go and see Mrs Gordon, when her husband's not around.'

Clement smiled. Good. 'You think she might tell you anything, though?' he asked, a shade sceptically. 'She's hardly likely to want to admit that her husband's been up to no good – always supposing he has been.'

Trudy sighed. 'We won't know that if I don't try,' she pointed out.

'Can't argue with logic like that,' Clement said cheerfully. 'Right then, off you go. And have a nice night with the pheasants.'

Trudy groaned. One of her fellow PCs had told her that their prime suspect in the Deering/McGillicuddy case often spent several hours at night with his game birds. And tonight was going to be bloody freezing!

Inside her house, Beatrice Fleet-Wright helped herself to a third glass of sherry, finding she was still prone to intermittently breaking out in compulsive giggles.

But she couldn't help it. It was just so *funny*!

And to think, she'd almost been on the verge of confessing it all. Every dirty, grubby little thing.

But then, like a lifesaver, that young policewoman had accused her of trying to cover up Gisela's suicide. And . . . oh! If only they knew how truly hilarious that actually was!

Again, Beatrice began to giggle and slapped a hand over her mouth in case the maid should hear her. Then, very carefully making sure she didn't spill a single drop, she finished the sherry in her glass and went to pour herself another.

Chapter Twenty-Four

Anthony Deering was glad to get out of the hospital. Although the doctors and nurses had been great, there was something about the clean white lines and antiseptic smell of places like that that always made him feel uneasy.

Now he was back home again, he was already feeling much better. Although he still felt stiff and sore from his bruises and was prone to sudden lightning strikes of unexpected pain when he made certain movements, he was hopeful that soon he'd be able to get back on his horse and ride around the estate. Just a gentle trot, to fill his lungs with clean, cold, country air.

But as he lay in his bed, staring up at the ceiling and trying to convince himself he didn't feel afraid, he couldn't help but worry – and finally start to face some hard, unpalatable facts.

This time, with the car, he'd been lucky. He hadn't been travelling that fast and he'd managed to slow the car down – his lovely car, now a total write-off – enough to make a difference. But still, no two ways about it. He *had* been lucky. And following hard on the heels of that thought was the inevitable addendum – *this time*! And again, following on inevitably from that, one thought now filled his mind.

What about next time?

As Anthony lay on his bed in his father's large country house, surrounded by his father's acres, he couldn't help but wonder – and not for the first time – just what his father had done. What unspeakable sin or act had he committed in the past to bring this vengeful madman to their door?

He sighed heavily then winced as pain lanced across his bruised ribs. With a second, carefully shallow sigh, he closed his eyes and told himself to go to sleep. Surely the police would get to the bottom of all this soon. The chap in charge, Jennings, seemed a competent sort of fellow. And Sergeant O'Grady, likewise, lent a reassuringly solid presence to the household.

But Anthony might not have been able to drift off into his nap quite so easily had he known what his father was doing that very moment, downstairs, in his study.

Sir Marcus Deering carefully watched Sergeant Mike O'Grady as the solid, sandy-haired policeman sat in the chair opposite his desk, rereading the latest letter. It had come in that morning's post, leaving the businessman feeling almost suicidal with despair.

O'Grady, though, was being careful to keep his face expressionless.

'I AM RUNNING OUT OF PATIENCE, AND YOU ARE RUNNING OUT OF TIME. DO THE RIGHT THING, SOON. NEXT TIME YOUR YOUNGEST SON WON'T BE SO LUCKY.'

Since the car accident, there had always been a PC on patrol outside the house, but that hardly seemed adequate, and now the older man asked testily, 'Is there no progress being made at all?'

Mike O'Grady hesitated. He couldn't, of course, reveal anything specific about their ongoing investigation, but the DI had told him to keep the businessman sweet.

'We *do* have a prime suspect, sir,' he said cautiously, then held out a hand to prevent Sir Marcus from bombarding him with questions. 'And we're keeping a very close eye on him.'

'Did he have something to do with the fire?' Sir Marcus demanded.

Again, O'Grady hesitated, then nodded slowly.

Sir Marcus slumped in his chair. In truth, he was rather surprised by that. 'I still can't understand it,' he said helplessly. For the life of him, he just couldn't see how anyone would blame him for that. It just didn't feel right somehow. And Sir Marcus had always been a great believer in listening to his instincts. But if this wasn't about the fire, what was it about? *What?*

For weeks now he'd been wracking his brains, but could think of nothing he'd done to deserve this plague that had fallen on his house. The frustration of not knowing what to do to bring it all to an end was almost killing him. Already, he'd had to go to the doctor's with suspected ulcers.

With a huge mental effort, he forced himself to calm down. As his GP had said, stress could bring on a heart attack and that was the last thing he needed right now. At all costs, he had to stay strong and focused.

He waved a hand at the latest letter. 'Well, it's obvious my piece in the *Oxford Mail* and the charitable donation weren't enough to satisfy him,' he said heavily.

'Apparently not, sir,' O'Grady agreed cautiously.

'You fellows *will* keep Anthony safe until all this is over, right?'

'Yes, sir,' O'Grady said. But he, like all policemen, knew it was almost impossible to guard a man day and night. Just ask the secret service detailed to keep the President of the United States alive. The simple fact was, if someone wanted you dead, and that person was reasonably intelligent, patient and deter-mined, sooner or later . . . well . . .

If only they could be sure Clive Greaves was their man. Unfortunately, this latest letter to Sir Marcus had been posted before they'd started keeping a twenty-four-hour watch on him. Still, the Sergeant thought with some satisfaction, if Greaves *was* their man, and he made another attempt on Anthony Deering, this time they'd be ready for him.

Chapter Twenty-Five

Glenda Gordon watched the young WPC coming up the garden path and felt a moment of near panic. When she'd returned from afternoon bingo that time and found Dickie talking to her, she'd sensed at once that something wasn't right.

Dickie insisting she only wanted to pick his brains about one of his old cases simply didn't ring true. Glenda had always known when her husband was lying, and was nobody's fool. The daughter of a coalman, she'd grown up working class and savvy. It hadn't taken her long, after marrying, to realise that her husband wasn't always as straight and trustworthy as she'd – perhaps rather naively – expected policemen to be. And she herself was honest enough to acknowledge that, with a large family to feed and times being so hard, the little bits of extra cash or unexpected goods he provided on an irregular basis came in very handy.

Like the bags of unpaid-for coal her father always used to bring home, she'd come to accept them as perks of his job. In Dickie's case it was the odd sofa that 'fell off the back of a lorry' that had badly been needed to replace their old broken one. The cash that helped pay the rent when the next pay cheque seemed a long way away. The boxes of small electrical goods that sometimes appeared and then disappeared from the garden shed.

Although she hadn't liked it, none of it had ever made her feel her husband wasn't a 'good' man at heart, or indeed not a 'good' husband. He provided for them, which was the main thing, and she'd always been able to keep them and the kids well fed and clothed.

But while that sort of thing was all very well, she'd always known that, just before he retired, something major had happened that had been out of the ordinary, and it had always worried her . . .

The knock on the door jerked her out of her reverie and she felt her heart pounding with trepidation as she walked through the hall to the front door.

Dickie was out on his allotment about ten minutes' walk away, and she had the feeling this WPC knew that. Telling herself not to start getting paranoid, she forced a smile onto her face and opened the door.

'Hello, Mrs Gordon. I don't know if you remember me?' the young girl said cheerfully.

Glenda looked at the pretty young girl and sighed. 'Of course I do, love. Come on in.'

Trudy thanked her and stepped inside.

'Come into the kitchen then, and I'll put the kettle on.'

'Thank you,' Trudy said, following her past a sunburst wooden clock hanging in the hall. Her mum had always wanted one of those! In the kitchen, a large new-model Bakelite radio was on, playing a repeat of a Tony Hancock comedy skit.

Quickly, Glenda turned it off.

'This is a lovely home you have, Mrs Gordon,' Trudy said, looking around admiringly.

Glenda, reaching over to switch on the kettle, felt herself tense.

She could still remember Dickie telling her, just before he put in his retirement papers, that they'd be moving from the council house to 'somewhere decent'.

At the time, she'd thought he meant a smaller place now the kids had grown and left. She knew the local council liked to keep the big, three-bedroomed places for young families, and had built some nice little bungalows for older couples, not far from their old place.

She could still remember her surprise and delight when he'd brought her here. Proud as a peacock he'd been. And, in truth, she'd felt like she'd won the pools herself. It had only been later that she'd begun to wonder how they could ever have afforded it – especially when she realised she didn't have to pay rent. Which meant Dickie had bought it outright. Which was unheard of – nobody in her family had ever owned their own house, and she was sure Dickie's family was the same.

But time passed and the sky didn't fall in on them, and he'd got that part-time job as a night watchman with such good wages, and she'd allowed herself to relax . . .

Now, this pretty young girl in her police uniform was here, looking around and no doubt wondering how they'd been able to afford it.

Glenda swallowed hard. Just what *was* this all about? She should have known things had always been too good to be true.

Her hand shook slightly as she poured out the boiling water and added three good heaped teaspoonfuls of tea leaves into the pot and stirred it thoroughly.

'I wanted to have a quiet word with you, Mrs Gordon, when your husband wasn't here,' Trudy began, surprising the older woman considerably by coming out with it so frankly. 'Because there's something important you need to be made aware of.'

Trudy could tell Glenda hadn't expected her to get to the point so quickly. But Trudy had already decided that shock tactics were probably the best ones to use, and she only hoped she was right.

For, in Glenda Gordon, she thought she'd seen echoes of her own mother. Both had been raised by the same sorts of families, in the same city, and had grown up with the same values and down-to-earth view of life. And she was gambling that, just like her own mother, Glenda would have her own way of thinking and doing things. For all that men liked to think the 'little woman' was always compliant and reliant, Trudy was well aware just how resilient and clever women like her mother actually were. She was willing to gamble that Glenda, too, was far more aware of what went on, especially in her own household, than her husband liked to think. And could be persuaded to act, even behind her man's back, if the occasion demanded it.

'Oh? I thought you'd be wanting Dickie,' Glenda said. 'Police business, and all that.'

Trudy smiled, and eyed the now very wary woman sadly.

'No. It's you I wanted to see.' Trudy took a long, slow breath. 'Can I ask, what did your husband tell you about my previous visit? About what it was I wanted?' she began cautiously.

Glenda sat down a shade heavily, and Trudy was aware she'd metaphorically pulled the rug out from under her. So she was right. Already the woman was suspicious. Which was good. It meant she already knew something was wrong, and might be persuaded that only she could fix it.

'Oh, Dickie never did talk about his work much,' Glenda said as casually as she could manage. 'He just said you wanted to pick his brains about something.' She took a sip of her tea, hardly aware it was still so hot that it almost burned her lips.

Glenda glanced at her visitor to see how that had gone down, and felt a wave of unease wash over her. She was so young and wet behind the ears. She hardly looked twenty! Whatever had brought her to the door, there was no reason to feel so scared, surely? After all, if it was something *really* serious her Dickie had got himself messed up in, they wouldn't have sent a young whippersnapper like this to sort it out, would they?

'Yes. It was about a young girl who died.' Trudy answered her question simply.

Glenda nearly choked on her next sip of tea.

'*Died?*'

'Yes. Your husband was called in when her mother found her dead in bed. This would have been nearly five years ago now. The coroner ruled her death as misadventure.'

'Oh . . .' Glenda let out a small sigh of relief. 'I think I remember that case. It was so sad. But here I was, thinking it was about something really bad. Not that a young girl dying isn't bad . . .' She tried to cover her slip hastily.

'But it *is* about something really bad, Mrs Gordon,' Trudy interrupted her firmly. 'Murder is about as bad as it can get.'

This time Glenda almost dropped her teacup.

'Murder?' she managed faintly. Hadn't she just said something about death by misadventure?

'Yes. We're currently investigating the murder of Jonathan McGillicuddy. You must have read about it in the papers?' Trudy said.

Now Glenda felt more confused than ever. 'Oh, yes. That poor gardener, you mean? Got hit over the head with his own spade, didn't he?'

'Yes.'

'But what's that got to do with Dickie? He's long since retired.'

'Like I said, five years ago he was the first on the scene when a young girl died. That girl was called Gisela Fleet-Wright.'

Glenda's eyes widened. 'But that's the same name as . . .' Abruptly, she shut the words off.

But Trudy was already nodding. 'Yes, we know. It's her father who owns the haulage yard where your husband now works part-time.'

Glenda blinked.

'Your husband took a job there right after retiring, didn't he?'

Glenda nodded, not trusting herself to speak now.

'And I understand his wages are . . . very good.'

Again, Glenda nodded numbly.

'And that you moved in here about five years ago. Not long, in fact, after Gisela Fleet-Wright died.'

Trudy could see her hostess was now as white as a sheet.

'I don't quite see what . . .' Glenda began, trying to rally, but her thoughts were ricocheting around all over the place. What on earth was going on? What had Dickie got them all into?

*

'Mrs Gordon,' Trudy said firmly. 'I really don't care what happened all those years ago.' She was lying like a trouper, hoping for once that she wasn't blushing and giving herself away. 'We know *something did*, and that your husband somehow profited from it.' And before Glenda Gordon could protest, she swept on firmly, 'But that's not what's at issue here. We're trying to catch a killer, Mrs Gordon.' Trudy held the older woman's eye and refused to look away. 'Someone, for some reason, cold-bloodedly bludgeoned a young man to death. He was a widower, you know, and left a little girl. And his mother is absolutely devastated. He was her only child.'

For a moment, the words hung heavily in the air and Trudy knew Glenda had to be thinking of her own children. Thinking of how things might have turned out for them if they'd lost both parents at a young age. And then, of course, how she'd feel in Mavis McGillicuddy's place.

'That's awful,' Glenda said, tears springing to her eyes. 'But you can't think my Dickie . . .'

'No, Mrs Gordon, we don't,' Trudy said hastily. If this woman thought her man was in any real danger, she'd clam up hard and then wild horses wouldn't get her to cooperate. 'We don't think he had anything to do with it. But we think he might know *something* about it.'

Glenda slumped back in her chair, struggling to process it all.

'Before Gisela Fleet-Wright died,' Trudy swept on, 'Mr McGillicuddy had been stepping out with her. And there's now some question over how and why she died, which is why the coroner is reinvestigating the case. And we're sure your husband knew something about that. Something to his advantage, as they say.'

For a moment, she let that hang in the air.

Glenda, her tea now forgotten, stared at the pretty young girl helplessly. Because, of course, she knew it was true. How else had they been able to afford to come and live here? Why else could Dickie get such a good job for really quite ridiculously high wages? Because the Fleet-Wrights had paid him off about something, she acknowledged glumly. That was exactly the kind of back-hander Dickie would have jumped at.

'We think the two incidents may be linked,' Trudy ploughed on. 'That Gisela's death and that of Jonathan McGillicuddy are somehow connected. What's more, it's possible that the killer of Mr McGillicuddy might not be finished yet.'

She didn't believe for one minute that Glenda could be unaware there had to be something questionable surrounding her husband's relationship with Reginald Fleet-Wright. But she certainly wouldn't be willing to talk about it unless she was given a really compelling reason.

'And it seems to us that anyone mixed up in these killings may be in danger themselves.' Trudy added her final bombshell carefully.

And she saw the moment it detonated in the sudden widening of Glenda's eyes. 'You think . . . *Dickie could be in danger*?' she gasped, her hand going to her throat in alarm.

Trudy sighed and spread her hands helplessly. 'We don't know, Mrs Gordon. But it's possible. And if you know anything about any of this, you need to tell us. It needs to be cleared up, before anyone else gets hurt. I'm sure you can see that?'

For a moment, Glenda's mind went to her husband's locked sock drawer upstairs. Ever since they'd moved in, he'd kept it locked. She knew he didn't keep socks in it. Of course, she'd pretended not to notice. And of course, she'd never once asked him about it; though, of course, she knew where he kept the key hidden.

But . . .

'I need to think about all this,' Glenda said faintly.

Trudy, knowing when it was time to back off, nodded. 'All right. But please, Mrs Gordon, think quickly,' she urged. Then she got up and left her untouched tea on the table. 'After all, just think how you'd feel if someone else were killed and you might have prevented it from happening.'

Glenda paled even further, but said nothing.

Trudy, feeling suddenly small and shabby, left the stricken woman and quietly let herself out.

Having hopped onto the back of one of the city's red buses with its distinctive thin green stripe, Trudy dug into her purse for the necessary pennies. Finding she didn't have enough, she had to hand over a tanner instead, making the clippie sigh. Had her father been driving this route, he might have asked the bus conductor to let her off with the fare, as he'd done in the past. Which made her wonder. Was that police corruption? Or just her dad looking out for her?

She shook off the thought and, all the way back into town, tried to reassure herself she'd done the right thing in trying to get Glenda Gordon to come clean about what her husband was up to. It was her job, and her duty, after all.

Even if the worst came to the worst, and former PC Gordon faced some minor corruption charges, the chances were good that the family would get to keep their nice detached house. And even if he lost his police pension, she suspected the Fleet-Wrights would still see him right.

No, all in all, they'd remain better off than most – certainly better off than her own parents. No, her conscience was clear, Trudy reassured herself.

She was still trying to convince herself of this when she walked into the station house. There, the desk sergeant lay in wait for her. And what he had to tell her promptly made her forget all about Glenda Gordon.

'Here, WPC Loveday.' Phil Monroe called her over the moment she stepped through the door. He was one of the few coppers who didn't tease her about her surname, calling her 'the lovely Loveday' (or other variations on the theme) behind her back, as that clown Rodney Broadstairs was wont to do.

'I've remembered where I heard that name before – you know, the one you and the old vulture are so interested in.'

Trudy quickly hustled over to him. 'Oh? Beatrice Fleet-Wright, you mean?'

'Yeah, that's the one. I knew I'd heard it before, so I looked up me old notes,' Monroe said.

All coppers kept their notebooks safe, meticulously up-to-date, and in chronological order, so they could be consulted whenever needed – which could sometimes be years down the line. You certainly needed them in good order when you had to testify in court. It was something that was drilled into you in training. So Trudy had no doubts that the desk sergeant's information would be accurate and reliable.

'And it turns out it was in the same summer she had all that trouble with her daughter,' Monroe said, flipping through his notebook. 'There was a young lad, Jack Braine, worked out of Boots, the chemist. Delivered prescriptions by bike. One day, he got knocked off and robbed.'

Trudy stared at Monroe avidly. 'Robbed of money, or the drug prescriptions he was delivering?'

'Both. The delivery boy didn't see much of what happened – one moment he was biking up the Broad, next he was flying over the handlebars and someone was making off with his bags. But a passer-by that witnessed the whole thing came up with a good description of the perpetrator. And that's where your Mrs F-W comes into it.'

Trudy felt her jaw drop. '*What!* Don't tell me the witness described *her*?' What on earth was a highly respectable, middle-aged, wealthy lady doing robbing . . .

'Nah, 'course not!' the desk sergeant said scornfully. 'Have some sense, young 'un!'

Trudy blushed and hung her head. 'Sorry, Sarge.'

'Nah, the witness described some young chap or other that he thought he recognised. I don't have many details, since I wasn't doing the follow-up on it. Apparently, the witness thought he knew this chap slightly, and thought he was the one doing the robbery. Only saw him side-featured, though, so he wasn't sure. Anyway, the suspect was brought in but it turned out it wasn't him and that the witness was wrong after all. Well, they often are, aren't they?'

Trudy nodded, knowing this was a sad fact. Ask any two

members of the public who'd witnessed the same event to describe a perpetrator, and the villain could be both fat and thin, dark and fair, tall and short, and wearing a black or red shirt.

'Anyway,' Monroe swept on, 'this bloke the witness fingered turned out to have a solid-gold alibi – from a very respectable member of the community who could place him elsewhere at the time – and so that was that.'

Trudy felt herself go hot then cold. 'Mrs Fleet-Wright?'

Monroe grinned. 'Give the girl a goldfish in a bag! Yup.'

'Can you give me the case-file number?' Trudy asked.

'Sure. Not that there'll be much in it. The case never got solved, that I *can* remember. I daresay the little sod that did it sold the drugs and spent all the money on fags and booze.'

He rattled off the case-file number, and Trudy quickly jotted it down in her own notebook. 'This is great! I'll head down to Records now.'

'No, you won't,' Monroe said with a grin. 'The old vulture phoned. He wants you down at his office sharpish.'

Trudy groaned. He probably wanted to know how her interview with Glenda had gone. 'Okay,' she sighed.

Even though she was desperate to find the file and learn what it was all about, it would just have to wait for a bit.

It simply didn't do to keep Dr Ryder waiting!

Chapter Twenty-Six

'Take a look at these photographs and tell me what you see,' Clement said abruptly.

They were sitting in his office, and a mild grey wind was once more throwing rain at the draughty windows. A fire was again roaring in the fireplace, and in the outer office, Trudy could hear the coroner's secretary busily tapping away on her Remington typewriter. It was all beginning to feel rather cosy and familiar. And she realised with a pang that she was going to miss all of this, once the case was solved and DI Jennings put her back on normal duties. It was, perhaps, a measure of just how much she had come to respect Dr Ryder that it didn't even occur to her now that they wouldn't get to the truth of how Gisela Fleet-Wright had come to die.

She reached forward and took the sheaf of black-and-white photographs from him. There weren't that many, and they showed various scenes of what was obviously a young woman's bedroom.

'Gisela's room?' she hazarded.

'Yes. The police photographer took them after photographing the body in situ.'

Trudy noticed that none of the photographs he'd given her showed the dead girl on her bed, and she was about to demand he hand those over too, when something stopped her.

Did she really need to see them?

Clement, watching the play of emotion on her face, said brusquely, 'I want to get another perspective on them – specifically, another young woman's point of view. Try not to look at them as a police officer so much as you would as yourself. Does that make sense? I've been studying them off and on over the years, but I'm not sure I'm seeing everything there is to see, because I don't have the mind of a young woman around Gisela's age.'

Trudy smiled. 'No,' she said succinctly. He certainly didn't! But she understood his point, so she settled down and began to study the photographs carefully.

The first thing that struck her was the size of the room – she could have fitted her own tiny bedroom, with its modest single bed, four times over into the bedroom depicted in the photographs. Gisela's bed had been large, and double – and she'd also had access to two large wardrobes and a dressing table, complete with a pretty, oval-shaped mirror. And still there had been room left over for a couple of padded chairs and plenty of space to walk between them, over what looked like a sumptuous carpet.

On the dressing table were five bottles of expensive-looking scent, a box of tissues, and a make-up bag that looked crammed full with the finest of cosmetics. She would bet one of the lipsticks alone would cost as much as five shillings. On her wages, that would be . . .

Then she told herself to stop being envious of what the other girl had had, and to start looking beyond all that. After all, the girl who had owned all these lovely things was dead and gone. Chastened by the thought, she took a long, deep breath.

Focus, Trudy! Was there anything *suspicious* in these photographs?

Carefully, she splayed them out in front of her on the coroner's desk, her mind darting here and there, looking for anything odd or out of place. She tried to put herself into the mind of Gisela Fleet-Wright.

More and more, Trudy found herself concentrating on the pretty pie-crust table that was positioned beside her bed. On it had been a crystal jug and matching crystal-cut glass – probably full of water, in case she got thirsty. Or, more likely, for use when she was taking all her medication. There was a vase of pretty freesias. Three bottles of pills were set neatly on a small silver tray. A hairbrush, another box of tissues, and what looked like a slender, jewel-encrusted, silver lady's watch. Had she taken it off when she'd lain down to sleep – a sleep from which she was destined never to awaken?

Shaking off the maudlin thought, Trudy frowned. 'It's all so very tidy, isn't it?' she said at last. 'I mean, from all we've heard about Gisela, she seemed to be an emotional mess. I suppose I expected her personal space to be as messy. But it's not. Even the vase of freesias looks perfect – as if they'd just been arranged.'

Clement reached for a photograph and studied it thoughtfully. 'Hmmm. Anything else?'

Trudy shrugged. 'I'm not really sure. But I'd have expected to see her diary somewhere on the scene. We know from her friends that she kept one.'

Clement's impressive silver head turned her way sharply. 'Do you keep one?' he asked curiously.

Trudy blushed, then jutted out her chin. 'Yes. One that locks.'

'And you think most girls would keep one?'

Trudy shrugged again. 'I think so. I know all my friends do.'

'There was no record of Gisela's diary being found in the police files?' he demanded. If any evidence had been kept back . . .

'No,' Trudy said at once. 'There was no record of a diary being found at the scene. And the exhibits officer wouldn't have missed it. At the time, nobody thought to ask Gisela's friends if she'd kept a diary. Why would they? It isn't something we thought to ask her mother about either, was it? But I'd bet Beatrice Fleet-Wright would have known that Gisela had kept one. It couldn't have been much of a secret if her friends knew.'

'Yes, I'm sure she would,' the coroner agreed wryly.

'When are we going back to speak to *Mr* Fleet-Wright?' she asked thoughtfully. 'By all accounts, he and his daughter were close. He might have some insights for us.'

Clement shook his head. 'He might well do. But I doubt he'd be willing to talk to *us* about them. I imagine he'd rather the whole business be left in the past and forgotten. Don't forget – we promised your boss we'd try to be discreet in our inquiries, and if we go to Reginald, he's bound to kick up a fuss. Believe me – wealthy men with a sense of self-importance like to be heard.'

Diplomatically, Trudy said nothing, although her eyes danced as she looked at him mutely.

For a moment, all was silent in the room. Then Clement sighed and tapped the photographs back into a neat pile. 'All right. You've given me some food for thought with these.' He waved them briefly in the air. 'Now suppose you tell me what's got you so excited?'

For a moment, Trudy stared at him blankly.

'When you first came in, you were clearly bubbling with some news?'

'Oh! Yes! The desk sergeant!'

Quickly, Trudy filled him in on Phil Monroe's unexpected revelation, and to her relief he seemed to share her excitement. He was certainly quick to agree that her next course of action should be to hunt down the file at once and learn all the details she could. Naturally, she was to make copious notes and come back with the results as soon as possible.

Chapter Twenty-Seven

Clive Greaves was a worried man.

He knew the police were watching him, and after being pulled in out of the blue as he had been, and interviewed by that canny sod, DI Jennnings, he'd quickly come to realise they suspected him of doing something really major.

But it had taken him a little while to figure out what it was.

Although he'd done his fair share of bending the rules (mostly selling rabbits and pheasants on the side to local butchers), apart from the odd pub brawl, Clive had never done anything that had brought him – seriously – to the attention of the men in blue.

Until now, that is. As he walked across a ploughed field to set up some netting traps to catch some wood pigeons for the pot (as well as to sell on to the cook at a nearby pub for her famous pigeon pie), he wondered how many pairs of eyes were watching him.

He'd spotted a pale-blue-and-white police panda car outside his local pub just the other night. So how much longer would it be before his neighbours started noticing it too? Or his landlady for that matter? The last thing he needed was to get kicked out of his room and have to try and find somewhere else local to rent.

When he'd taken the job as gamekeeper on, he'd hoped it might come with a tied cottage, but the estate owner wouldn't stretch to that. A stockbroker from the city, he only wanted someone to make sure there would be enough birds to shoot six or seven times a year, when he invited his cronies to come up to his 'shooting lodge' to form a party.

Playing the part of Lord Bountiful wasn't on the agenda.

Now Clive wondered how long it would be before he found out that his gamekeeper had come 'to the attention of the police' and gave him the boot. With his scarred face, it had always been a struggle finding employment –which was why his current position suited him so well. He was out in the fields nearly all day, where nobody had to look at him. And the wildlife didn't care what he looked like.

Cursing DI Jennings under his breath – and cursing Sir Marcus Deering even more – Clive began competently setting out the netting and weights. Finally, he secured the small explosive charge and timer that would detonate later on and propel the net about twenty-five feet over the area of newly sown winter wheat, when the pigeons had come down to feed.

His scarred face scanned the open field thoughtfully. With a bit of luck he could get up to fifty pigeons a pop. If he only sold them at sixpence a bird, he'd be on to a nice little earner.

He didn't know it, but PC Rodney Broadstairs, watching him from the cover of a small copse of trees, was making an excited note of his use of explosives in his official police notebook.

Back in his office, Clement Ryder studied the photographs for some minutes after Trudy had left. Then he nodded. Yes, everything did look rather tidy now he thought about it. Maybe even a bit staged? Of course, it could be that, in spite of what you might expect, Gisela Fleet-Wright had just been a tidy girl. But he didn't think so.

If Trudy thought there should have been a diary, he was inclined to trust her judgement. He smiled as he considered the young WPC, who was shaping up nicely. What a pity she'd soon have to go back to doing dead-end duties for that idiot Jennings.

Shaking off the thought, he turned his mind back to the conundrum of the dead girl. It made sense, given what they knew of Gisela's personality, that she'd keep a written record of her doings. Drama had clearly been meat and drink to her and, as she'd been studying English, the written word would have been her obvious medium, enabling her to pour out her emotions and reinforcing her self-image. And of course now it had been confirmed, from questioning her friends more thoroughly, that she had been a keen recorder of her life and emotions.

So why hadn't the diary ever turned up?

As he reached for the photograph showing her bedside table, his hand began to shake. He glared at the evidence of this latest tremor in distaste and got up to walk to the window, stuffing his hands firmly into his trouser pockets.

But out of sight was hardly out of mind.

As a doctor he knew only too well that, as the disease progressed, things would gradually worsen. His movements would become slower – or, as his esteemed colleagues would describe it, he would begin to show signs of bradykinesia. His steps would become shorter and shorter as he walked. He might even begin to drag his feet.

He could expect more and more moments of stiffness. In fact, his muscles could become stiff and downright painful.

But he wasn't there yet. Not by a long chalk! So far, nobody suspected a thing, and while that held true, he *could* and *would* carry on working.

With that in mind, he returned to the desk, took a small measure of brandy from a slender hip flask he kept concealed in his jacket pocket, and then gathered up the photographs, intending to slip them back inside their large, brown envelope.

Perhaps because he was now looking at them with fresh eyes, as his gaze fell on the topmost photograph he noticed there was something slightly odd about the arrangement of articles on the table. That there seemed to be a significant void on the side of the table nearest the bed. The vase of flowers was centred at the back, near the wall and out of the way, which made sense – you didn't want to accidentally knock it over while getting into bed. The tray was next to it, again flush to the wall. The hairbrush had been pushed to the far left-hand side.

Which left a space in the middle, where it looked as if something should have rested. A square-ish space, of just the right proportions to fit in a book of some kind. And yes, he was sure there was a square-shaped mark in the very slight layer of dust, just barely visible. As if a book-shaped object was missing. Which, given the fact that Gisela had been reading English at the time, wouldn't have been surprising.

But perhaps it hadn't been a volume of poetry or a book by Hardy that had rested there, but a diary?

Trudy went straight back to the station house and down into Records, her heart rate accelerating in anticipation. Luckily, the main offices were all but empty, the majority of her colleagues no doubt having being assigned to ensure that Anthony Deering and the rest of his family were safe, or out following their main suspect, or otherwise working elsewhere on the McGillicuddy murder inquiry.

But, for once, Trudy didn't feel envious at being left out and passed over for such interesting duties.

With all her experience in admin, it didn't take her long to find the file on Phil Monroe's case of petty larceny. Although a delivery boy getting knocked off his bike and robbed didn't rate high on the list of crime statistics, the fact that the victim had been delivering drugs from a chemist *had* ensured it was thoroughly investigated.

The filing cabinet for 1955 was towards the back of the Records Office, and after filling in the forms and chatting to the clerk for a few minutes, she was quickly jotting down all the relevant details from the dusty file.

The chemist's lad, Jack Braine, turned out to be not so much of a lad, being at the time of robbery already thirty-five years of age. Reading between the lines, she got the impression that Mr Braine, who was the brother of the chief pharmacist's wife, wasn't the brightest button in the box, but had worked as a delivery boy for them for some years. According to the investigating officer, the delivery boy had been considered trustworthy and reliable, and had been popular with his customers. Most of whom, she noted, were the elderly or infirm, and thus couldn't get to the pharmacy themselves.

Fortunately, Mr Braine had sustained only scrapes and bruises after being knocked off his bicycle, falling to the side of the road rather than in the middle of it – which could have resulted in real tragedy had he gone under the wheels of a passing car or lorry. Unfortunately, though, he hadn't been able to give any sort of description of his assailant, since, after he'd picked himself up and brushed himself down, the perpetrator had already grabbed the satchels of drugs and small amount of cash he'd been carrying, and made off.

That task had fallen to the main witness in the case, listed in the file as one Mr Malcolm Finch, with an address in Cowley.

Trudy, with a frown of disapproval, noted that it had taken Mr Finch nearly a week to come forward with this information. He'd given the excuse that, at the time of the incident, he'd been in a hurry to make an important appointment, which had been scheduled for only ten minutes later. He'd gone on to say that, since the robbery victim was clearly all right, he'd not stuck around with the rest of the crowd to watch the aftermath of the drama. It was only later that his conscience started to bother him, leading him to come into the police station five days after the robbery and make a statement.

With a sigh over the vagaries of the general public, Trudy read his belated testimony with some interest. He stated that he'd been walking down Broad Street during his lunch hour in order to buy stockings for his wife. He had seen the incident, and thought he'd recognised the assailant as being a man he knew only vaguely, when he'd done some gardening work for a neighbour.

As she read these words – and for a giddying moment – Trudy felt as if the office was abruptly closing in around her. *Gardening work?*

Feverishly, her eyes scanned the neatly typed incident report, ignoring the police jargon and hunting out the name . . .

And there it was.

Jonathan McGillicuddy.

The man who had robbed Mr Braine of his money and drug prescriptions had been Jonathan McGillicuddy!

Chapter Twenty-Eight

Anthony Deering wondered if taking Darjeeling out so soon after coming out of hospital had been a good idea after all. Even though he'd kept his mount to a steady walk, he knew the old boy was longing to go for a good run and who could blame him? But every movement felt slightly uncomfortable, so he kept his horse under tight control, denying him his urge to canter.

The horse showed his displeasure at this by tossing his handsome head and prancing about impatiently, making Anthony tighten the reins and curse him fondly from time to time.

Still, for all the discomfort – and even with the old boy playing up – it was nice to get out of the house. The weather had turned mild, if still damp, and the fresh air was certainly doing him good. What's more, Sergeant O'Grady hadn't objected when he'd said he wanted to go out, leaving Anthony with the distinct impression that the police had their eye on someone and were confident they knew where their suspect was and what he was doing.

Which was very good news. Before, he now realised, he'd been inclined to be a shade cavalier about the whole thing. But there was nothing like a brush with death to teach a chap a lesson!

'Come on, lad, settle down,' he told his horse as they approached a cattle-grid, set between two old gateposts, designed to keep his father's sheep from straying into a field of newly sown winter barley. He knew Darjeeling hated crossing cattle-grids, and he couldn't say he blamed him. Horses hooves and tightly spaced parallel iron bars didn't make for a good match. 'Want to jump it, lad?' he muttered.

Then he considered what such a manoeuvre would do to his bruised ribs and sighed. 'Sorry, lad, not this time. You'll just have to pick your way across.'

Which, as it turned out, was a pity. For, had Anthony Deering but known it, he would have been far better off taking the grid at a jump and then enduring the painful jolt of the landing on the other side. Because, as Darjeeling snorted and unhappily began to negotiate the grid, his right forehoof hit a near-invisible strand of fishing wire that had been stretched between the two gateposts, low down near the ground. This then released a short metal pin that had been attached to a small black box, containing a standard bird-scarer, which subsequently let out a large, shot-gun-loud bang.

Darjeeling, already unnerved by the cattle-grid, let out a whinny of terror, launched himself into the air, and bolted madly. Leaving behind his master, who'd fallen heavily across the metal grid and was now screaming in agony.

'Don't you see? It has to be murder!'

Trudy was pacing up and down in front of the coroner's

desk, her face flushed with excitement and glowing with pride. Her WPC's cap lay tossed carelessly on the desk in front of him as she continued to pace, reading rapidly from her notebook.

'It says right here,' she continued, talking so fast that Clement could barely follow her, 'that when Mr McGillicuddy was brought in and put in a lineup, the witness, Malcolm Finch, said he was almost certain it was him he'd seen rob Jack Braine. Though he didn't really want to testify to it. But then, witnesses often don't.' Trudy put in the aside with such a world-weary sigh that it sent the coroner's lips twitching in amusement.

'And from this you deduce that Gisela was murdered?' he asked mildly.

'Yes, and I'll tell you why!' Trudy insisted, scrabbling through her notes. 'You're a medical man. Half the names of the drugs that were stolen I can't even pronounce, let alone spell. But I copied them down carefully, and then I went back to the case files from the coroner's court and . . . here . . . See?'

She all but slapped her notebook down, opened at the spot where she'd meticulously listed the stolen items from the Braine robbery, and pointed to one multisyllable word. Then, in the Fleet-Wright court transcripts, she put another finger on the same word.

'It's the same medication! Gisela was on this . . . this . . .' She stuttered over the tongue-twisting chemical formula. Obligingly Clement read it out loud for her, the word flowing easily off his physician's tongue.

'Yes. It's the exact same course of medication Gisela was on! Don't you see?' she demanded, glowing with excitement. 'Jonathan stole it in order to kill her with it.'

'And her mother gave him an alibi?' Clement mused, watching her with an almost fond smile. She was so excited she was almost coming out of her skin!

But there was no doubting the young WPC had come up with a real golden nugget of information. He just wasn't quite sure, yet, precisely where and how it fit into the jigsaw they were trying to put together.

'Of course! They were in it together. See, here . . .' Again, Trudy frantically bent down and riffled through her notebook. She was standing over the desk, so close beside him that the material on the arm of her uniform actually touched his sleeve. For a moment, as she searched through her notes for the relevant information, she was close enough to smell his breath.

And distinctly smelt alcohol.

As a police officer, she knew the smell well. More often than not, most Saturday nights she and Rodney Broadstairs spent a vast amount of their night shift escorting unruly drunks to the cells.

For a moment, the surprising revelation that Dr Clement Ryder was taken to drinking during the day distracted her. She hadn't heard any rumours that the old vulture liked to drink, had she?

But she was too excited with what she'd found out to pay much attention to that intriguing – and worrying – little snippet just now. Though she did file it away to be duly considered and mulled over later.

'Here. It says that after Jonathan was brought in, and after Mr Finch made his positive identification, he was closely questioned by the sergeant in the case, who gave him his due caution and told him he was likely to be charged with robbery and assault. But when he was asked where he was at the time of the robbery, Jonathan McGillicuddy immediately said he had been gardening for Mrs Beatrice Fleet-Wright.'

Trudy stood up in triumph. 'But we know, by this time . . .' She tapped the date of the robbery significantly. ' . . . That Jonathan hadn't been employed as the Fleet-Wright gardener for quite some time! And this less than a week before Gisela died, mind.'

'If I remember, he left just before breaking up with Gisela.' Clement offered thoughtfully. Which made sense. If you knew you were going to stop seeing a girl, you'd make sure you weren't going to be hanging around, doing the family garden.

'Exactly. So Beatrice must have been lying when she gave him that alibi! And just look at the date of the robbery,' she crowed. 'Mr Braine was robbed just three days before Gisela died! That *has* to be significant.'

Trudy stared at the older man, wondering why he wasn't looking more excited by all this. Surely, this was the break-through they were looking for?

'All right,' Clement admonished, 'let's just sit down for a minute and calmly and rationally think this through.'

Reluctantly, Trudy forced herself to sit on the edge of her chair.

'You're saying Jonathan McGillicuddy robbed the chemist's lad in order to get his hands on this specific batch of medication. The same medication he knew Gisela used?' he began quietly.

'Right.'

'And he did so in order to give her a fatal overdose of it?'

'Yes.'

'And that Mrs Fleet-Wright had to be a party to this, either as an accessory after the fact, or as an active participant, because she provided him with a false alibi when he needed it?' he continued patiently.

Trudy, by now, was becoming a shade impatient with all this measured, careful talking. She knew the coroner was a very educated and clever man, but did he have to be so pedantic all the time? 'Yes. Surely that's obvious?' she demanded.

Clement Ryder smiled patiently. 'Is it, WPC Loveday?' he asked gently. 'Why did Jonathan need to steal the drugs at all? Her mother had access to Gisela's own supply whenever she wanted it,' he pointed out with devastating logic.

Trudy opened her mouth, and then closed it again. She thought for a second, and then said slowly, 'Well, perhaps it was just Jonathan on his own? He'd left Gisela by then, and didn't work in the gardens any more, so he wouldn't have access to her room. Which meant he needed to get some of the pills for himself. He'd have known what brand of pills she took, wouldn't he?'

'All right,' Clement conceded patiently. 'Say that's true. He steals the pills. How does he get her to take them? There were no marks of violence on her body, remember, and nobody saw him in the house the day she died.'

'Oh, come on! He could have sneaked in easily. And Gisela would have been so glad to see him!'

'So glad that she'd let him feed her pills?'

Trudy stared at him angrily. She was beginning to feel foolish now, because she had the appalling feeling she was making a spectacle of herself. She could feel herself deflating by the second. But some inner demon wouldn't let her give up her lovely theories without a fight!

'No. But she would have taken them from her mother!'

'So we're back to Beatrice and Jonathan being in it together then? In which case, my previous question still stands. Why did he need to rob the chemist's lad?'

Trudy slowly slumped back in her chair. It didn't make much sense, did it? Unless . . . 'What if they only got together to conspire about things *after* Gisela died?' she hazarded. Yes – that was better. 'Let's just say Jonathan *did* steal the drugs, and *did* somehow get Gisela to take too many. And afterwards, for some reason, Beatrice found out about it. And, again for some reason we don't know yet, agreed to cover it all up. The scandal or something . . .'

Her voice trailed off as she saw the coroner's white eyebrows slowly beginning to rise at all the 'ifs' and 'maybes' she was scattering around.

'Oh, I know that's a bit lame – but she might have wanted to avoid the scandal, mightn't she?' Trudy persisted, a shade plaintively. 'They are Roman Catholics, and Dad always says the rich are different from everybody else – that they don't think the same way we do. Or she might have been . . . well . . . rather fond of Jonathan herself.' She put forward this second offering a shade timidly.

It made her blush to think of a woman her mother's age being interested in a man so much younger, but she knew such things happened.

'All right, let's go with that hypothesis for a moment,' Clement said, pretending not to notice her sudden unease. 'Jonathan killed Gisela and, for some reason, knew he could rely on Gisela's mother to be his ally. Let me ask you one simple question.'

Trudy tensed, sensing a trap. 'Yes?' she said uncertainly.

'Why did Jonathan McGillicuddy murder Gisela?' Clement asked simply.

Trudy blinked. 'Why? Well, because . . . because . . . he loved her. Or hated her. Or because she was making such a nuisance of herself – take your pick!'

But already Clement was shaking his head. 'No, that simply won't do, WPC Loveday, and you know it. Men kill women out of passion or jealousy, yes. But we already know that Jonathan was the one to end their relationship. So he was hardly still in love with her. And at the time of her death, he'd been free and clear of her for several months. He had no reason to need her dead. So why go to all the trouble and risk of killing her?'

'But we know Gisela was determined to win him back,' Trudy insisted gamely. 'We *know* she kept on trying to talk to him, even followed him around. And she wasn't very stable, was she? Perhaps he was scared she might . . . I don't know . . . do something *really* crazy and embarrass him. Or perhaps she'd begun to behave so oddly he feared she might present a danger to his mother – or his little girl!'

Clement nodded. 'Yes, that might do it,' he finally conceded. 'But we have no evidence that that was the case, do we? And if any of that *had* been true, and he *had* been worried about it, why didn't he simply go to the police? Or seek legal advice? Or go to the girl's family, and tell them something needed to be done or he'd have her committed? Don't forget, by all accounts, Jonathan McGillicuddy was a plain, simple, law-abiding lad. Do you really think his first thought would be to commit an act of murder? Without at least trying some of those alternatives?'

Trudy blinked.

'Or that the girl's mother, her *mother*, Trudy, would connive with him to murder her only daughter?' he continued.

'DI Jennings said most murders happen in the family,' Trudy said stubbornly. But, in truth, she now felt totally confused.

When she'd read the Braine file, she'd thought it provided the answers to all their questions. Now she didn't know *what* she had uncovered. Except, perhaps, more confusion.

For a while she simply sat in a somewhat sulky silence, annoyed the old vulture was being such a wet blanket, but slowly coming to terms with the fact that he was probably right. And going over things again, this time with less excitement and more care, one thing was becoming more and more abundantly clear.

She simply didn't have the brains for this job.

Right away, Dr Ryder had seen the problems that came with this new evidence, but she hadn't had a clue!

'I'm not good enough to do this, am I?' she finally blurted out miserably.

'Nonsense! Don't go all self-pitying on me, Constable,' Clement snapped bracingly. 'I'll warrant you've got more brains in your little finger than most of your colleagues at that station house have in their entire bodies. And certainly more than that vain little twerp I notice admiring his good looks in the window glass every time I see him.'

In spite of herself, Trudy laughed at this clear description of Rodney Broadstairs.

Then she felt the smile fall away. 'I thought I'd found the answers, though. I thought I had it all figured out. But I was wrong.'

Clement smiled wryly. She was such a contradiction, this young woman. Bright but naive, innocent yet savvy, determined and stubborn, and yet so quick to blush. She was still so inchoate and unformed she sometimes worried him. And yet, there was no denying he found her a useful sounding board, helping him to order and examine his thoughts more clearly. And in spite of all the odds being against it, he felt they had the makings of a really good team.

'So, tell me, what do you think you've learned by this episode?' he asked, rather enjoying the role of being an educator again.

'Not to jump to conclusions,' Trudy said at once, and with some bitterness.

'And in learning that, do you think you've probably learned more than you did in all your months of police training? What else?'

Trudy blinked, thought about it for a moment, and then nodded. 'To think things through logically. To ask and answer questions. To keep a clear head and question everything.'

'Even more valuable lessons learned,' he nodded approvingly. 'And you think you're not cut out for this job?' he scoffed.

'You're just trying to cheer me up.'

Clement snorted. 'Young woman, let me assure you, I have better things to do with my valuable time than pander to your ego. So, let's get on with the important stuff, shall we?' He rose from his chair and slipped on his raincoat and favourite homburg hat.

'Where are we going?' Trudy asked blankly, quickly gathering her accoutrements together and putting them into her leather satchel. Fixing her cap on top of her head, she hastily tucked a few strands of escaped hair neatly underneath it.

'To talk to Beatrice Fleet-Wright again, of course,' Clement said, looking at her sharply. 'Where else?'

Chapter Twenty-Nine

Beatrice Fleet-Wright didn't look particularly surprised to see her two recent visitors returning to her home again after only a few days, but there was a close, shuttered and wary look lurking behind her polite smile as she greeted them.

She ushered them into the same lovely, lifeless room as before, but this time there was no offer of tea. Such an unthinkable lack of hospitality on her part was clearly an indication of just how nervous she truly was beneath her veneer of polite enquiry, if it could make her so forget her duties as a hostess. Either that or it was a deliberate ploy on her part to make it clear just how brief she expected this second visit to be, a not-so-subtle indication that she expected them to make themselves scarce in short order.

But Trudy rather thought it was the former.

Although she had been too young to really remember the war years, she had clear memories of the dreary years of rationing that had followed, and could recall she hadn't, for instance, even tasted her first sweet until she was twelve. Even though people had had so little to eat or drink themselves, somehow this had only served to make respecting the laws of hospitality become even more ingrained. One time, her mother had shared her last spoonful of tea with an elderly woman who had come collecting for an orphanage. And for the rest of the month, the family had had to drink something so foul (and made from dandelions) that even the family dog refused to lap it up when she'd emptied it into his bowl.

'I'm sorry to bother you again so soon, Mrs Fleet-Wright,' Clement Ryder began with a brief smile, cutting into Trudy's reminiscences. 'But when we talked to you last about Mr McGillicuddy and your dealings with him, we think perhaps you might have forgotten to mention something?'

For a second, Beatrice – looking very chic in a soft, heather-coloured twinset, with a pearly grey blouse – froze in place. Then she allowed a slightly baffled frown to appear on her face.

Her make-up, Trudy noted idly, was minimal but flawless. And just a faint scent of violets wafted in the air whenever she moved. It made it almost impossible to believe that this well-heeled, respectable, middle-aged woman could in any way be mixed up in even one murder, let alone two. Always supposing her daughter's death hadn't been quite so accidental as the coroner's court had ruled.

'Oh? I don't think so,' Beatrice said politely. 'I'm sure I answered all the questions you asked me correctly.'

Clement bit back a small, appreciative smile. Yes, that was a very clever answer, he acknowledged wryly. But then, he was beginning to get the feeling that Mrs Beatrice Fleet-Wright was a very clever woman.

'Perhaps the fault was ours,' he conceded amiably. 'Let me be more clear and precise. We have since learned that, around the time of your daughter's death, you were, in fact, on at least one occasion, in close contact with Mr McGillicuddy. Is that not so?'

Even on a grey day in the darkest depths of winter, and with limited light coming in through the windows, Trudy could clearly see that the older woman had gone rather pale. She also swallowed visibly.

'Really?' Beatrice murmured. 'It was so long ago . . . And my memories from that time were . . .' Her hands fluttered helplessly. 'I was given sedatives to take by my doctor around that time. I'm afraid my recollection might not be quite so clear. It was a traumatic time, you understand. I try not to think about it.'

Trudy blinked at this disjointed sequence of sentences. There were too many excuses, mixed up with so much rationalising. And all for nothing, since it was clear as crystal that she was lying.

'But the occasion we're referring to would have had reason to stand out, Mrs Fleet-Wright,' Clement persisted, gently but ruthlessly. 'It can't be very often, after all, that a member of the public is asked to provide an alibi for a young man accused of daylight robbery.'

'Day . . .' For a moment, Beatrice's face went genuinely slack, and a blank look came into her eyes. Trudy felt a cold trickle run down her spine. For, whatever it was Beatrice had expected them to accuse her of, it had certainly not been that.

Which immediately make her wonder. What *had* this woman thought they'd been talking about? What *other* contact had she had with her daughter's former beau?

'Oh . . . Oh, yes. Now I remember! That silly nonsense about Jon . . . Mr McGillicuddy . . . stealing money and . . . things . . . from a chemist, wasn't it?' Beatrice said with a light little laugh.

She'd said things, not drugs, Trudy noted, which was surely the most obvious thing to have said. But clearly Mrs Fleet-Wright didn't like mentioning prescription drugs, which wasn't perhaps so surprising. They were bound to be a sore topic for her, given her daughter's dependence on them and the fact that they had – somehow – been responsible for her death.

She shot the coroner a quick glance to see if he'd picked up on the telltale mistake, and thought he probably had.

'Was it such nonsense?' Clement asked calmly.

'Of course it was!' Beatrice said quickly, rushing to defend him. 'Mr McGillicuddy was a hard-working and respectable man. He'd never been in trouble with the law in his life – as I'm sure you must be in a position to know.'

Trudy nodded. There had certainly been no 'previous' incidents that had brought the murdered man to police attention.

'So you had no doubts that he couldn't possibly have been the man who robbed the chemist's delivery boy? Even though he was identified by someone who knew him slightly?' Clement swept on quietly.

For a moment, an extraordinary expression flitted across Beatrice's face, but it was gone so quickly that Trudy couldn't quite place it. She was certain, though, that there was anger in it – and perhaps fear? Or was it . . . regret? Sorrow? Something negative, anyway.

'Clearly that was a mistake on the witness's part,' Beatrice said flatly. And at that point, she drew in a rather long breath. Clement noted, with a doctor's detached observation, that she was in danger of hyperventilating if she carried on like this. Clearly she was in a very highly charged emotional state (with her nerves at absolute stretching point) if she was forgetting how to breathe properly.

'Luckily for him, then, that he was able to provide such a solid alibi,' Clement acknowledged smoothly, looking at her expectantly.

'Yes, yes, I suppose it was,' she agreed faintly. 'When the police called, asking about it . . . The thing was . . . my magnolia tree had been in dire need of attention for some time. And I didn't really trust the gardener we had hired after Jonathan . . . er . . . left us to treat it properly. So I'd asked him if he wouldn't mind pruning it for me. Just a one-off job – and it happened to be on that day.'

Beatrice paused once more for a much-needed breath.

'That was quite a coincidence,' Clement said, with absolutely no inflection in his voice whatsoever.

Beatrice merely shrugged. 'Coincidences *do* happen, though, don't they, Dr Ryder?' she challenged him mildly. 'So, naturally, when the police contacted me and asked if I could confirm Mr McGillicuddy was working here in the garden when that poor man was being knocked off his bicycle and robbed, I had to say he was.'

'Naturally,' Clement said dryly. 'And that was the last time you saw him?'

'Yes.'

'And your daughter died, in fact, only a few days after the robbery?'

Beatrice again swallowed convulsively and stared down at her hands. 'Yes,' she said faintly.

'Mrs Fleet-Wright,' Clement said gently. 'Are you sure you don't know who killed Mr McGillicuddy?'

Beatrice went white. Her head shot up. And then she stared at him levelly for quite a number of silent, tense seconds. 'Dr Ryder,' she eventually said calmly, 'I can assure you I have no idea at all who killed Mr McGillicuddy.'

'Or why?'

'Or why,' she repeated firmly.

'So do you believe her?' Trudy demanded as they walked outside and climbed once more into his Rover.

'About what? Her giving your murder victim an alibi, or not knowing who killed him?'

'About the alibi,' Trudy said.

'No. I think she was lying through her teeth about the whole thing.'

'So do I!'

'Especially since, when she was called upon to give him his alibi, her daughter had been dead for only two days.'

'What? No, it was just before . . . Oh. Oh, of course!' Trudy breathed. She'd forgotten about the reluctant witness. Mr Braine had been robbed two days *before* Gisela died, but Mr Finch had only plucked up the nerve to come in and tell what he had seen five days *later*. By which time, Gisela had been dead for two days.

'Would a woman still reeling from a shock like that really be thinking about her magnolia tree?' Clement asked with a snort. 'And, for that matter, is the middle of summer even the time to be pruning one of them?'

Trudy, who was no gardener either, had no idea. Not that

it mattered. Clearly, Beatrice Fleet-Wright would have been in no fit state to even be thinking about her precious garden. Much less asking her dead daughter's former boyfriend to attend to it. Which made the alibi she had given Jonathan McGillicuddy even more outlandishly false.

'And yet, for all that, I'm not so sure she wasn't telling the truth about the rest of it,' Trudy said after a moment's thought. 'When she said she didn't know who had killed Jonathan, I got the feeling she was being honest.' Then, not wanting to be teased about 'women's intuition' (which was something her male colleagues liked to deride with much male condescension), she added firmly, 'But of course, my personal opinion is neither here nor there. It's facts and proof that we need.'

How many times had both Sergeant O'Grady and her DI drummed that into her?

'Yes, that always helps,' Clement said dryly. 'But a good detective should always listen to their inner voice too. We often pick up things, especially as we gain in experience, that can't always be quantified in terms of specific data. Sometimes instinct is a good starting point.'

Taken rather by surprise at this unscientific observation on the part of her colleague, Trudy fell thoughtfully silent as he drove them back to the station house.

She hadn't been inside long, however, before she was brought quickly up-to-date on Anthony Deering's latest near-miss.

'He's been able to stay at home, which is good,' Rodney Broadstairs told her, sweeping back his golden hair with one hand and reaching for his notebook with the other. 'His GP didn't think anything was broken, so there was no need for the poor sod to have to go back to hospital. But on top of all his other injuries, getting these latest cuts and bruises must have hurt like the devil. You wouldn't catch me riding no horse.'

Trudy, fighting back the urge to laugh as she instantly pictured Rodney on horseback, sighed. 'So what's been happening?'

'The DI has had Clive Greaves brought back in for questioning. He's grilling him now, down in the cells. I mean, it stands to reason he must have done it, don't it?'

'Does it?'

'Yeah. I told you – the horse was spooked by one of them things you hear in the fields going off bang every now and then, to keep the pigeons and crows and what-have-you off the seed. And our man Greaves is a gamekeeper, yeah? On a farming and hunting estate. Stands to reason, he'd have access to one of them, and know how to use 'em.'

Trudy frowned. 'But almost anybody could get hold of one, couldn't they? The hardware shops would sell them. And they can't be that hard to use, surely?'

'Nah, Jennings is convinced he's our man,' Broadstairs said comfortably. 'One – he got burned in that fire.' He ticked the points off on his fingers. 'Two, he's right here in the area. And now, three, this latest attempt to bump off Deering's precious son and heir with a piece of farming kit? Got to be Greaves, ain't it? Anyway, at least while he's in here being grilled by the Sarge and the DI, the likes of me and you won't be needed to pull any more night duty on obbo, watching his comings and goings.'

Well, at least that was true, Trudy thought, with a bright smile. She didn't particularly relish having to spend any more freezing nights watching Mr Greaves stagger home from the pub to his lodgings.

But the next morning, when Sir Marcus Deering received what was to turn out to be his final anonymous letter, it seemed she might not have to worry about following Clive Greaves around ever again.

For the letter came first class, and after certain exhaustive inquiries at the Post Office were made, it became clear the letter had been posted at 2.30 p.m. the preceding day. At which precise time, Mr Clive Greaves had been 'helping the police with their inquiries' at St Aldates' nick.

So unless he had an accomplice – or had managed to be in two places at the same time – DI Jennings had to concede he couldn't possibly have been responsible for sending the latest letter.

On first receiving the envelope from his tremulous, sympathetic secretary, Sir Marcus had immediately phoned Jennings, who, along with Sergeant O'Grady, had motored over to his home. Now all three men were gathered in his study, and a sense of dread was palpable in the air.

'So it's come right down to it at last, just like I knew it always must!' had been Sir Marcus's first, trembling words to them on their arrival. His face looked dreadful – haggard and drawn, and he had a defeated slope to his shoulders.

With a look of fear and despair on his face, he handed the note over.

YOUR TIME IS NOW UP.

Sir Marcus slumped back into his chair, looking distraught. 'What can I do?' he asked desperately. 'I must do something to save my son! Do you think if I offered to make restitution it would keep Anthony safe? Yes, I can do that, can't I?' he babbled eagerly. 'I can put an advert in the paper saying I'm going to give the survivors of the fire some compensation? You'll help me find them, right?'

Jennings half-heartedly agreed, sympathising with the man's desperation, and said all the usual platitudes and comforting things; that he was confident it was now only a matter of time before they found out just who had murdered Jonathan McGillicuddy. But he wasn't feeling particularly sanguine about it.

Chapter Thirty

Glenda Gordon walked nervously down the street, glancing over her shoulder every so often, as if expecting to see her husband's furious face as he came charging down the street behind her.

Of course, he did no such thing. He was once again on his allotment, where at this time of year he spent more time in his shed, drinking whisky-laden tea out of his thermos with his little coterie of old cronies, than doing any actual digging.

She marched up to St Aldates police station before she could lose her nerve and bolt back home and then glanced quickly around. Luckily, on such a drab January afternoon, everyone was too busy scuttling about on their own business to pay any attention to her and her doings.

Nervously, she stepped inside and looked around furtively. She'd never been inside a police station before. Clutching her handbag tightly in front of her, she approached the desk sergeant – who looked like a kindly sort of individual – and gave what she hoped was a confident smile.

*

Phil Monroe watched the approaching member of the public with professional detachment and mild curiosity. Good-quality coat, nice enough shoes, a typical housewife. Pale face, big, anxious eyes. Timid. As he greeted her, he wondered what it was she wanted to report. Lost cat, or peeping Tom?

'Yes, madam, how can I help you?'

'Is WPC Loveday here, please?' Glenda asked, glancing through the open inner door to the main office, as if expecting to see a bunch of ravening wolves fighting over a deer carcass. 'I was wondering if I could talk to her privately?' she added anxiously. She didn't know if any of Dickie's former colleagues worked here, and she absolutely didn't want her visit to the station getting back to him.

Phil nodded, lifting up the flap behind his desk and stepping out of his domain with a comforting smile. 'Nothing easier, madam,' he assured her. 'This way, please.' After getting her name, he deposited her in an interview room, then left very smartly to fetch his favourite constable, guessing that Trudy Loveday's witness might do a runner if she was left alone for any length of time.

She had the look of a frightened rabbit about her.

'Hello, Mrs Gordon,' Trudy said brightly, the moment she stepped inside.

'I've been thinking about what you said before,' Glenda Gordon began quickly, wanting to get the words out before she could change her mind. 'I don't know what it's all about, mind,' she said, somewhat confusingly, 'but I know my Dickie and his little ways, and I know he can't have done anything *really* wrong, otherwise I wouldn't be here.' She wanted to make that clear.

She then pulled from her handbag a small, padded brown envelope. 'He always keeps his little secrets locked in his sock drawer, you see,' she carried on. 'Silly, really, because I know where he keeps the key. Usually he just keeps a flask of best brandy in there and some . . . er . . .' Here she broke off abruptly. There was no need to tell this pretty young girl about the harmless, but rather smutty, pictures Dickie liked to drool over. 'Anyway, I think this might be what you wanted,' she said hastily, thrusting it towards a slightly startled Trudy.

'I'll need it back, mind, when you've finished with it,' Glenda rushed on. 'I want to get it back into his sock drawer before he knows it's gone.'

Trudy blinked as she took the envelope, her heart rate accelerating as she saw the initials the former PC had written in pencil on one side. G F-W.

The diary! It had to be. But even as she thought it, Trudy realised it couldn't be Gisela's missing diary that was inside. The envelope was far too light. In fact . . . She peeked inside and saw only a square of pale paper, encased in a plastic evidence bag.

'How soon can I have it back?' Glenda demanded, luckily distracting her from her first impulse, which was to snatch it out and read it. But, of course, she couldn't do that. She had to maintain the integrity of the evidence.

Trudy looked back at her visitor and thought quickly. 'How about tomorrow?'

But even as she said it, she realised she no idea whether or not it would be possible to let Glenda have it back so soon. After all, she'd have to take it to the coroner, and then they'd have to study it, and maybe even send it away for tests. And if it did turn out to be vital evidence of a crime, she'd probably never get it back.

But Trudy didn't think Glenda would willingly part with it if she said as much.

'Oh, that's fine,' Glenda said now, looking so relieved that Trudy felt instantly guilty. 'Like I said, I don't know what it is. I didn't look.'

'So you never took it out of the plastic bag?' Trudy asked sharply. When the older woman vigorously shook her head, she smiled with relief. Good. That would be one less set of fingerprints they needed to worry about.

'After what you said about . . . murder . . . and things . . . I've been lying awake all night, worrying,' Glenda went on. 'I hope . . . I hope . . . Nothing's going to happen to my Dickie, is it?' she wailed, her nerves finally failing her.

Trudy instantly went to her and put a comforting hand on her shoulder. 'I really don't think your husband is in any imminent danger from the killer, Mrs Gordon,' she said, mentally crossing her fingers that she was right about that. 'And I promise you, I'll do everything I can to make sure you and your family don't suffer for this either,' she added, giving the envelope a little jiggle.

Once again, Trudy hoped she'd be able to make good on that promise as well. But she was very much aware that, as a lowly WPC, her opinions would count for nothing. On the other hand, she was confident that DI Jennings and his superiors wouldn't be in any hurry to bring the force into disrepute if they could avoid it – and that if they could keep Richard Gordon's name out of things, they would be happy to do so.

With more assurances that Trudy knew she really shouldn't

be making, she gently ushered the pale-faced woman back into the outer hall, where Phil Monroe watched them thoughtfully.

'That's not a happy lady,' he said in massive understatement, once Glenda, casting a final, anxious look over her shoulder, had hurried through the front door and scuttled away.

'No,' Trudy agreed. She was itching to look inside the envelope, but decided, very reluctantly, that she should wait until someone superior to her had seen it first. For a second, she was torn – should she take it straight to DI Jennings, or to Clement Ryder?

But once she thought about it, there was no question which of them she trusted most. If she gave it to DI Jennings, he'd simply take it off her and dismiss her, and she'd probably never even get to read it, whereas Dr Ryder actually seemed happy to be working with her, and was far more likely to share his thoughts.

She quite liked being useful, and being asked for her opinion. In spite of his sometimes-frightening intelligence and arrogant manner, she was beginning to rather like the old vulture.

'I'm just off to Floyds Row,' she told the desk sergeant.

'Fine. But don't be late for the afternoon briefing,' Phil called after her with a grin. 'You know the DI likes to observe the rule book!' he warned sagely.

'I won't,' Trudy called back gaily.

Phil Monroe shook his head in wonderment. Clearly the young lass was getting on well with that crusty old sod, the coroner, after all. Now who'd have thought that unlikely pair would make such a good team?

Chapter Thirty-One

Trudy quickly requisitioned a bicycle from the police bike shed, not wanting to walk even the short distance, so eager was she to show Dr Ryder what she had. She was also mindful of the desk sergeant's warning, and if the contents of the envelope were interesting, and the coroner kept her late, she'd need the extra few minutes the pedal-power would give her to get back in time for the debriefing.

She knew Dr Ryder wasn't sitting in court that afternoon, since he'd made sure she had a copy of his schedule. By now his secretary was so used to seeing her face that she ushered Trudy through without even bothering to consult his diary or look disapproving at her rushed, cheerful greeting.

Had Trudy but known it, she was one of a very select few who didn't need an appointment to see the eminent man.

Unaware of this honour, however, she simply rushed into his office and found Clement sitting behind his desk and frowning over the autopsy report from his last case of the week – the unexpected death of a 32-year-old television repairman.

He looked up as Trudy barrelled in. Her cheeks were flushed and she was breathing hard (she'd pedalled like fury) and Clement felt a momentary pang of something nostalgic as he looked at her. How long had it been since he'd been in such a hurry? Or had felt so excited his eyes shone, as hers did now?

'WPC Loveday,' he said dryly. 'I take it you have something interesting?'

'Yes! Well, I think so,' Trudy temporised, as a sudden, horrible thought hit her. What if there was nothing of interest in the envelope, after all? What if Glenda had merely stumbled on another of her husband's minor peccadilloes that had nothing to do with their case?

Quickly, she recounted the gist of Glenda Gordon's visit, and then placed the envelope on the desk between them. She felt, suddenly and absurdly, as if she was some sort of gundog proudly bringing him a fallen pheasant and placing it at his feet.

But then the flash of resentment this thought brought rapidly faded as the coroner reached into his desk and drew on a pair of thin rubber gloves, and pulled the inner, plastic envelope free of the outer brown paper one. Carefully, he removed the sheet of paper from its protective covering and opened it out.

Eagerly, Trudy moved around his side of the desk so she could read it. This time, she was pleased to note, she couldn't smell alcohol on him, which was a relief. She hadn't liked to think that the old vulture might be a secret tippler or a bit of an old soak on the sly. Somehow, that would have diminished him irreparably in her eyes.

And that would have made her feel very sad.

The small, rectangular piece of paper that was now lying on the desk in front of them was pale lavender in colour, and the flowing feminine handwriting that covered it had been written in black ink. It was dated July 28th, 1955, and the printed letterhead bore the Fleet-Wright address.

Trudy's heart beat faster as she read the few, simple lines.

'I'm so sorry, but this simply can't go on. I haven't enough strength or courage. I only hope my family can forgive me. But life is simply no longer worth living.'

It was signed, simply, Gisela.

'So it was suicide, after all!' Trudy said, not sure whether to feel disappointed or elated that they had finally got to the truth of the matter.

For a long while, however, Dr Ryder said nothing. He reread the few lines a number of times, then sighed softly, and carefully put the piece of paper back into the plastic evidence bag.

Trudy watched him, feeling vaguely dissatisfied. She knew he wasn't the most demonstrative of men, but she had expected him to be a little more animated than this. Maybe even just a little bit complimentary? She had, after all, just brought him the solution to the case on a platter, hadn't she?

But she should have known better than to expect praise, she thought crossly. She was just going to have to get used to the fact that nothing she did would ever be good enough for her superiors – be they DIs, sergeants or civilians!

Then, telling herself that self-pity was unattractive, she distracted herself by confessing just what she had promised Glenda Gordon.

As expected, he didn't approve, and showed no compunction about showing it. Oh, that's typical, Trudy fumed silently. You do something *wrong* and they didn't hesitate to jump on you like a ton of bricks.

'You shouldn't have done that, Constable. There's no way Mrs Gordon can have this back tomorrow,' Clement said, waving the letter briefly in the air. 'And you'll just have to tell her so.'

Trudy nodded glumly. It wasn't a task she was looking forward to. 'So what are you going to do with it?' she asked curiously, nodding at the letter. 'I suppose you can close the case now? And should I tell DI Jennings?'

'Not just yet,' Clement said, a shade sharply. 'He'll only re-assign you to something useless and asinine, I have no doubt! And I don't want to lose you just yet. There are still a few loose ends I need to tie up.'

'Oh?' Trudy said, feeling ridiculously pleased, but also puzzled. 'Like what?'

'I want you to find that witness who identified Jonathan McGillicuddy for a start. His details will be in the file, won't they?'

'Yes, they should be,' Trudy agreed vaguely. 'But why?'

'I want you to find out all you can about him and ask him about that day. I'm curious as to why he thought it was Jonathan he saw robbing the delivery boy.'

Trudy sighed. She couldn't see how that was relevant now, but she was game. Anything was better than walking the cold winter streets looking for bag-snatchers. 'All right.' She glanced at her watch. 'Is there anything else? Only I need to get back. Did I tell you our prime suspect, that gamekeeper I told you about, doesn't look like such a sure thing any more?'

She was about to explain, but Clement dismissed her with

a vague wave of his hand and she could see he clearly had other things on his mind. In fact, he seemed to be thinking very hard about something. She was beginning to recognise the look. And so, feeling vaguely disappointed, and with a definite sense of anticlimax, she left him to it, and pedalled, rather gloomily, back to the station house.

In his office, Clement sat in his chair, thinking furiously.

There was something glaringly wrong about that suicide note, and young Trudy, once she'd had a chance to think it through properly, would almost certainly come to the same conclusion. With a small grunt, he got up from the desk and headed towards the filing cabinet where he kept his briefcase. As he did so, he felt his foot snag on the rug in front of the window and stumbled forward slightly.

He glanced down, wondering if he'd started to drag his feet. Watching them as he continued walking to the cabinet, he decided he was walking just fine. He'd just tripped, that was all.

He retrieved his briefcase and hunted through it, finally finding what he was looking for, which was the postcard Gisela had sent her friend, and which he'd asked to keep when he and Trudy had interviewed her last week. Experience had taught him that it never hurt to accumulate as much evidence as you possibly could – even the kind that didn't seem particularly promising or useful at the time. Because you never knew when it could suddenly become very significant indeed.

He looked at the card thoughtfully as he went back to his desk. It was of the usual seaside view, and Gisela had written the usual short lines of platitudes. But the light-hearted phrases didn't matter – the handwriting did.

And although, when he compared the two examples side by side a minute later, they looked the same to his eyes, he willingly admitted to himself that his eyes were not those of a handwriting expert.

But this was Oxford, after all, and it took him only a few minutes on the telephone to find an obliging Don at St Cross College, who said he would be happy to compare them and give his expert opinion right away.

As he left the office with the two pieces of evidence in his hand, Dr Clement Ryder was smiling gently, the smile of a fox on the scent of a rather juicy, plump little partridge.

As he made his way to St Cross College, he wondered how WPC Loveday would get on with the little task he'd set her. Because, unless he was very much mistaken (and he hardly ever was), she was going to find locating and talking to the witness to the theft of the drugs rather more interesting than she'd ever supposed.

The following morning, Trudy grew increasingly annoyed with herself. She'd been given such a simple task, and with her very good, if reluctantly acquired, clerical skills, it should have been a snap. And yet, she simply couldn't find Mr Malcolm Finch anywhere. Or any evidence he'd ever existed, for that matter.

First, she'd gone to his last-known address in Cowley, which he'd given in his witness statement, but the landlady there had firmly denied any knowledge of him. At Trudy's gentle suggestion that she might have forgotten him, the good lady had puffed up like an indignant cat and told Trudy her memory was razor-sharp. To prove it, she'd even gone and fetched her record book for July 1955 and showed her the neat, handwritten ledger, wherein the name of Malcolm Finch was most definitely not to be found.

Fully vindicated, the triumphant landlady had seen her off, and Trudy, feeling a little shamefaced and vexed, had returned to the station and started out on a veritable blitz of paperwork.

But of Mr Malcolm Finch she could find no sign. She quickly discovered he had *not*, in fact, been employed in the place of work he had given in his official statement, and neither was he listed in any local census. He wasn't registered to vote in the area and she could find no birth certificate for him that matched the date he'd given as his date of birth.

In short, it was quite clear that Mr Malcolm Finch, as a person, did not exist.

'What the hell's going on?' Trudy muttered, slamming down the telephone on the water board, which had been the last company she'd contacted, to see if they'd issued any utility bill to a man of that name.

It was ten o'clock in the morning, and by now Trudy had the sneaking suspicion that Dr Ryder had known just what she would have to report back to him. That he had, in fact, deliberately sent her off on what he had known – or at least strongly suspected – to be a wild-goose chase.

With a growing sense of anger that she'd been taken for a mug, Trudy stalked out of the station house and set off for Floyds Row.

It was time she and the old vulture had a few words!

But when she got to his office, her nicely worked-up steam of self-righteous anger was unceremoniously nipped in the bud before she'd even had a chance to utter a single word. Because the moment she walked into his office, Clement looked at her and cried jubilantly, 'It's a fake!'

He was even openly grinning – something Trudy had never witnessed before. The crusty old coroner, actually looking happy!

'What?' Trudy said blankly.

Clement reached for the now-familiar evidence envelope, with its square of lavender notepaper. 'This so-called suicide note,' he scoffed. 'It's a fake. *Gisela didn't write it.*'

Quickly he filled her in on his visit to the handwriting expert at St Cross, as Trudy slowly sank down onto the chair opposite him, wide-eyed and quivering.

'And he was quite sure that, although the writing resembled that on the postcard,' Clement concluded, 'it was *not* the same hand. Though he did think it bore naturally occurring similarities – which is rather suggestive, don't you think?' Clement said pointedly.

But, for the moment, the point was clearly lost on her, because all she said was, 'So it *was* murder, after all!'

'Not necessarily,' he muttered. But apart from giving him a sudden, sharp glance, Trudy didn't comment. In truth, she was beginning to worry she would only make a fool of herself if she said anything else. All along, as the case had progressed, she'd become more and more aware that this clever man was always one step ahead of her. Which only made her more determined than ever to raise her game. After all, she didn't want to play the bumbling Doctor Watson to his Sherlock Holmes forever!

Take this latest development, for instance. Surely, if the suicide note was a fake, Gisela hadn't written it. And if she hadn't written it, then someone else had. And if someone else had, they'd done it in order to make her death look like a suicide. Which left only murder, didn't it? Given all they'd learned, it had to be murder, right? To her, the logic seemed impeccable. Yet Dr Ryder didn't seem to think so – or else why make such a cryptic comment?

For a while she sat in simple, miserable silence. Because no matter how she twisted the facts, she still couldn't see it – whatever *it* was. And, boy, did that make her feel cross!

Clement, looking at her over the width of his desk, felt his lips twitch and had to fight back a sudden desire to laugh. She looked so forlorn, and yet slightly simmering underneath – like a wet hen, contemplating a good pecking of somebody's ankles.

It was clearly time to snap the young miss out of her self-pity and doubt, so he said briskly, 'Now you've had time to think about it, did anything strike you as odd about the note? Not that it was a forgery,' he added quickly, as she looked about to erupt angrily. 'There was no way you could have known that. I didn't know it myself until I'd had an expert check it. I mean, was there anything about the note itself you didn't like?'

Trudy sighed. 'Yes. When I was in bed last night thinking about it,' she admitted wearily, 'I realised it was rather short, and not very well written. Or dramatic. I mean, Gisela was a student of English literature, and I'd have expected her last words to be more . . . I don't know. But certainly not so prosaic and *ordinary*.'

Clement nodded. Yes, he'd known the girl would get there. She was really quite intelligent – just green and inexperienced.

Give her time, and she would make quite a good detective. If that fool of a boss of hers ever woke up to the fact and gave her something decent to work on, that was.

'Go on,' he encouraged.

Trudy straightened slightly in her chair. 'I would have expected the note to either go on and on about her feelings, justifying herself and her actions because of how desperate she felt, or maybe be angrier and more accusing. Putting the blame for her fate on someone else – her mother, Jonathan, anyone,' Trudy said.

'Yes. That's what struck me too.'

'And that's why you thought it must be a fake?'

Clement shrugged. 'I wouldn't say it was as definite as that,' he temporised. 'Let's just say, I thought it would be prudent to find out one way or the other. So . . .' he said briskly, glad to see she'd got a little sparkle back in her dark-brown eyes. ' . . . Let's recap. Your PC Gordon . . .' Trudy winced at being grouped together with the bent police officer, but said nothing. ' . . . Arrives at the scene and finds a young girl dead in her bed. On the table beside her – or on the bed, or somewhere nearby – he finds a suicide note, and sees the medication bottles by her bed. He instantly leaps to the obvious conclusion. Agree with me so far?'

'Yes,' Trudy agreed warily, sensing a trap and then telling herself off for being so paranoid.

'He might feel a little sorry for the girl, or he might be so jaded by now that he couldn't care less.' Clement waved a hand in the air to show just how moot this point was. 'But either way, he sees an *opportunity*.'

Trudy again winced but said nothing. She knew it only took

one rotten apple to spoil the barrel. But she still stubbornly believed that most of her fellow police officers were as straight as they came. Certainly the Sarge was, and she couldn't see even that vain idiot Rodney Broadstairs really being on the take either.

'He's approaching retirement, he's only got his pension to look forward to, and here he is,' Clement swept on, 'in this big, fancy house, with its wealthy occupants, and some silly little girl who doesn't appreciate what she has, who has gone and done away with herself. So why shouldn't he make the most of it?' Clement leaned back in his chair, picturing the scene in his mind. 'He walks that beat, so he knows the family – or at least enough about them to know they're Catholic, and wealthy. And, as such, won't be happy to have it get out that their precious daughter killed herself. So he pockets the evidence of suicide and, when the time's right, approaches the father.'

'The father?' Trudy said sharply. 'Not the mother?'

'No, no,' Clement said firmly. 'The man of the house is where the power lies – and where the money is.' He smiled grimly. 'So, he approaches the stricken father and shows him the suicide note. And being two reasonable men of the world, they come to a civilised agreement. There's no need for an even worse scandal to come out of an already tragic event, is there? The poor young girl merely made a mistake with her pills.'

'And later, when PC Gordon retires, he's able to buy his own little place and work three nights a week on double the customary salary in Mr Fleet-Wright's haulage yard,' Trudy added bitterly. 'Yes. Very nice!'

'Except Gisela didn't write the suicide note,' Clement said.

'No,' Trudy sighed. But she refused to ask him who he

thought had written it – because she had no idea. Surely, though, the candidates had to be few and far between? Jonathan McGillicuddy, or a member of Gisela's family? Or a cold-blooded and very clever killer, who Trudy – being so stupid – hadn't yet even begun to suspect?

'So, what do we do now?' she asked instead.

'Let's go and ask the person who *did* write it, of course,' Clement said.

Trudy's lips thinned. She known it all along! She'd just known the old vulture would know. 'And who would that be?'

Chapter Thirty-Two

Mavis McGillicuddy suddenly remembered where she'd seen the woman before. The woman who'd kept coming up to her gate just after her boy had been taken from her, but couldn't work up the courage to come to the door.

She was sitting at the kitchen table, darning Marie's school socks, when the memory simply popped into her head. One day, years ago now, when the sun had been shining brightly – the woman and Jonathan in the garden shed out in their tiny back garden, earnestly discussing something.

Clearly, she'd been one of Jonathan's clients or had been asking him for gardening advice. Such a simple, irrelevant thing, but her subconscious mind must have been working at it all this time, trying to place her.

When it didn't really matter at all.

Mavis sighed and stuck the needle rhythmically into the white sock. Perhaps she'd been one of Jonathan's regular customers and had wanted to come and give her condolences, but hadn't wanted to intrude. People could sometimes be so kind.

With that little mystery solved, Mavis continued to darn her granddaughter's socks and pretend everything would be all right soon.

It was the only way she could get through the day.

Clive Greaves sat in his ramshackle shed in the woods on his employer's estate, placidly plucking pigeons. He'd known the coppers would have to see sense sooner or later, so long as he kept his head down and his mouth shut.

Luckily, he still had his job.

And pheasants didn't care what his face looked like.

Beatrice Fleet-Wright was nipping the outer, shrivelling leaves off a poinsettia plant in the conservatory when she saw them walking up the garden path. The rather fine-looking and intelligent coroner and the fresh-faced, pretty WPC.

So they were back. Again.

Her heart leapt to her throat as she wondered what they could possibly want now. She'd hoped she'd seen the last of them, but deep down inside she'd known she hadn't. Now she walked to the front door, aware that her palms were feeling moist. Nervously she wiped them on her grey worsted skirt as she opened the door to their polite knock.

She smiled, feeling as if her face might crack as she led them back to the front room. This time she remembered to ask if they wanted tea, but this time they both declined.

'Mrs Fleet-Wright,' Clement began, reaching into his inner coat pocket and withdrawing a piece of lavender-coloured paper ensconced in a plastic bag.

Her eyes went to it, and her mouth went totally dry. She

recognised it at once, of course. But how . . . *How could that be?*

'This is a suicide note, signed by Gisela, which was, until recently, in the possession of PC Gordon. He was the first police officer on the scene after your daughter died,' Clement explained, slowly and clearly. 'We believe he took it from your daughter's bedroom and used it to blackmail your husband into giving him a large sum of money, and thereafter has continued to extort money from your husband, on a regular basis, in the form of a so-called "salary". But you were aware of all this.'

He made it a statement rather than a question, leaving her no room to deny it.

After a moment's frantic thought, Beatrice realised it would be pointless to do so. Instead, she stared down at her hands and said simply, 'Yes.'

Her mind was racing. How much did they truly know? And how much could she still keep from them?

'You knew your daughter had committed suicide right from the start, in fact,' he continued calmly.

Trudy, sitting, listening, marvelling, felt her heart thumping loudly. She also felt slightly sick. Something momentous was going to happen, she just knew it – could almost feel and taste it. The culmination of all their hard work and investigation was about to pay off. She felt almost afraid to breathe.

'Yes,' Beatrice responded to his question, her tone flat and verging on uninterested.

'And your husband persuaded you to stand up in the coroner's court and lie about that day.'

'I thought I should do that.'

'To say you might have accidentally been responsible for your daughter taking more pills – or that, between the two of you, and through an unfortunate lack of communication, circumstances contrived to ensure that your daughter consumed a fatal dose of her medication.'

'It's what happened, after all.'

'But you knew it wasn't true?'

'Who can say what's really true?'

'Would you care to tell us what really happened that day?' Clement demanded purposefully.

Beatrice blinked and took a long, slow, breath. If she was careful, if she was *very* careful indeed, perhaps she could end all this here and now. As long as this insistent, frightening man *thought* he'd got to the truth of the matter, surely he'd leave them all alone? All she had to do was keep her head, and not let slip anything they didn't already know. And, of course, keep the deep, dark, ugly truth firmly buried.

'Most of what I said was true,' she insisted, her voice little more than a whisper. 'I remember it was a lovely summer's day – the school holidays had just started, so both of the children were at home. I'd been due to go to a charity meeting, but at the last minute I changed my mind. I just didn't feel like it. Gisela had been acting really oddly all day – even more tense and wound up than usual. So I decided to stay at home.' She paused and stared down at her hands in her lap. 'About three o'clock I went up to her room to check on her. At first I thought she was sleeping. And then I saw . . . I saw her pill bottles were all opened and some were scattered around . . . I went to the bed and shook her, but even as I did it, I knew . . . She was so still. So pale. So . . . somewhere else. I sat beside her. She wasn't breathing . . . I just knew it was all too late.'

Trudy felt herself swallow hard.

'My poor, lovely, *ill* daughter . . .' Beatrice cried. 'And then I saw it.' She nodded at the lavender piece of paper, still held lightly in Clement's hand. 'I read it and couldn't . . . I just couldn't . . . I ran downstairs and telephoned my husband. He told me to call our doctor. And when he came, he called in the police.'

'Did he see the note?' Trudy spoke for the first time.

And, for the first time, Beatrice looked a little disconcerted. Her mind raced. What should she answer? *Was it a trick? What would they most readily believe?* 'I'm not sure,' she said eventually, hedging her bets. 'If he did, he never said anything to me.'

Clement smiled grimly. Well done, WPC Loveday, he thought. First blood to you.

'Anyway, the policeman came,' Beatrice continued quickly. 'I was . . . in a daze. At some point, they came and took my lovely Gisela away. And then my husband was talking to me about . . . the neighbours. Our priest. The scandal. And of course, once it all sank in, I agreed with him totally,' Beatrice rushed on. The quicker she could get the story out, the sooner they'd leave. 'We couldn't have it said that Gisela killed herself. It was a mortal sin. The church wouldn't have allowed us to b . . . bury her . . .'

For a moment it looked as if the woman was finally going to break down and cry at last, but she caught herself in time. Her shoulders stiffened, and her back straightened. She stared sightlessly out of the window and gave a small, tremulous smile.

'So I agreed to say . . . what I did,' she finished.

'Even though it meant you would be taking the blame for something you didn't do?' Trudy said softly. 'In open court. Knowing everyone would blame you for all but killing your own daughter?'

'Yes.'

'But you must have known you'd be reviled. Or pitied?' Trudy said. For a woman such as this, who put respectability before all else, that was such a massive sacrifice. Trudy couldn't help but admire her for it.

Beatrice shrugged fatalistically. 'Better that than having them talking about Gisela as if she was . . . My daughter was *ill*, don't you see?' she said, with sudden ferocity. 'It wasn't as if she could help herself . . . Her mind was . . . I had to protect her! I was her mother!'

Clement nodded. 'Yes, I understand that.'

Beatrice turned to him eagerly. 'Then you do see?' she cried.

'Oh, yes, I think I do,' Clement said. 'You needed to protect your daughter from herself.'

'Exactly!'

'Because she wasn't responsible for her actions.'

'Yes! You and I, we're normal. Our brains are normal, we think rationally.' Beatrice pleaded her cause passionately, leaning forward a little on her chair now, her eyes fixed with burning intensity on Clement Ryder. 'We have checks and measures, we have a good, working conscience. We think with a clear head and see things as they really are,' she swept on passionately. 'But Gisela wasn't like that. She was ill! You're a medical man – oh, you must understand?'

Clement nodded. 'And that's why you did what you did, after finding her dead.'

'Yes, I . . . what do you mean?' Beatrice asked sharply. 'I didn't do anything after I found her dead. I told you. I just sat beside her and wept.'

'Oh, no, Mrs Fleet-Wright,' Clement said, his voice becoming a shade harder now. 'You may well have sat beside her and wept. But that was only the beginning. Because of what you saw in your daughter's bedroom that day – when you found her dead and saw what she'd done – you had a lot of covering up to do, didn't you?'

Both Beatrice and Trudy were now staring at the coroner intently. And because they were, neither one of them noticed the door to the parlour very gently ease open. Only Clement saw it, and was momentarily thrown.

Then, when the door remained simply ajar, Clement decided to carry on. But even as he spoke, he was alert, his quick brain weighing and assessing all the possibilities.

'I think it's time you told us the truth now, Mrs Fleet-Wright,' he said firmly. And perhaps a shade more loudly than before, 'And let's start with this, shall we?' He gave the piece of lavender paper a little shake. 'Because you wrote this, didn't you? The handwriting expert who confirmed it was a forgery said it was a very good effort. In fact, he even went so far as to say that Gisela's writing and that of the forger had a lot of naturally occurring similarities. As might be expected, if the daughter had been taught to write by her mother.'

Beatrice gazed at him helplessly. After a long, fraught moment, Trudy saw the older woman's shoulders slump in defeat.

'Yes, I wrote it,' Beatrice said.

'Why?'

For a moment, it seemed that hope flared briefly in her eyes, and Trudy could almost see her brain whirring. Could she think up a lie? Could she still somehow salvage something from the wreckage?

But Beatrice could clearly see from the expression in Clement Ryder's eyes, as could Trudy, that it would be pointless.

'You already know, don't you?' Beatrice whispered, all hope now clearly lost.

'I can guess,' Clement corrected her. 'She wanted him hanged, didn't she?' he said simply. 'And you couldn't let that happen.'

Trudy felt her jaw drop.

What? Who? *What . . .?*

Chapter Thirty-Three

Rex had begun creeping down the stairs the moment he'd heard his mother's voice in the hall, alerted to the fact that she was clearly agitated by the excessively polite tone of her voice. By the time he'd reached the front room, he could guess who the visitors were. The same pair as before – the nosy coroner and his pretty WPC sidekick.

Having them in the house again made him smile.

Once in the hall, and by placing his ear carefully against the door to the parlour, he could catch about half of what was being said. But as the conversation became progressively more and more interesting and exciting, he'd become frustrated at missing key bits of it and so had risked opening the door a fraction.

Rex was glad, for now he could fully appreciate how the wily, silver-haired coroner was grilling his mother. He found it impressive the way he wasn't letting her get away with her usual tricks. Not many men managed to get the better of his mother – certainly not his father, that was for sure. In fact, Rex was fully confident that his dear Pater understood very little of what went on under his own roof.

Now, as he heard the last chilling accusation, he felt his breath catch in his chest. Although he wanted to burst in and tell the old man to keep his filthy opinions about Gisela to himself, another part of him couldn't help but feel elated, and a wide smile stretched across his face. At last! After all the lies, and the long, dreary, tedious years without his sister, things were livening up again. All the pretence was about to come tumbling down around everyone's ears, and the consequences were going to be glorious!

Oh, if only Gisela were here to share the fun.

He clamped his hand over his mouth to prevent the chuckles of glee bubbling up inside him and listened with ever more intensity.

Just how would his dearest mama react to that latest cannon shot across her bows?

Inside the parlour, everything had gone preternaturally quiet.

Beatrice opened her mouth, then closed it again, like a landed fish. Trudy felt pretty sure she was doing the same thing, and then wondered, with a lance of horror and despair, if Clement Ryder was drunk.

It was the only thing she could think of that might account for his last outlandish statement.

'I don't . . . I don't . . .' Beatrice stuttered helplessly.

Clement, seeing Trudy's wide-eyed look, shot her a brief, hard glare that told her plainly to sit still and shut up.

Sitting still, and shutting up, Trudy glared back at him.

'Come on, Mrs Fleet-Wright, we're not stupid, you know,' he chided her impatiently. 'And I have to tell you now that

WPC Loveday and myself haven't been investigating Jonathan McGillicuddy's murder, as such, as we may have led you to believe earlier. In fact, we have been re-examining your daughter's case. And in the course of our investigations, we've uncovered many illuminating facts that, had they seen the light of day in the original coroner's court proceedings, would have resulted in a very different verdict being handed down.'

Beatrice had now gone so pale she had begun to look positively ethereal.

'So, let's start again, shall we, and this time without any lies?' Clement suggested briskly, his eyes flitting briefly to the still-open door. Perhaps it had just clicked open and come ajar in a draught? Or were inquisitive ears listening closely?

'When you found your daughter that afternoon, it was clear she'd taken her own life. She'd left plenty of evidence to that effect, hadn't she? In fact, far too much?' Clement began firmly and confidently. 'Let me see – we know she must have left certain pill bottles somewhere easily found. Pill bottles that shouldn't have been there?'

Trudy blinked. The stolen pills? But . . .

'And then there was her diary. We know she kept one. Now that, I'm sure, would have made for some very interesting reading, wouldn't it?' he swept on.

Slowly, Beatrice lowered her face into her cupped hands and moaned softly.

'Then there was the curious fact that she had, in fact, left no suicide note behind at all – as most young girls who commit suicide nearly always do. And certainly not this trite little fancy of yours.' He indicated the lavender missive with disdain.

Beatrice drew in a ragged breath. *They knew*. Somehow, this awful man had found it all out.

'Yes,' she said helplessly.

'Yes *what*, Mrs Fleet-Wright?' Clement said, indicating furiously to Trudy to start taking down notes. Flustered, but quickly organising herself, Trudy began to do just that.

Beatrice leaned back in the chair and let her hands lie limply on the armrests. She didn't think she had the strength to raise them so much as an inch. She felt curiously boneless. And cold. And utterly weary. And, in some odd and curious way, also relieved. It was as if so much weight had left her, she could have floated up and away and drifted off into outer space, never to return.

In truth, she had simply gone, in the matter of a few minutes, from a state where everything mattered and must be protected to a universe where nothing mattered at all.

'Oh, yes to all of it,' she agreed wearily. 'When I found her, the pills were there, but they weren't her own usual prescription. The name on the bottle wasn't even hers. I couldn't understand it. And then the diary was right there, lying out in the open . . . That was really the first thing that caught my eye.' Beatrice frowned slightly, staring vaguely at a vase of dried grasses on the low coffee table. 'Normally Gisela was so paranoid about her diary. She was always so very careful to keep it locked – it had one of those pretty little brass-banded frames around it with a heart-shaped lock. She'd always been adamant it was private and that nobody must ever read it.'

Beatrice gave such a wry smile that it sent chills down Trudy's spine. 'Now, of course, I know why.'

'You read it that afternoon?' Clement pressed her more gently now.

'Yes. Not all of it, it was too long and detailed. But enough to understand . . . At first, when I picked it up and decided to read it, it was because I just wanted to understand why . . . why . . . she'd done such a thing. And if there had been any clues I had missed or something I should have seen . . . anything at all that I might have done to prevent it all. I expected to read that she'd been steadily losing her fight against the "Black Dog" of depression that had plagued her all her life. Or, perhaps, to find out what final straw had broken her . . . Instead . . . instead . . .'

But Beatrice simply couldn't continue.

'Instead, you read a very careful, cunning, cold-blooded account of how she'd come to suspect that her former lover wanted to kill her,' Clement finished for her softly.

Trudy, furiously getting everything down in her neat, hard-learned Pitman's shorthand, found her pencil stalling. Her head shot up.

But Beatrice merely shook her head – not in denial of his words so much, as to indicate her continued inability to understand it. 'It was awful. More awful because I knew none of it could possibly be true. At first, when I began to read it, I thought . . . perhaps . . . it *was* true. That for some reason Jonathan had fooled us all. But then . . . then I read parts where she'd said Jonathan had done something, and I knew he hadn't. Or she'd give details of a conversation they'd had, when I knew Jonathan hadn't even been in the gardens that day. And other things . . . impossible things. Oh, I don't want to go into all that.'

Clement knew she would have to, at some future point, but for now he didn't want to push her too hard. Not when she was finally beginning to admit the truth.

'I imagine that at some point,' he mused, 'it must have said something about how, if she were to be found dead, the police should look to Jonathan McGillicuddy for the blame?'

Beatrice groaned.

Trudy gasped. 'You mean, she actually killed herself, but only so she could make it look as if she'd been murdered! As if Jonathan had murdered her?' She looked aghast at Clement for confirmation, and he gave it with a curt nod. 'She hated him so much, she was so obsessed with him, that she was willing to die in order to make him suffer? Her ego was that monstrous? But how on earth did she think she could get away with it?'

'Imagine how things would have looked if her mother hadn't interfered,' Clement advised her grimly. 'The police would have found a young woman dead of an overdose, but with no suicide note. They'd have read her diary, a no doubt very convincing document, outlining her growing horror and suspicion that McGillicuddy wanted her dead. Don't forget – we know Gisela was a very intelligent and erudite young lady. It wouldn't have been hard for her to paint a convincing picture. Jonathan had grown jealous of *her*. *She* had been the one to break off the relationship, even though he'd gone around telling everyone it was him. And she had let him keep his pride and gone along with this fiction, in the vain hope that it would appease him. But it hadn't and his bitterness and anger grew and grew. Am I right, Mrs Fleet-Wright?' He suddenly threw the question at Beatrice, who merely nodded helplessly.

'Yes. It went pretty much like that. She wrote that he'd started to follow her around, to threaten her with what he'd do if she didn't come back to him. She claimed he'd sent her death threats she'd destroyed because she didn't want me, her mother, finding them and being upset.'

Beatrice sighed heavily. 'But none of it happened. I've always been the first to get the mail and sort it out. There were no letters for her. And I was used to watching her, to seeing she was all right. There was no way Jonathan could have done any of the things she claimed he did, and for me to not know.'

Clement nodded. 'But you would have had a hard time convincing the police of that,' he mused. 'Especially when they would have had the evidence of the pill bottles to consider.'

'When I read the diary . . . when I'd had time to absorb it . . . I was still in shock. But I couldn't really believe . . . I thought she'd just been ill, that the whole diary was a fantasy of her own making. But then I remembered that the pill bottles on her bedside table were wrong. Different. That they weren't her own.'

'No. Because they'd been stolen a few days earlier from a chemist's delivery boy,' Clement said flatly. 'No doubt by someone she'd paid very handsomely to do just that. They were to be the final nail in Jonathan's coffin.'

Trudy's pen literally flew over the paper. But even as she took down every word, she wondered. How on earth could they prove any of this?

'She must also have paid someone else to give false witness,' Clement went on smoothly, 'claiming to have seen Jonathan McGillicuddy actually commit the robbery. A witness, you won't be surprised to hear, who now can't be found, since he'd given a false name, address and place of employment.'

Yes, Trudy thought grimly. No doubt Gisela had paid him a lot of money to testify to that in Jonathan's subsequent murder trial. But there, she'd seriously underestimated the concept of honour among crooks, which was perhaps not surprising for someone like Gisela, who seemed to live in a fantasy world.

She might have fondly believed that, after her death, he'd honour the contract they'd made, but in reality, whoever Finch had really been, he'd never intended to stick his neck out and perjure himself in court during a murder trial. Or else he'd have made sure to be available to the police and wouldn't have disappeared so quickly after making his initial statement.

Beatrice lifted her face from her hands and shook her head. 'I don't know all the details about that,' she said simply. 'But it doesn't surprise me.'

'No,' Clement said flatly. 'Your daughter wouldn't have wanted to leave anything to chance. After all, she was making a huge gesture – the most final, dramatic and irrevocable of all gestures. She was going to die! And she wanted to make damned good and sure she was taking him with her. That was the whole point, after all. He'd rejected her, and for that he had to be made to suffer and pay.'

The condemnation in his tone chilled both women, and large tears finally trickled down Beatrice Fleet-Wright's cheeks. 'You have to understand! Gisela was devastated when Jonathan left her. She truly loved him. And she loved so desperately, as she did in all things. She was fully committed, heart, body and soul, in a way that was truly terrifying. Her emotions weren't the same as yours and mine – they were heightened, all-consuming. Her subsequent despair and rage were all-consuming too. I watched her growing more and more desperate, more and more disbelieving, more and more furious, as the truth sank in during those summer months. He'd left her and wasn't coming back. She couldn't believe it. She just . . . couldn't . . . accept it.'

Beatrice sighed and shook her head. 'Oh, it's no use, is it? I can't expect you to understand. Or to forgive,' she muttered dejectedly.

'But you *did* understand. And you *did* forgive her,' Clement said softly. 'Because you were her mother, you had to save her. So you destroyed the diary and removed the pills. You faked her suicide note. You ensured, in fact, that she didn't become a posthumous murderess.'

Beatrice began to cry quietly and Trudy found herself swallowing a hard lump that had risen in her throat. 'You make it sound so easy, but it wasn't!' the older woman cried. 'Don't you understand? Our family is Catholic. And the thought of suicide is utterly abhorrent to us, and goes against all our teachings. And yet I had to reveal that Gisela had indeed taken her own life. It was yet another betrayal of her. It was all so horrendous. I felt so guilty!'

'They must have been the worst few hours of your life,' Clement said compassionately. 'First you find your beloved daughter dead. In spite of all your efforts, and the lifelong battle to look after her, she had defeated you. And then, as if that shock wasn't enough, you read her diary and understood what fate she'd intended for Jonathan. Because, as sure as eggs are eggs, any jury being presented with the victim's own fears and suspicions in a diary, coupled with the evidence of the stolen drugs, would have convicted him and had him hanged. I take it she made sure he'd have no alibi for that afternoon?' he added, almost as an afterthought.

'Yes,' Beatrice said on a sigh. 'Later, Jonathan told me that, on the day she died, he was gardening alone at a house where the owners were in Corfu for their summer holidays. So he had no witnesses. Which is something Gisela could have easily found out. I knew she watched him, sometimes, you see. Kept track of his movements.'

In fact, she'd been guilty of stalking him, instead of the other way around, Trudy mused grimly.

'You must have thought you'd managed to contain the situation, though,' Clement said softly, and not without sympathy. 'You'd got rid of all the incriminating and false evidence, and had cleverly faked a suicide note. All was in readiness, in fact, to present a neat, safe scenario. A young girl with a history of mental illness kills herself. Everything would play out as it had to, and then you could start to get on with your lives. It would be hard, but achievable. Then along comes greedy little PC Gordon and puts a spanner in the whole works by taking the note. You must have been terrified.'

Beatrice managed a snort of laughter. 'I couldn't think, at first, what had gone wrong. Our doctor didn't seem to notice the note, but I knew the police would find it. After they'd taken . . . Gisela from the house, I waited and waited. I thought, at any moment, someone would tell me she'd committed suicide and that the note had been found. Instead, my husband called me into his study and told me he'd fixed everything. That we'd say it was all accidental.'

Beatrice again smothered a laugh. 'I almost . . . well . . .' She shrugged fatalistically. 'It doesn't matter now, does it?' she asked rhetorically. 'And after I'd had a chance to get over this latest shock and think about it, I realised it didn't really matter whether we presented Gisela's death as a suicide or an accident. So long as the truth was never discovered.'

'Tell me about the day you had to give Jonathan an alibi for the robbery,' Clement asked briskly, knowing it would be cruel to let her dwell on the fact that the truth had been uncovered anyway. And after all she had suffered to keep it buried.

Glad to change the topic, Beatrice drew in a deep, wavering breath.

'The day after Gisela died, I realised I simply had to tell Jonathan about all I'd found out,' Beatrice said. 'Not because I wanted to – my instinct was to keep it totally secret, with me the only one ever knowing. But the more I thought it over, the more I realised Jonathan had to know as well, just in case he was still in danger somehow. I couldn't be sure what other plans Gisela had made. And if something else were to come to light that threw suspicion on him, he needed to be warned beforehand. I really didn't want to do it, I'm sure you can understand that,' Beatrice said, almost with a laugh. 'I wanted her memory to remain . . . But . . . I suppose those pill bottles worried me. They seemed to me to be like a ticking time bomb, just waiting to explode. As it turned out, I had good cause to be worried. Anyway, I rang him at his house and told him I needed to meet up with him. We met at a small pub nearby, and I told him about her diary and what it said.'

'He must have been very worried,' Clement said dryly.

'Of course he was! We both were. He wanted to go to the

police, but I persuaded him it would only make matters worse. Things were already so complicated. Besides, as I pointed out, going to the police might serve to cast suspicion on him, whereas, as things stood, he was in the clear.'

Beatrice shook her head. 'I promised him that if anything were ever to happen or come up, I'd make sure he didn't suffer because of it. Which was the least I could do. And sure enough, when he phoned the very next day, his first words to me were that he was at a police station and that someone thought he might have robbed a chemist's delivery boy. And could I please come down and tell them he'd been working in the garden that day?' Beatrice shrugged graphically. 'Well, it was as clear as day what I needed to do.'

'So you went and gave a false statement,' Clement said mildly.

Beatrice blinked. And oddly enough, it was only then, for the very first time, that she fully realised how culpable she was in the eyes of the law, and that she might actually be prosecuted for all these lies. Before, she'd always thought of herself simply as a mother protecting her child – and had never seen her actions as being in any way illegal or even wrong. What's more, she'd always comforted herself with the fact that what she'd done had brought harm to no one but herself. But now she wondered. What was the penalty for perjury? And was it perjury if you lied for someone, when that person had been falsely accused? But then, she reminded herself wryly, she'd also lied under oath in a coroner's court.

She was probably going to go to prison.

Such a thought, ten years ago, would have been unthinkable. Absurd. Nonsense. Things like that simply didn't happen to people like her – people who'd been brought up to respect the law. Respectable, normal, law-abiding citizens. But now . . . her neighbours would watch her being taken away in a police car! But the truth would come out now. Reginald would know what his daughter had done. Rex's life would be made a misery. The scandal . . .

And yet, Beatrice couldn't really find anything left inside of herself to worry about even that. It was as if she was running on empty now. She had no more pain or worry left to give.

'What happened then? After you'd made your statement giving Jonathan his alibi and left the police station?' The coroner's words distracted her from her bout of self-contemplation.

'What? Oh, we just went to the nearest park and talked things over. And we wondered if she might have done something else that proved his guilt. But it was Jonathan who actually figured it out,' Beatrice acknowledged. 'He said Gisela would want to prove, beyond all doubt, that he was behind the robbery. So perhaps she had hidden the rest of the stolen drugs or money somewhere compromising, where the police would be sure to find them. Anyway, we went to his home, intending to search it from top to bottom. But when we got there, Jonathan said his mother was always at home all day, so he didn't think Gisela would have risked trying to get into the actual house itself. She would almost certainly have been seen or caught out. First, he checked his gardener's van. But there was nothing there – which made sense, when we thought about it,' Beatrice said, her voice now so exhausted she was nearly slurring her words. 'Gisela didn't have a key to his van. And then we went to the shed in the McGillicuddys' back garden. It was the only place left to look.'

'And you found them?' Clement guessed pityingly.

'Yes. We found them in his toolbox. The rest of the stolen drugs haul and some money.'

Beatrice hung her head in remembered shame. 'He was so kind to me then. He had every right to be angry. To be really furious, in fact, after what Gisela had done to him. But he wasn't. He told me he'd burn the drugs and we'd say nothing about it.'

'And then there was only the inquest to get through,' Clement said flatly. 'And the lies you both told.'

'Yes.'

'And that was that. Gisela was buried, and her lover was spared the noose,' Trudy said wonderingly, feeling almost as emotionally wrung-out as Beatrice.

'*Yes!*' Another voice, young and shockingly loud, suddenly soared into the room, making them all jump in shock as the door slammed open and the furious, red-faced, wild-eyed figure of Rex Fleet-Wright stormed in. '*And that should never have happened!*' he shouted into his mother's astonished face.

'Gisela deserved that he should die, damn him!'

Chapter Thirty-Four

'Rex!' Beatrice gasped, looking up at her son in blank-eyed shock. 'What on earth's got into you?'

Trudy, who had leapt instinctively to her feet when the young man threw himself into the room, caught Clement Ryder's surreptitious gesture that she should sit back down, and warily subsided back into her seat.

Not that Rex Fleet-Wright noticed, as he was too fixated on berating his mother. Now, he bore a marked resemblance to the photographs they'd seen of his sister – he was also lean, with thick, dark-brown hair and vivid green eyes, and had a triangular-shaped face that was almost feminine. His lips, though, were currently twisted into a most unattractive snarl as he loomed over his mother. His face was flushed, and he was so emotionally over-wrought, he was virtually spitting as he talked.

'You had no right to interfere! How dare you, you, you worthless, *stupid* woman!' He was practically vibrating with repressed fury, and his fists clenched and unclenched at his sides.

Now Trudy finally understood what it meant when someone was described as 'being beside themselves with rage'.

'Rex!' Beatrice cried.

'Oh, why did you have to go and spoil it all?' he wailed. 'I knew something was wrong that day she died. I just *knew* you'd been up to something, but I thought you only . . .' He stopped suddenly, and swayed a little.

Dressed in black trousers with a knitted Fair Isle sweater in deep cream, he suddenly went as pale as his jersey and reached out and steadied himself against his mother's chair. 'If only I'd known what she wanted . . .'

'Why don't you tell us about the day your sister died, Rex?' Clement interposed gently. 'You were here at home that day, weren't you?'

The question seemed to pull him back to the present, and he turned to look at the coroner scornfully. 'Oh, yes, I was here,' he admitted with a grim smile. 'Mother thought I was out playing somewhere with my friends. But I wasn't.'

'Do you have many friends, Rex?' Clement asked curiously, watching the young man closely. He was breathing hard and clearly struggling to keep very strong emotions in check. Obviously the same malady that had so dogged his sister had found another victim to torment. Hereditary, perhaps?

His mother shifted uneasily in her chair, suddenly sensing that the worst was not over yet, but unable to put her finger on exactly where the danger lay. But that didn't hinder her instinct to try and protect her child. 'Rex,' she warned softly, but her son moved abruptly away from her, as if she was tainted, and flung himself down onto a hard chair near the window, where he could watch all the occupants of the room with a baleful eye.

'No, not really,' he finally answered the old man's question.

'Is that because they don't like you, Rex?' Clement asked dryly. 'Or is there just nobody good enough for you, that you want to hang around with?'

Rex snorted. 'The latter, of course! Only Gisela really understood me.' Then he laughed. It was a rather high-pitched laugh that instantly grated on Trudy's nerves – a bit like when someone scratched a blackboard with their nails. 'And the former too, I expect,' he owned sourly, with what Clement thought was probably a rare moment of insight for the boy.

Clement smiled and nodded. 'Not that it mattered, right? You were quite happy being on your own.'

'Oh, yes. I liked to read – science fiction mostly. And ghost stories sometimes.' Rex shrugged. 'It took me away from all this . . .' He waved a hand around the room. ' . . . Dull suburbia. You have no idea how we hated it.'

'We? You mean you and your sister?'

'Gisela didn't belong here any more than I did,' Rex stated scornfully. 'She belonged in Monte Carlo, winning a fortune at the baccarat tables. Or in Hollywood, vamping James Dean. She adored James Dean. She always thought that oaf, McGillicuddy, looked a bit like him.' Rex snorted again. 'I tried to tell her he wasn't good enough for her and that she was wasting herself on him.'

He looked petulant now, and Trudy began to wonder, a shade uneasily, if he was, as her old gran would have put it, 'playing with a full deck of cards'.

'But Gisela wouldn't listen to you,' Clement guessed softly.

'No. I . . . I couldn't make her see it,' he agreed miserably. 'She only saw his good looks. And went on and on about how he'd been touched by tragedy – marrying young, being widowed young, and nobly bringing up that little brat of his.'

On her chair, Beatrice again shifted uneasily. 'Rex, you know you don't have to answer this man's questions. In fact, I think . . .'

'I don't care what you *think*, Mother,' Rex interrupted rudely and brutally, his blazing green eyes radiating utter scorn. 'Neither did Gisela. In fact, we both used to sit up in her bedroom laughing at you. At both of you. Father was just as bad.'

Beatrice flinched.

'You and your sister were close,' Clement swept on, taking advantage of the boy's inability to listen to good advice when it was offered to him. He knew he needed to keep the boy talking before Beatrice had the chance to rally sufficiently and chuck them out. 'How *you* must have suffered when *she* suffered,' he added sympathetically.

'I did! I did! And I tried to help her when that brute, that utter *bastard*, McGillicuddy dropped her,' Rex ranted. 'But I couldn't reach her. I couldn't help her or stop her from slipping down and down.'

'Why don't you tell us about that day she died,' Clement said softly.

'No!' Beatrice said sharply.

'I saw her,' Rex shouted, overriding his mother's objections and instead fixing his stare on the old man. He at least seemed to understand the gross unfairness of what had been done. 'I saw her lying on the bed – so quiet and still and beautiful. I had been reading comics in my bedroom but I had the door ajar, and saw Mother go into her room. And it stayed so quiet.

I couldn't hear them talking, so I was curious. And when I saw Mother leave a long while later and go downstairs – in order to telephone Father and the doctor, as it turned out – I went into her room.'

'Oh, Rex, no. You never said!' his mother wailed.

Ignoring her totally, his eyes still fixed on the coroner, the young man slunk back a bit in the chair, his eyes taking on a dreamy look. Clement risked a quick glance at Trudy, relieved to see she was still busily taking everything down that was being said.

He gave a brief, sharp nod. Good. They were going to need her notes later.

'I saw her lying there and I just knew she was dead. And then I saw the note. *A* note, I should say, and one I now know she didn't even write. Oh, hell! I should have realised at once she hadn't written it,' he said with utter self-disgust. 'I was such a fool! Such a stingy, emotionless, drab little note!' he glowered at his mother bitterly.

'I couldn't even cry for her, not then,' he went on quietly. 'I just stood there, looking down at her. Knowing she was gone. Knowing I'd never hear her voice or see her smile. She meant everything to me – she was the only thing that made living in this hellhole of a world worthwhile,' he declared, oblivious of the absurd melodrama he was spouting. 'I wanted to shout at her and shake her and ask her why she hadn't taken me with her. That's what hurt the most, you know,' he added, almost conversationally, turning to glance at the old man to make sure he properly understood. 'I'd have done it, you know,' he said, shouting once more into his poor mother's appalled face. 'If she'd told me what she was going to do, we could have gone together.'

'A suicide pact?' Clement sighed, shaking his head.

'Why not?' Rex insisted savagely. 'Instead, there I was, left there all on my own. She could be a selfish little cow sometimes,' he said, but his tone of voice was admiring more than annoyed – as if he approved of such self-absorption.

'And how old were you then?'

Rex shrugged the question aside, as if his youth had been of no importance. 'I heard Mother coming back and scarpered just in time. I slipped out of the house when the doctor came and pretended to come back home not long after Father.' Rex suddenly laughed. 'Later, when I heard the version of events she gave to the police, I knew she and Father had been up to something, concocting some stupid story, because they made no mention of the suicide note. It only took a little while to figure out they were covering it up because they didn't want a *scandal*!'

He shouted the last word at his mother with such hatred and vitriol that even Trudy recoiled. 'As if she wasn't *worth* a scandal. As if she didn't *deserve* to be talked about and mourned and fêted and . . . I'd have shouted it from the rooftops if I could. She was dead! Gisela was dead and the whole world should have mourned. Instead, her parents came up with this pathetic little story about too many pills taken accidentally. Talk about going out, "not with a bang, but with a whimper"!'

He shook his head, his eyes glittering with what looked, to Trudy, to be utter madness. 'I thought at the time it was all so pathetic! But now I know just how truly and to what extent Gisela was robbed. By you!' He sprang up, his fists clenched, as his mother shrank back in her chair. 'You had no right to do that! Don't you see, even now, you utterly worthless fool, what you did? What she had planned was *glorious*! It was clever and so perfect! If you'd just let well enough alone, that man would have hanged for what he did to her! But, oh no! You had to go and spoil it all! You had to let her down! *Like always.*'

'But *you* didn't let her down, did you, Rex?' Clement said, raising his voice to almost a shout now as he saw the boy was about to throw himself at his mother. Trudy tensed, waiting and willing to spring into action if he went so far as to attack Beatrice.

But the coroner's words got through to him, and instead he turned and stared at the old man, wild-eyed. Clement nodded. 'It's obvious you were the only one here to really understand her,' he said soothingly. 'You were like kindred spirits, you and Gisela, am I right? We've spoken to her friends and they all told us how close you were.'

Trudy thought back to some of the descriptions they'd been given of Gisela's twisted and unhealthy relationship with her younger brother, and shuddered. But she was wise enough not to speak.

'We were close. She loved me – she was the only one who did,' Rex whispered.

At this, Beatrice gave a small moan of pain, but Clement was sure, even now, that she still didn't realise the true horror of what was to come.

'And when she died, you weren't going to just leave it at that, were you, Rex? Let the family cover it up and bury her, almost guiltily, as if she was worth nothing.'

'Hell, no! If only I'd known what her plan had been, I'd have helped her!' he cried. 'I'd never have let Mother ruin it all. I'd have made sure he paid, just like she intended.'

'But you were only young,' Clement said gently. 'A boy, still. There wasn't much you could do. Not then.'

'No, you're right. I had to wait.'

'And not just wait,' Clement said gently. 'You did some serious thinking, didn't you, Rex? All these years, you've been making your plans. And very clever plans they were too. Plans to avenge your sister.'

'What?' Beatrice said faintly.

Trudy shot the coroner a quick look.

Rex began to smile widely. 'Oh, yes. I made plans,' he agreed dreamily.

'You weren't going to let your sister's murderer get away with it, were you, Rex?' Clement said. 'Because that's how you thought of him, wasn't it? As far as you knew, she'd killed herself for love of him, and he'd never been worthy of her. And he couldn't be allowed to get away with it, could he?'

'No, of course he couldn't,' Rex agreed, sounding petulant and impatient at such a silly question.

'So what did you do? Just how did you figure it all out? Start with Marcus Deering,' Clement encouraged. 'That was really clever. How did you even know about him? That he was Jonathan's real father, I mean?' As he spoke, he glanced at Trudy, glad to see that, once again, she was scribbling away furiously.

'Oh, that was easy. Gisela was curious about everything concerning her beloved Jonathan,' Rex sneered. 'And she couldn't stand it that he was so incurious about the father he'd never known. I don't think she ever believed his mother's story that he was some ignorant toiler on the land, stupid enough to let a tractor roll on him and kill him. She always told me Jonathan had a "noble" head, and too much breeding to be the offspring of two poor specimens like his mother and some mere peasant. And she was right!'

Clement nodded. 'She snooped around his home, I suppose?'

'Yes. At first she found a clue in his mother's bankbook. Going back years, a regular amount being paid in. Clearly it had to be for child maintenance. And then, she found some love letters in a hidden drawer in Mrs McGillicuddy's jewellery box. Letters Deering had written to her years ago, when he was still smitten.'

'And Gisela told you all about it, her confidant and beloved little brother?' Clement nodded.

'Oh, yes, she had to crow about it. And what's more, she only told me! She didn't even tell *him*! I think she planned to surprise him with the knowledge later, when she felt the time was right. But then he left her! Just how stupid *was* he? How could any man leave her?' he raged. 'Anyway . . .' He took a deep breath, smiling in reminiscence. 'She bragged about it to me for ages after she found out. I said big deal – it hardly made him little Lord Fauntleroy, did it? Sir Marcus was only knighted for services to industry. But she said it proved her point – that Jonathan had inherited his father's brains and gumption. Hah! He was running a penny ante gardening business. But Gisela still insisted on seeing him as Prince Charming.'

Clement nodded, needing to move things on quickly before they lost momentum. 'So, once you'd grown up a bit, and had time to make your plans, you decided it was time to avenge Gisela.'

'Yes.'

'But what made you think of the anonymous letters?' Clement said.

Trudy's heart fluttered. Was it possible . . .?

'Oh, that was simple,' Rex crowed. 'Once I'd looked into Deering, I got my first idea of how I could kill McGillicuddy and get away with it. It was so ridiculously simple – misdirection!'

Beatrice stared at her son as if at a stranger. Luckily, though, for the moment she seemed incapable of speech.

'Misdirection?' Clement echoed quickly, knowing it was vital he keep the boy talking, and boasting, about his cleverness. 'Like a magician? Get everyone looking in the wrong place? That way, when McGillicuddy was murdered, nobody would be looking at *your* family. As they might have done otherwise. After all, McGillicuddy didn't have any other enemies, did he? He'd only wronged you and yours.'

'Exactly. You're a clever man, Dr Ryder,' Rex complimented him. 'I needed to make sure, when McGillicuddy died, that the police were looking in the wrong place for his killer. So I began writing the anonymous notes to Sir Marcus, threatening to kill his son if he didn't do the right thing. Naturally, I knew everyone would assume the notes were referring to his legitimate son, Anthony.'

'But when Jonathan died, you knew his connection to Sir Marcus would be made, and then everyone would think they were looking for a killer with a grudge against the Deering family,' Clement said, forcing an admiring smile onto his face. 'Yes, that was very clever. And that thing about the warehouse fire was a gift, wasn't it? It trailed another smelly red herring right across the case.'

'Oh, that!' Rex laughed. 'You know, I never even knew about that until I saw that piece of Deering's in the local paper. Going on about how sorry he was about it!'

'I'm not quite sure I follow,' Clement said.

Rex sighed, as if disappointed he wasn't keeping up. 'When I wrote the notes, I needed something that was pointed enough to sound threatening, but vague enough to mean anything. And "do the right thing" was just something I came up with.' He laughed. 'After all, the man had risen from virtually nothing to become a bigwig millionaire. You don't get to do that without doing *something* that might tweak your conscience a bit, right? All these fat-cat entrepreneurs are the same. Ruthless, money-grabbing parasites.'

'Ah, yes, I see.' Clement almost gave a genuine smile at this little bit of cynical – but accurate – psychology. 'And so, with all the police attention focused on them and on protecting Anthony, the actual killing of Jonathan presented no problem for you at all, did it?' Clement put in silkily. 'In fact, I was wondering if it might not have felt like a bit of an anticlimax?'

Rex nodded and gave a smile that made Trudy feel slightly sick. 'You know, you're quite right. All I had to do was follow him to that garden that day and, when the time was right, creep up behind him, pick up his spade from the ground and . . .'

'Oh, Rex, no!' Beatrice wailed.

Her son merely shot her a cynical, dismissive smile.

'Did he even know it was coming?' Clement asked casually.

'No,' Rex said, looking almost shamefaced for the first time. 'I wanted him to!' he said fiercely, 'But . . . I wasn't sure, you see, if it came to a straight fight, that I would win. He was bigger than me, and with all that manual work he was used to doing . . .'

Rex shrugged.

'Ah . . .' Now Clement understood why the young man had temporarily lost his cocky, crowing attitude. 'So, in the end, you had to settle for a rather ordinary method of dispatching him. How disappointing for you.'

Rex flushed sullenly.

'So you hit him on the back of the head and, after he went down, hit him another couple of times, just to make sure he was dead? You were careful not to leave any fingerprints,' he mused, ignoring the scornful snort Rex gave, 'and you probably disposed of the clothes you were wearing, just in case?'

'Burned them on a bonfire,' Rex admitted cheerfully. 'So there were no giveaway blood splatters or little clues. I *have* read Agatha Christie, you know. Not even Hercule Poirot could find the evidence to prove what I'd done.'

'And with the police still looking for a killer interested in Deering, nobody was even looking your way,' Clement finished. 'Yes, it was all very clever. Congratulations,' he added dryly.

Beatrice Fleet-Wright began to cry bitterly as her world finally and irrevocably came tumbling down around her.

Her monstrous son eyed her without pity.

'I expect you'd like to make a full statement now?' Clement said briskly. And as the young man visibly hesitated, taken aback by his matter-of-fact manner, Clement smiled widely. 'After all, Rex, you've been *so* clever that unless you confess, it might all get swept under the carpet again.' He pointed at the broken woman weeping in her chair. 'If the police can find no evidence against you, your parents will make sure of that. They'll hire some clever legal types and nobody will ever know you committed the perfect murder. But, more importantly, nobody will ever know what Gisela did. Just think of it, Rex,'

Clement growled softly. 'Standing up in open court, with all the newspaper reporters there, hanging on your every word. How she would have loved the drama of it! And you, telling them how magnificent she was – how utterly out of the ordinary. After all, how many of them, all those dull little trolls sitting in the public gallery, or even working from the defence or prosecution benches, would ever have been able to do what she did?'

. Rex's face began to shine. 'You're right! They wouldn't have had a clue!'

'Exactly. But she was magnificent, wasn't she? She was even willing to go through with the ultimate sacrifice – to actually die! It's like something from a Thomas Hardy novel,' Clement said. 'The beautiful young tragic heroine, undone by love. Her wicked parents' despicable scheme to hush up the scandal. And the triumph of her young brother, the only man who truly loved and appreciated her, coming to her rescue and avenging her honour.' Clement shook his head. 'It'll be spectacular.'

'Yes! Yes!'

'But first, you must let WPC Loveday arrest you. And then you must make a full confession, mind,' he warned, his voice almost chiding now.

Rex nodded, but he was so caught up in the sick fantasy world the coroner had just described for him that he barely gave a nod of consent. Already, he was mentally preparing his speeches for the trial.

Trudy, in something of a daze, responded to the significant stare the coroner gave her, and, standing up on legs that felt distinctly wobbly, reached for her handcuffs before, with some trepidation, approaching Rex Fleet-Wright.

She was, in truth, rather afraid of him. He was clearly mad. But then her backbone stiffened and her chin came up. She had her duty to do, and she was damned well going to do it!

But she needn't have worried. As she reached him he impatiently held out his wrists for her, his eyes, shining in madness, already somewhere far away.

Trudy took a breath and forced herself to recite the familiar caution. 'Rex Fleet-Wright, I must caution you that anything you say will be taken down and may be given in evidence.'

But as she spoke, all she could think – and with some wonder – was *I'm actually arresting a man for murder.*

Chapter Thirty-Five

When they arrived back at the station, the desk sergeant was the first to notice them. Phil Monroe took one look at Trudy's stunned but triumphant face, the coroner's rather bleaker expression, and their prisoner, who was looking around rather like someone inspecting a second-class restaurant, and reached straight for the telephone to inform DI Jennings he was wanted.

The Inspector met them at the door to his office, and when he saw the young man in cuffs, looked questioningly at his WPC. Trudy swallowed hard. 'Sir. I've just arrested Mr Rex Fleet-Wright for the murder of Jonathan McGillicuddy.'

For a second, her superior looked stunned, then thunderous. 'You've done *what*?'

Rex giggled.

'I think you also need to arrest him for the assaults on Anthony Deering,' Clement put in dryly, cutting off Jennings before he had a fit of apoplexy. 'Isn't that right, Rex?' he asked mildly.

Jennings, wide-eyed, shot a look at the young man, who nodded complacently. 'Oh, yes. I fixed his car all right. It was easy – I read up on it in a car manual. And I set the wire with the booby trap so he'd fall off his horse. I stole the bird-scarer from a farmer's shed. I can show you where if you like,' he offered helpfully.

Jennings, clearly flustered, pulled himself together and nodded brusquely. 'I see. WPC Loveday, perhaps you'd like to get Mr, er, Fleet-Wright settled down in an interview room. Dr Ryder . . .' He shot the coroner a fierce glare. 'Perhaps you'd like to brief me? *Thoroughly!*'

Trudy, glad to get away from her simmering DI, quickly set about processing her prisoner, enjoying enormously the look on the booking officer's face as she read out the charges. She had barely filled in the paperwork and got Rex settled in the interview room when the door opened.

She wasn't surprised to see DI Jennings and Sergeant O'Grady come in. The Sarge gave her a broad grin behind the DI's back.

'You can go, Constable,' Jennings said, dismissing her abruptly, and Trudy, without a qualm, made herself scarce. She had never been naive enough to think she'd ever be allowed to sit in on the formal interview, let alone play a hand in it, but she didn't care. After all, she'd heard it all anyway!

Instead, she made her way to her desk, receiving curious looks from the rest of the constables in the room as she did so. Clearly, the rumour mill had already been hard at work, and the range of looks she was being given ranged from scepticism, to envy, to amusement.

*

Clement Ryder found her ten minutes later, sitting in splendid isolation and furiously tapping away at her typewriter as she transcribed the notes from her notebook. She had no doubt DI Jennings would be demanding them soon.

With the coroner's approach, though, she left off typing and smiled at him wearily. 'Is the DI very cross with me?' she asked.

Clement shrugged carelessly as he slipped into the seat opposite her. 'So-so,' he drawled. 'But I did point out to him that you *had* been keeping him updated on what we were doing, as requested, but that the culmination of the case unravelled so quickly and unexpectedly that it was hardly your fault it ended as it did. It wasn't as if we could stop our interview in mid-flow and call him in, was it? Mrs Fleet-Wright would almost certainly have taken the time to pull herself together and call a solicitor. And, as I pointed out to him, given our lack of evidence, we needed to get Rex's confession down as a matter of some urgency.'

Trudy sighed heavily. 'And he agreed with you?'

Clement's lips twitched. 'In the end. And reluctantly.'

Trudy nodded glumly.

'Cheer up,' Clement said with a smile. 'Soon he'll have cleared up his murder case, his superiors will be off his back, and he'll have earned the everlasting gratitude of Sir Marcus to boot. He'll be feeling positively mellow.'

Trudy didn't feel particularly confident that any of this joy would filter down to her. In fact, she was pretty sure that, come tomorrow, she'd be back to walking her beat and looking for flashers in the park.

To take her mind off that, she looked across at the coroner

thoughtfully. 'Just how much did you know? Or guess?' she demanded. 'Before we went to talk to Mrs Fleet-Wright, I mean? Only it strikes me that you seemed to have it all figured out even before we set foot in the house.'

Clement gazed innocently back at her. 'Well, I was pretty sure about the part Beatrice had played in covering up her daughter's scheme. Once I'd asked myself why the woman would fake a suicide note and then stand up in court and take the blame for her daughter's death, it was pretty clear something pretty drastic had to be behind it all.'

Trudy sighed. 'Even so! Figuring out Gisela's plan to frame Jonathan for her murder was some leap.'

'Well, there *were* clues,' Clement said modestly. 'And the robbery of the chemist's lad was a big one. But mostly, it was what we learned about the dead girl's character that provided the biggest insight into what must have happened that afternoon.'

Trudy shook her head. The old man was amazing. Then her eyes narrowed. 'And Rex? Did you know about him too? Killing McGillicuddy?'

Clement hesitated briefly. In truth, he hadn't really started putting all that together until the young man had burst into the room, all but frothing at the mouth. But it hadn't been that hard to see how the land lay, especially as the lad himself had been so accommodating.

'Well, it was clear *someone* had killed Jonathan,' Clement pointed out. 'And if we swept away all that Deering business, and asked ourselves *who* would have a good motive for wanting Jonathan dead, then the little brother became the obvious suspect. We know he adored his sister and must have been devastated by her death,' he pointed out. 'We know, since it was the holidays, that he'd have been in or around the house on the day she died. And, let's face it, once he started talking, it wasn't that hard to steer him into admitting it all, was it?'

Trudy shuddered, remembering Rex's gleeful boasting. 'He's not right in the head, is he?' she said, after a moment's thought.

'No, I don't think he is,' Clement agreed quietly. 'Which is perhaps just as well.'

Trudy gave him a puzzled look and he said softly, 'Do you really want to feel responsible for seeing a man hanged, WPC Loveday?'

Trudy went pale. It wasn't something that, until that moment, she'd actually thought about. But she *had* arrested him. And she *had*, along with the coroner, been responsible for collecting the evidence against him. So just how would she feel if, in a year's time, say, he was led to the gallows . . .

She felt sick.

'As it is, he's bound to end up in an insane asylum some-where,' Clement pointed out quickly, seeing her go rather pale. 'It's been my experience that when that type finally blows, they unravel pretty fast. It won't take the trick cyclists long to get their hands on him and declare him unfit to stand trial – you mark my words.'

Trudy let out a huge sigh of relief and then smiled. 'So he won't even get his day in court, like you promised?'

Clement shrugged. 'No. How sad.' He grinned. Then he slapped his hands on his thighs in preparation for getting up and leaving. 'So, when you've finished for the day, I take it that you and your fellow officers will go out and celebrate?' he asked, glancing around the room. 'I believe that's traditional, isn't it?'

Trudy nodded. In truth, though, she was feeling so wrung-out that all she really wanted to do was go home to her mum and dad and let them fuss over her and take care of her. Not that she was going to tell anyone here that!

'Yes, probably,' she said casually.

The old vulture smiled, then stood up. 'Well, it's certainly been interesting, WPC Loveday,' he said, and held out his hand to her. After a startled second, she jumped up and shook it warmly.

'Yes, Dr Ryder, it has,' she agreed. And felt a shaft of sadness lance through her as the old man turned to go. She was going to miss him, as aggravating and annoying as he could be.

Then, just as he was about to step away from her desk, he swung back to look at her, his eyes glittering. 'Mind you, now that DI of yours has set a precedent, there might be other cases that cross my desk that I'm not happy with.'

Trudy blinked, then began to smile. 'That's certainly a possibility, Doctor,' she said cautiously.

'And if that happens, I might need to have a police liaison again.'

'I can see how that might be necessary, sir,' she agreed with growing confidence.

'And if I do, DI Jennings might be reminded of just how well it worked out the last time he appointed you to that office.'

Trudy looked less sure.

'Especially if I made it clear to him just what a nuisance I might make of myself if he were to fail to give me what I wanted,' Dr Clement Ryder added modestly. And reaching for his hat, he placed it squarely on top of his head.

Trudy could have kissed the old vulture. Instead, she merely inclined her head and said crisply, 'Until next time then, Dr Ryder?'

Acknowledgements

With many thanks to Mr Ken Wells (police officer, retired); Mr N. Gardiner, from the Oxford Coroner's Office, and The Oxford Bus Museum.

Karin
Slaughter's
Killer Reads

Exclusive to
ASDA

EXCLUSIVE ADDITIONAL CONTENT

Dear Readers,

Set in 1960s Oxford, an era where cracking the case relies on old-fashioned detective work and clever interviewing rather than DNA testing and technology, *A Fatal Obsession* is the perfect novel for those of you who like to try and solve the crime as you read.

It's five years since twenty-one-year old Gisela Fleet-Wright died, but her former boyfriend has just been found murdered, and the case has been reopened. Together with coroner Clement Ryder, WPC Trudy Loveday is sent to investigate – her very first murder case. The only female police constable in her station, Trudy has always been overlooked by her colleagues, but she and Clement make a surprisingly effective team and they soon begin to unravel the truth behind Gisela's death.

With poison pen letters, family secrets and a truly twisted motive, *A Fatal Obsession* had me completely swept away to sixties Oxford. I couldn't put it down until I reached the ending – and what an explosive ending it is!

Karin

READING GROUP QUESTIONS

(Warning: contains spoilers)

1. Discuss the setting of the book in 1960s Oxford, where there is no DNA testing or technology, but a reliance on instinct and old-fashioned policing. What did you think of this setting?

2. Ryder and Loveday are from different backgrounds with very different personalities. Did you think they worked well together? Did you find yourself identifying with one more than the other?

3. Trudy is the only WPC in her station and underestimated by her superiors. How do you think this impacted her as a character?

4. Clement's role as a coroner rather than a police officer means he had a unique view on the case. How did this influence the investigation?

5. Clement is keeping his health issues a secret. How did this revelation change your view of him?

6. How did your feelings about Gisela change over the course of the novel? Did you suspect the truth about her death?

7. Beatrice destroyed the diary and faked the suicide note to prevent Jonathan being accused of murder. Do you think her actions were justified?

8. Did you find the twist at the end effective? Were you satisfied with the reveal of Jonathan's killer?

A Q&A WITH
FAITH MARTIN

**Readers have particularly enjoyed your 1960s
setting, and its impact on both the investigation
and Trudy's experiences. Why did you choose
this era?**

I was born in the 1960s – yes, I know, a total give-away
about my age – and I've always loved a great many
things about that era. It was such an iconic age in so
many ways; even now I think most people agree it had
the best pop music (and performers) ever! Then there
was the revolution in fashion: who didn't gulp at seeing
their first Quant dress or mini-skirt? It was also a time
of immense political and social change – the Summer
of Love, the Vietnam war, etc. – that even now, from a
distance of fifty years, it still seems to have an almost
magical vibrancy about it. Even the political scandals
were somehow more epic and scandalous, like the
Profumo affair, so all in all it seemed a perfect time for
the setting of a crime novel. Especially since so many
people feel a great nostalgia for those seemingly more
simple and innocent days, giving them a unique appeal in
our far more technology-oriented age.

**The novel is set in Oxford and the city's
landmarks feature heavily. What made you
choose Oxford as a setting?**

Mostly because it's the only city I know! On a more
serious note, Oxford is also world famous for its
beautiful colleges and other buildings, its breadth of

history, and the wealth of its academic knowledge and status as a place of learning. It was also made so famous by Inspector Morse (and Lewis!) that it would have seemed churlish, not to mention downright silly, *not* to set my books there. Especially since a lot of my readers would probably have already gained a strong sense of the place and its atmosphere after seeing it featured on television programmes, or from reading other books set there. Over the years, many authors have set books in Oxford – including the golden-age author, Edmund Crispin, who wrote *The Moving Toyshop*.

There are two protagonists in the novel, Clement and Trudy. What made you decide to write a novel with two lead characters? Was it difficult to balance the two?

My previous series have always featured just one main character – DI Hillary Greene, Jenny Starling, Monica Noble – and I wanted to challenge myself to try something new and different, thus giving my readers a new experience as well. Creating a partnership of two very different people seemed ideal. In order to make the dynamics of their pairing work, however, I quickly realised that they needed to have very clear and separate roles within the novel. Furthermore, these roles had to both complement one another, but also allow the reader to see the storyline progress from two very distinct and (sometimes) opposed points of view. So a young WPC fresh out of police training, with a lot to learn and a lot to prove, and a middle-aged, professional, powerful man fighting different demons of his own, fit the bill!

Trudy's role as a WPC underpins her character. Why did you decide to write about a WPC and how did you research what her experience would have been like?

Having written about the very experienced DI Hillary Greene for many years, I wanted to explore the other end of the spectrum and create a character who was very green, very young, and still had a vast amount of learning to do. Since I'd already decided to set the series in the 1960s I knew that she would have many work-place and social challenges to face, since, at that time, although female officers were a part of the constabulary they were not exactly in the majority! So I wrote to the Thames Valley Police's PR department who put me in touch with a wonderful retired officer who was very helpful indeed. He explained how a young WPC in those days would have been trained, what the police procedures for promotion were, how she would have been outfitted (with a satchel and all her accoutrements) and what duties she would likely have been given. As for her character, she came straight from my imagination, and how I thought a young, working-class girl would have lived and been raised – and from a certain amount of memory!

Much of Clement's narrative is concerned with his attempts to hide and compensate for his growing health issues. What made you decide to write a character who struggled in this way?

I wanted to make Clement interesting by giving him issues of his own – but not go 'over the top'. So many crime novels I read (and thoroughly enjoy!) seem to me to have lead characters with almost too much heavy baggage to carry. As a writer and a reader I wanted to make his problems believable and feasible, without being overwhelming: something personal that would add human tension and drama to the murder cases they were investigating, but not distract from them. And when I thought about him, a man in his fifties, health issues seemed the way to go. It also seemed to go well with his character – a previously fit, active and important man, with a high-powered job as a surgeon and a healthy dose of ego, would certainly find illness a challenge.

What led you to start writing crime novels?

My parents had a bad car crash when I was just nineteen, so I was their carer for over twenty years. Staying at home, I needed something to do and, since I'd always loved reading books, I thought I'd try my hand at writing some. As you do! Of course, it took a lot of practice, and it was five years before I got my first publishing contract. I began writing modern romantic thrillers in the 1990s under the pen name Maxine Barry, but as I got older (and more cynical!) found that I preferred writing crime novels. Since I'd always loved reading Agatha Christie and all the other golden-age authors, I chose to write classic-style whodunits (the Jenny Starling and Monica Noble books). Then I wrote the modern-day DI Hillary Greene police procedural novels. But the Ryder and Loveday books are, I think, a great mixture of both genres: although they do have a police officer in them, their setting in the 1960s means she doesn't have a mobile phone, a computer, or even motorised transport! Which means she and Clement Ryder have to use much more Sherlockian skills in order to catch the killer.

How do you come up with the ideas for your novels?

I come up with a basic premise: A kills B because of C.
I then work out how the killing took place and why.
Then I come up with other suspects, clues, red-herrings
and sub-plots. When I've done that, I do a complete
character profile of all the main protagonists, then a basic
timeline, and from that, a chapter-by-chapter synopsis,
roughly incorporating the entire story line from start to
finish. Then I do the research. Then I write the book.
(Well, you asked!) Alas, I have never yet had a plot come
to me in my dreams. But I live in hope!

What is your writing routine?

I used to write a chapter a day for many years, but
recently I've had to reduce that significantly after being
diagnosed with problems in both my eyes. This means
I can only work on a computer for one short period
a day – which is somewhat inconvenient! I eventually
came to the conclusion that it was nature's way of telling
me to slow down (I have written close to 60 novels in
my career so far). I'm duly slowing down! So to all my
readers who urge me to write more novels, I am writing
as fast as I can!

THE
LAST WIDOW

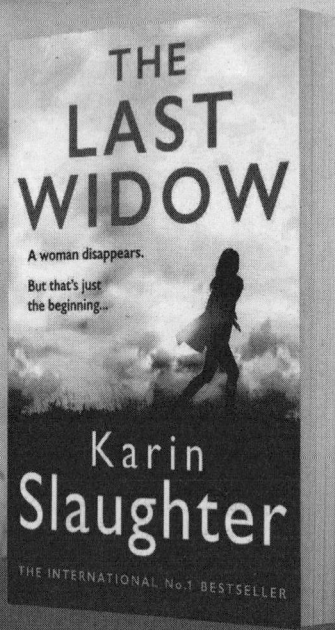

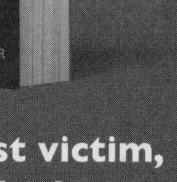

She might be the first victim, but she won't be the last.

Three...
A woman is abducted in front of her child.

Two...
A month later, a second is taken in explosive circumstances.

One...
But the web is bigger and darker than anyone could imagine.

The clock is ticking to uncover the truth.

THE
SILENT WIFE

He watches.

A woman runs alone in the woods. She convinces herself she has no reason to be afraid, but she's wrong. A predator is stalking the women of Grant County. He lingers in the shadows, until the time is just right to snatch his victim.

He waits.

A decade later, the case has been closed. The killer is behind bars. But then another young woman is brutally attacked and left for dead, and the MO is identical.

He takes.

Although the original trail has gone cold – memories have faded, witnesses have disappeared – agent Will Trent and forensic pathologist Sara Linton must re-open the cold case. But the clock is ticking, and the killer is determined to find his perfect silent wife….

ONE PLACE. MANY STORIES

Bold, innovative and
empowering publishing.

FOLLOW US ON:

@HQStories